# THE
# CERTAINTY
## OF
# CHRIST

Confident Faith in a Confused World

# Ken Dew

**THE CERTAINTY OF CHRIST**

Confident Faith in a Confused World

Author: Ken Dew

Copyright © 2022 by Ken Dew. Ken.Dew@EveryNation.org
ISBN: 978-1-9565670-1-4
Library of Congress Control Number: 2022949457
Design & Layout by: Douglas DoNascimento
Published by: Briggs & Schuster
            BSA.IM


Printed in the United States of America

# REVIEWS

"Dr. Ken Dew insightfully outlines the intellectual challenges Christians face in our increasingly secular society, and he provides a highly accessible overview of how to defend the truth of Christianity from science, history, and philosophy. Ken's book is sure to help people understand and better defend their faith against the various objections coming from the culture. I would highly recommend his book for anyone desiring a quick overview of the reason for the faith we hold. Ken's work provides a solid foundation to then explore more technical works on more specialized topics."

### Dr. Brian Miller

Ph.D. in physics from Duke University, Research Coordinator for the Center for Science and Culture at the Discovery Institute, and head researcher for the book, *God's Not Dead*.

"We live in uncertain times when, paradoxically, the very existence of truth is questioned even while unquestioning allegiance to shaky dogmas is demanded, not only in political matters but also in scientific ones! In, *The Certainty of Christ*, Pastor Ken Dew argues persuasively concerning our era's dire need to embrace Him who is Himself... the Truth."

### Dr. Michael Behe

Michael J. Behe is an American biochemist, author, and a brilliant advocate for the intelligent design argument. He serves as professor of biochemistry at Lehigh University in Pennsylvania and as a senior fellow of the Discovery Institute's Center for Science and Culture.

"I've served in collegiate ministry for over 30 years and during that time I've witnessed college students become less and less certain about "who Jesus is" and "what He came to do." That's why I believe this book is absolutely essential for us to take hold of; not only for ourselves but for the sake of the next generation. Dr. Ken Dew, is called for 'such a time as this' to equip Christians to both defend their faith with boldness, and also navigate the minefield of cultural confusion with grace & truth. He's one of the greatest evangelists I've ever known. I've watched him faithfully labor on college campuses across the world. In fact, Ken reached my wife with the Gospel when she was a college student at the University of Florida! Ken has trained and inspired hundreds of our Hope Church Movement leaders to defend their faith and I believe this book will equip thousands more to do the same!"

**Pastor Brian Smith, Sr.**
Hope Church Movement
Hopechurchmovement.com


"This book will embolden Christians and answer some difficult questions for those seeking answers. Ken has managed to condense the expansive field of Christian apologetics into an easy-to-read work. I was very encouraged reading it and found it provided interesting facts that paint a more complete picture of why we believe what we believe."

**Dr. David Westmark**
Ph.D. Physics
Florida State University

# ACKNOWLEDGEMENTS

I am deeply indebted to my wonderful wife Renee who has been a constant source of encouragement and wisdom while I have been writing this book. Renee also helped me with hours of proof reading and editing my drafts over the past months. A special thanks to my daughter Dr. Rebecca Ann Westmark for her help and insight in assisting with the layout and content of this book. Thank you too Dr. David Westmark, for being a wonderful support to your wife while she assisted with the development of this book and for your wisdom and advice in simplifying the subject matter for readers.

A special thanks to my son Benjamin and his wife Ashley, and my two daughters Rachael and Abigail for their constant encouragement urging me to complete this work. Rachael and Abigail were instrumental in helping to select the specific artwork and font style of the book cover that I eventually used for this publication. Thanks Abigail, for your creative insight in helping me with the illustrations used for this book. I want to extend my sincere appreciation to both Mary Ann Peterson and Gina Becker for helping proof read, edit, and bringing great suggestions in making this book more readable, interesting, and impacting to the potential audience.

Finally, I want to acknowledge Pastor Ron and Cindy Miller and the Every Nation Tallahassee Church for supporting this writing endeavor while our church was in the midst of a busy time of new growth, program evaluation, and ministry expansion. I am deeply indebted to you all for helping this book to become a reality. Thank You!

To God Be the Glory.

# FOREWORD

I have known Ken Dew for over thirty years. We both attended Tennessee Tech University where we participated in varsity sports. Ken was on the football team and I played on the golf team. I had just become a Christian and I happened to be in the meeting where Ken heard the truth and submitted his life to Jesus. I was privileged to watch him quickly become a bold, intelligent teacher of scriptural truth and a willing debater on university campuses. Ken and I both work for Every Nation, a global organization that plants churches next to university campuses worldwide.

Ken impressed me, early on in our friendship, as a seeker of truth. Ken is a natural evangelist and church planter, but in recent years he has developed into a gifted cultural apologist and defender of the Christian faith. Ken has traveled as an evangelist, missionary, and apologist to over forty countries around the globe and has lectured on over 130 universities in North America and around the world.

Ken has benefitted from living overseas and traveling globally. Because of that, he writes with a broad perspective and well-thought-out ideas. Ken has done a masterful job in identifying and dismantling many of the cultural objections that are being used to discredit and marginalize Christianity in our secular society.

This book accurately addresses the current trends of culture, but it is not trendy. This is a solid defense of objective truth… Read this book! It is timely, informative, challenging, and uplifting. My hope is that *The Certainty of Christ* will inspire a new wave of bold truth-tellers who can defend the Christian faith worldwide. Great job Ken!

**Dr. David Houston**
Every Nation Ministries
Nashville, TN

# CONTENTS

# INTRODUCTION

"Have I not written you excellent things of counsels and knowledge, to make you know the certainty of the words of truth that you may correctly answer him who sent you."
**- Proverbs 22:20-21**[1]

It was a bright sunny day when my family boarded a ferry in the Auckland viaduct to sail across the Waitemata harbor to a beautiful tourist destination called Waiheke Island. Renee and I had recently moved our family from Brentwood, Tennessee to Auckland, New Zealand to establish a new church plant in the city.

Waiheke Island is one of the most picturesque of sites, located about thirteen miles off the coast of Auckland in the Hauraki Gulf. The island is surrounded by the beautiful turquoise waters of the South Pacific Ocean. Waiheke is famous for its wineries, local artists, and of course, sheep grazing on the slopes of the green hills. There are ice cream parlors, outdoor cafes, an assortment of boutiques, restaurants, and great English-style fish and chips.

I still remember how excited our four children were to ride the ferry across the harbor to this "faraway island, way out in the ocean." The ride took about forty minutes of travel time. As the boat got closer to the island, our youngest daughter Abigail, about six years of age at the time, started yelling out, "Look Daddy! The island is getting bigger and bigger!"

We could now make out the big yachts anchored in the Waiheke marina, as well as people fishing and walking on the pier. The kids shouted, "We are almost there! See! The people are getting bigger and bigger!" Yes, the harbor and people did appear to be getting larger, but it wasn't the island or the people on it that were changing. The island was at a stationary, fixed point, marking our final destination for that day. Our boat had sailed to what was now a large piece of land rising out of the Pacific Ocean.

As we left the ferry, we felt a sense of security as our feet stood on solid ground. The children soon realized that what had first appeared to be a tiny volcano, was actually 12 miles long, and 6 miles wide, with 6,000 people living on it! In one form or another, people all over the world search for that same solid ground, a fixed point of certainty upon which to anchor their lives.

The seventeenth-century mathematician, Blaise Pascal offered an interesting analogy that described morality and the human perspective aboard a ship in the ocean: "When everything is moving at once, nothing appears to be moving, as on board a ship. When everyone is moving towards depravity, no one seems to be moving, but if someone stops, he exposes the others who are rushing on, by acting as a fixed point."[2] *Sometimes it takes a single action to make a change in a person's perspective.*

Events in the last decade have brought about social changes and cultural issues that are mind-boggling and deeply disturbing in some cases. When it comes to sexuality, gender identity, and morality, personal preference has replaced ethical truth and objective facts. Premarital sex is no longer viewed as immoral or discouraged by society but is openly accepted and encouraged by educators and public consensus. This cavalier attitude increasingly glamorizes sexual deviance and rebellion, without considering the spread of sexually transmitted illnesses and unwanted pregnancies, and the emotional damage done to the individuals involved.

In a Barna study of Generation Z (people born between 1995 and 2015) regarding their views about gender identity, it was discovered that today's teenagers are much more open to the idea that gender is determined by how they *feel*, and not by one's *birth sex*. One out of three teens think personal feelings should override your biological sex, and forty percent of teens say it's okay to be born one gender and change one's body to become another gender.[3]

The current battle in America over the morality of late-term abortion and neonaticide exemplifies the relativistic mindset towards morality in general. Nearly everyone agrees that the deliberate killing of a newborn baby is murder, but there is intense debate about the morality of terminating an early, middle, or late-term pregnancy.

Phillip Johnson, former California Berkeley Law professor, wrote regarding the abortion issue, "In the face of such disagreement the liberal rationalist's position is 'prochoice,' as it presumably will be if one day a substantial body of opinion - especially articulate and well-educated opinion - develops in favor of *infanticide*. How could it be otherwise, if morality rest ultimately on a human decision rather than external authority?"[4]

In support of gay marriage, the Defense of Marriage Act (DOMA) was introduced by President Bill Clinton in 1996. By the end of the Obama administration, gay marriage had become a right guaranteed by the U.S. Constitution. Unsurprisingly, the LGBTQ+ movement was not satisfied with just being tolerated by the rest of society. They are now demanding wholesale cultural endorsement of the gay lifestyle as being a *good thing* and want *preferential treatment* from federal institutions. Behavior that for millennia was viewed as emotionally harmful and morally deviant is now being publicly endorsed and celebrated.[5]

## Finding A Fixed Point

We are faced with a big dilemma. If there are no fixed laws, no overarching points of reference, then truth can be whatever an individual or group says it is! If all truths and ethics are fluid and transient, how does one navigate the societal issues of the twenty-first century? In all changing things, there must be something unchanging by which to measure progress and change.[6] If there is a fixed basis for law, there must exist an absolute point of reference upon which moral judgments can be made.

People of all cultures have believed that fixed points or transcendent laws along with a Giver of such laws had to exist.[7] With absolute standards established, our confidence in the law is made secure. These fixed reference points in our changing world are rooted in God's eternal truths found in the Bible. God's truth is universal in its scope and application. Fixed laws remain constant, placing the same expectations on every person of every age. Without at least one timeless, transcendent fixed point, there can be no way to determine right from wrong, up from down, or the moral from the immoral.

Jesus promised His followers, "If you hold to my teaching, you are really my disciples. Then you will know the truth and the truth will set you free" (John 8:31-32, NIV). As Jesus said, truth is something that anybody, anywhere can rationally and objectively know. God's truth about life and reality is liberating and empowering - not oppressive, discriminating, or unjust. History bears out that individuals who try to live contrary to God's fixed moral laws will encounter difficulties in this life, and according to Scripture, experience devastating consequences in the next.

The western pursuit of personal peace and affluence summarizes what most people believe will make them "happy." This elusive quest for happiness has proven to be a moving target that is extremely hard to hit, and when achieved, offers only fleeting and shallow satisfaction. And yet, for many their personal feelings negate and trump real-life facts. Individual preferences sabotage the human conscience, numbing the moral law written on the human heart. When this happens to a culture, truth is lost.

## Drifting from the Truth

George Orwell was the author of the dystopian novels *1984* and *Animal Farm*. Orwell wrote about a futuristic totalitarian government that controlled the population through surveillance and propaganda. In his book 1984, "Big Brother" was the name of an oppressive centralized government, which constantly kept its citizens under surveillance. In *1984* the citizens were reminded of this by the slogan "Big Brother is watching you." The story unfolds as people are monitored by a tyrannical central government as a means of controlling individual thought, ensuring *groupthink*, and thereby controlling the masses. Orwell intuitively understood something about the oppressive nature of Big Government in modern culture. To control and manipulate the population, free speech and the free exchange of ideas had to be restricted. Orwell wrote, "The further a society drifts from the truth, the more it will hate those who speak it." I would say, this especially holds for us today.

4

American colleges are supposed to be bastions for the exercise of free speech, academic inquiry, and the robust exchange of ideas. These pillars form the very basis of a Liberal Arts education, which were intended to foster freedom of individual inquiry. Today, on many American campuses, anyone asserting moral truth is often confronted with contempt, name-calling, and even physical assault. Social progressives argue that it is arrogant and bigoted to push your truth claims on others.

## Cancel Culture

On more and more university campuses of America, many students trying to express a Christian ideology have been shouted down and labeled offensive, bigoted, or intolerant by other students, as well as by, faculty members. There is a tangible pressure to conform one's ideas and speech to the "Group Think" of the secular, progressive culture. All ideas are welcome... except those ideologies that make absolute truth claims!

Philosopher J. P. Moreland wrote, "In much of our culture, reason has given way to rhetoric, evidence to emotion and real substance to catchy slogans."[8] Cancel Culture labels many ideas as dangerous or intolerant. They demand those ideas be censored or expunged from any public speech, Twitter feed, or Facebook posts. The stated reason is that certain ideas or assertions are deemed offensive. The freedom of speech and expression guaranteed in the First Amendment of our Constitution applies to them but, it would seem, not to individuals who might express contrary ideas. Recently we have seen the rise of draconian *political correctness* that has anointed itself solely as the guardian of free speech. All speech is acceptable as long as that speech is in-step with the prescribed ideology and secular narrative.

The denial of biblical truth as our fixed point of reference has not only resulted in personal confusion for the individual, but it has also produced a dangerous environment for our whole society. In an age where tolerance and diversity reign supreme in the minds of secular progressives, Christians must be willing to take a stand, defend biblical truths, and if necessary, be labeled as intolerant, bigoted, or hateful for the sake of truth.

Paul the Apostle wrote to the church in Rome:

For the wrath of God is revealed from heaven against all ungodliness and unrighteousness of men who suppress the truth in unrighteousness, because that which is known about God is evident within them; for God made it evident to them. For since the creation of the world His invisible attributes, His eternal power, and divine nature, have been clearly seen, being understood through what has been made, so that they are without excuse. For even though they knew God, they did not honor Him as God or give thanks, but they became futile in their speculations, and their foolish heart was darkened. Professing to be wise, they became fools (Romans 1:18-22).

Paul describes the truth as a mirror reflection revealed through the created order people can see in nature. The God who made the cosmos has made all of humanity accountable to this obvious knowledge so that we are without excuse. Something happens when we are confronted with the uncomfortable reality of truth, especially when it conflicts with our present lifestyles. We are faced with a dilemma: either conform to the truth or ignore and suppress the truth. But just like the proverbial beach ball at the swimming pool, truth, even though it is pushed down under the water for a little while, will sooner or later come rushing to the surface again.

In God's world, the knowledge of the Creator is forever popping up, reminding skeptics that objective reality exists. Paul assures his readers that truth exists and can be understood by those who are confronted with it. In other words, truth is rational and comprehensible. Today, just like in Paul's day, truth is being suppressed and even denied by individuals who refuse to conform to truth's dictates.

God's handiwork, demonstrated in His creation, demands that we acknowledge the Creator. As the English philosopher, Francis Bacon argued, "God never wrought miracles to convince atheism, because his ordinary works convince it. It is true that a little philosophy inclineth man's mind to atheism; but in depth philosophy bringeth men's minds back to religion."[9]

As I will demonstrate in later chapters, the physical creation offers overwhelming proof of God's existence. God doesn't need to perform more miracles to convince mankind that He exists. Scientists and most rational people agree with logical evidence offered by the order seen in the physical world. Suppressing the truth about God is not an easy job. We are constantly reminded of God's existence through the revelation of what we see in creation. It takes a lot of mental energy to pretend that complexity and order in the form of biological life are not designed, but just appear to be that way. Accordingly, many people have put their faith in a magical idea of "Mother Nature" and have rejected the reality of a Father God.

C.S. Lewis talked about the reality of God becoming obvious:

> It is after you have realized that there is a real Moral Law, and a Power behind the law, and that you have broken that law and put yourself wrong with that Power - it is after all this, and not a moment sooner, that Christianity begins to talk. I believe in Christianity as I believe that the sun has risen: not only because I see it, but because by it I see everything else.[10]

## Finding Solid Ground

Christian scholar and philosopher Francis Schaeffer once remarked, "Modern man has got both feet firmly planted in mid-air." Never has a phrase better described our present condition. Civil governments are necessary for any civilization to flourish. The rule of law is the basis of order and civilization. Authorities are instituted by God for the good of everyone, to restrain evil. The Bible teaches that governments are ordained by God to punish the wrongdoer and to commend those who do right (Romans 13:3-4; 1 Peter 2:14). The problem is, if evil is not identified as *being* evil, then it cannot be restrained by civil authorities.

Even politicians and secular pundits who talk about social justice and human rights are speaking nonsense if there is no common ground to define justice and rights. Ideas have consequences, and the idea that there are no transcendent moral reference points has set twenty-first-century humanity adrift, floating helplessly in a sea of relativism. In our current situation, we need to overcome this cultural confusion and grab hold of something eternal and solid.

In the course of this book, I will put forward four statements for us to consider if we are to find certainty. These four truth assertions will help blow away the smokescreen of confusion and doubt, putting us on solid ground.

1.  God Exists.

2.  Truth is Knowable.

3.  Miracles Do Occur.

4.  The Bible is God's Self-Revelation and is Reliable.

The Bible exhorts us, "Buy the truth and do not sell it, get wisdom and instruction and understanding" (Proverbs 23:23). Notice in the verse, how wisdom and understanding always accompany the acquisition and application of truth. The supreme truth recorded in the Bible and confirmed by overwhelming historical evidence is that God is the Creator and He became a man in the person of Jesus Christ. As God incarnate, Jesus lived on earth as a perfect, sinless man, was crucified by Pontius Pilate, was placed in a borrowed tomb, and on the third day resurrected from the dead. After 40 days He appeared to his disciples (Mark 16:14). On these historic facts rest the reality and foundations of Christianity's truth claims.

First, it is my deep desire in writing this book to help people find the only absolute fixed point to reference and direct their lives. I trust this journey will take you to a place of personal stability and spiritual confidence in your Christian walk and your quest for ultimate truth. You can know with certainty that the God of the Bible is the Author of all truth. In the course of this book, I will provide an apologetic overview of some of the most common objections that many skeptics and atheists use to dismiss or ignore the truth claims of Christianity. Although I will be writing from a Christian perspective, my critique of secularism, atheism, relativism, and postmodernism, as well as other worldviews will not be limited to quoting proof texts from the Bible, although I do believe the Bible is infallible and inerrant, serving as a reliable guide of God's revelation to humanity.

In today's culture, many Christians are intimidated about sharing their faith with others primarily for two reasons. They are afraid they won't be able to answer the person's objections to Christianity, or they are afraid of looking foolish in front of their friends or colleagues. We must not forget Peter's admonition to the church, being ready to give a defense for the hope within us with meekness and fear (1 Peter 3:15).

This book is intended to inspire Christians to develop the capacity to engage others in evangelism by answering objections in the "post-truth" culture. My intention is to help equip and embolden Christians by what they learn in this book. In later chapters, I will demonstrate that there is reasonable evidence available to all believers for them to give a sensible answer and intelligent defense to anyone who asks about their Christian faith.

Secondly, I hope this book will appeal to all those readers who are sincerely skeptical or unsure about Jesus' life, death, and resurrection. I trust you will hear and feel my sincerity in communicating truths that have transformed and shaped my life over the past forty years. Finally, I hope this book opens up the possibility for you that truth is indeed real, and that you will see it revealed in the person of Jesus Christ of Nazareth.

**Just Follow the Evidence**

In the course of answering objections to Christianity's truth claims, I intend to use the famous formula that the late Dr. Antony Flew coined for discovering the truth: "Go wherever the evidence leads." Flew was the best-known academic atheist of modern times to be convinced of the existence of God. Before his death he wrote the book, *There is a God: How the World's Most Notorious Atheist Changed His Mind.* Flew was finally convinced about the existence of God because he could no longer deny the evidence and keep his intellectual integrity.[11] In 2004, Antony

Flew publicly renounced his atheism, concluding that the case for God's existence, Who possesses characteristics of power and also intelligence is now stronger than ever before.[12] The simplest recipe for discovering the truth, *follow the evidence to wherever it leads.*

Later on, in chapter five, I will address the *reliability of the Bible.* I will present various arguments that try to attack and discredit Christianity and the Bible. This book will offer evidence from textual criticism, history, and archaeology that will validate the truth claims of the Bible as being factually reliable. I intend to use the rules of logical proof regarding both natural science and philosophy to establish the veracity of the Bible's claims. I will also examine the supernatural predictions of biblical prophecy to confirm those claims as being historically accurate in regards to what they predicted would come to pass.

I will call upon several classical apologetic arguments, rather than using only Scripture to answer objections to Christianity's validity. Many people are not familiar with apologetics. *Apologetics* is the branch of theology that offers a rational defense for the truthfulness of the divine origin and authority of Christianity.[13] It comes from the Greek word *apologia*, which means to give a reason or a defense. Scripture encourages the use of apologetics by all believers. Apologetics is sometimes called "pre-evangelism" because it can help remove intellectual obstacles in the way of faith. Classical apologetics stresses rational arguments for the existence of God and historical evidence supporting the truth of Christianity.

While I acknowledge that people can only receive salvation, as the Holy Spirit draws them by grace to believe and trust in Jesus Christ alone, I am also convinced that many people will not consider the truth of Christ without being exposed to a convincing argument that offers persuasive evidence. Christian apologetics serves much like a *bulldozer* clearing the way of debris, enabling skeptics to objectively hear the gospel message, as well as, consider the evidence that supports it. I intend to address many of the contemporary objections that have been raised against theism in general and Christianity particularly.

This book will offer an apologetic for the deity of Jesus through the historical reality of Jesus' virgin birth, crucifixion, death, and resurrection. I will also address the topic of "theodicy," which deals with the problem of evil, investigating the question, "If a good and loving God exists, why does He allow evil and suffering in the world?" This book will further contrast various world religions, allowing for a defense of the uniqueness of Christianity by identifying and substantiating Christianity's exclusive claims. I will also examine the various worldviews that have tried to suppress ethical-monotheism and cast doubt on the Judeo-Christian God of the Bible.

I write this book with the conviction that absolute, objective truth both does exist, and can be known! Jesus openly claimed to be "the Truth" (John 14:6). If we follow the author of truth, we can have confident faith while living in a very confusing world. Because God exists and His truths are available to us, we can anchor our lives on the solid rock of Christ. "Therefore, let all of the house of Israel know for certain that God has made Him both LORD and Christ this Jesus whom you have crucified" (Acts 2:36). Thanks to God's revelation to people down through the ages, He can be known, believed, and trusted by ordinary people.

# CHAPTER ONE

## Whatever Happened to Right and Wrong?

"Truth is sacred because departure from the truth is a departure from God."

**- Mark Rutland**

I have many exciting opportunities to speak on university campuses about the existence of God and the reliability of the Bible. Many times, I start seminars by asking students, "Do you believe in true north?" All of the audience acknowledges there is indeed a geographical location known as true north. True north's existence is never in question, but its correct location can at times be in question. I then ask the audience to close their eyes. Once their eyes are closed, I instruct the audience to extend their right hand straight up into the air while keeping their eyes shut. Finally, I ask them to try to point to where they think true north is located. Against the background of giggles and sighs, hundreds of students begin pointing to where they believe true north is located, the majority of them being wrong.

When I ask the audience to open their eyes while maintaining their arm position without fail, the room erupts with laughter. Why? Because the audience opens their eyes to discover hundreds of fingers pointed in every direction imaginable. I then ask them a question. Is *everyone* in the room correct in their guess about the geographical location of true north? They all agree, "No!" They all acknowledge that true north is found *only at one* geographical point on the earth. At that moment, I get out my smartphone and activate my trusty compass App. Magically, I can locate true north.

Most of the time, only a few of the people in the auditorium are pointing towards geographical true north. What is the point of this exercise? If there was confusion regarding the reference point of true north, it would be impossible to reliably travel in any other direction. Trying to successfully navigate through life without a fixed point is impossible. Morally our culture finds itself wandering, steeped in confusion over what is actually real and what is imaginary.

According to the Gospel of John, before His crucifixion, Jesus of Nazareth stood trial before Pontius Pilate accused of treason because He claimed to be King of the Jews, "Therefore, Pilate said to Him, 'So You are a king?' Jesus answered, 'You say correctly that I am a king. For this, I have been born, and for this I have come into the world, to testify to the truth. Everyone who is of the truth hears My voice'" (John 18:37). Jesus proclaimed himself to be both the total *embodiment* of truth and the *source* of all truth.

Pilate, intrigued by Jesus, asked Him, "What is truth?" Was Pilate trying to appease the Jews and settle the political unrest in Jerusalem that night? Or was he entertaining the possibility that Jesus was the promised Messiah and King of the Jews? Whatever the motive, Pilate foolishly dismissed a golden opportunity to embrace the *essence* of truth. Just like Pilate, much of the world continues to search in vain for truth without embracing the Author and source of all truth. The ramifications of truth can be very personal, and require change. Sadly, self-interest and self-justification have become the real objectives for many people. Well then, what exactly is the truth? Most people know the truth when they see it, but philosophically it can be a slippery concept to grasp. The Greek Philosopher Socrates would have probably answered Pilate's question by posing three more questions himself:

1. Is Truth absolute?

2. Is Truth knowable?

3. Does Truth correspond with reality?[14]

Jesus' answer would have been, "I am the way, and the truth, and the life; no one comes to the Father but through Me" (John 14:6). The Greek word for *truth* primarily used in the New Testament is *Alethia*.

Alethia can also be translated to mean genuine *reality*.[15] What we might say in the common vernacular is, "truth is *really real*."

For truth to correspond with reality, we must begin by being honest about our finiteness. Honesty brings us into the correct relationship with the highest level of reality; truth. The issue of truth is absolutely crucial to what we believe to be objectively real.[16] Currently, many are stuck in a moral vacuum, held in the grips of a relativistic society that cannot or will not recognize the reality of truth claims.

The concept of truth has come under fire through the guise of *cultural relativism*. One Barna report finds that Millennials (people born between 1981-1996) sport a carefree notion of *live* and let *live*, or *you-do-youism*.[17] The elusive search for "the self" has caused many in this generation to dismiss or distort traditional values and biblical truth claims, while at the same time exalting personal preferences and individualism. This *self-authenticating* mindset has become the foundation and the filter that many people use to define their meaning and purpose in life. There are a great many voices across the educational and political landscape that are happy to accommodate all individual claims, with the condition that they are considered situational and subjective.

The battle over truth claims can be a volatile topic. We are living in a time where sensitivities are on the surface and many people are ready to attack at the slightest provocation. "Religiously, you can believe in almost any deity, just as long as you don't bring Jesus Christ into it."[18] This is because Christianity, by its truth claims, cannot be reduced to just another option, floating in a pluralistic sea with other religions from which to choose.

There are a few questions that we must ask ourselves: What is really at stake for us, our families, our world, and future generations? Who gets to be the final authority to say what is really right or wrong? If a fixed point of reference is found, is there any guarantee that people will acknowledge it and adhere to it?

Let's take a step back into our nation's history. In the nineteenth century, American educators believed in an idea called the "unity of the truth." They taught that *all truth is one and inseparable*. This unity of the truth encompassed two important premises:

1. All truths agree and can be related to one another in a single system.

2. Knowledge has a moral dimension.

According to these premises, to know the truth is to know the good. Our forefathers agreed that knowledge and ethics are inextricably linked together. The early American colleges, including Harvard, believed and taught their curriculum according to this "unity of the truth" principle. They asserted that all knowledge ultimately illuminated the Divine essence found in and through obtaining knowledge.[19] Taking a step back even further into history, the Old Testament Scripture instructed how the nation of Israel was to govern itself once the Israelites entered the promised land (Deuteronomy 28:1-14). Israel had two presuppositions they maintained while conquering the land of Canaan:

- God is the King.

- God is the Ultimate Lawgiver and Source of Justice.

These ideas place sovereignty outside of human volition and fly directly in the face of twenty-first-century individualism and the idea of situational ethics.[20]

## Truth Matters

In 2012 our family moved to Brisbane, Australia, and established a church in that beautiful city. On the campus of the University of Queensland stands the Forgan Smith Building. UQ, as it is called by locals is one of the most beautiful campuses I have ever visited. My eldest daughter, Rebecca, studied and earned her Ph.D. there. This stately sandstone building offers a majestic entrance onto this campus, but it was not the impressive architecture of the building that grabbed my attention. What struck me was the university's motto inscribed on the building's entrance: "Great is Truth and Mighty Above All Things." According to the founders of this institution of higher learning, truth alone is the most magnificent resource to obtain and is supremely valuable when embraced.

Here are a few prominent academic institutions that openly acknowledged and sought to obtain this commodity known as *truth*.

- Harvard University: *Veritas* and *Christo et Ecclesiae*, "For Truth" and "For Christ and Church."
- Oxford University: *Dominus Illumination MEA*, "The Lord is my Light."
- California Institute of Technology: *The Truth Shall Make You Free*.
- Yale University: *Lux et Veritas*, "Light and Truth."
- Columbia University: *In Lumine Tuo Videbimis Lumen*, "We will see the light in Your light."[21]

Reading these mottos, it is clear that at the founding of these prestigious institutions the proclamation and dissemination of truth was their core mission. Their stated goals were to pursue the truth through all disciplines of education. How tragic that the foundation of education, the dissemination of truth, is now distorted by many as being either unknowable or subjective.

If God and His word are not established as the timeless, transcendent point of reference to determine objective truth, then there can be no standard or absolute sense of right and wrong. All ethics will quickly deteriorate into subjective chaos. Philosopher Gordon H. Clark argues for beginning one's pursuit of truth with two necessary presuppositions: God exists and the Bible is infallible. Clarke insisted that human rationale and sense perception lead only to skepticism. Certainty comes only through the Bible and Godly reason.[22] Any culture that adopts situational ethics and fallible human reason as its ethical foundations is asking for conflict, confusion, and eventual social breakdown. American writer, and political commentator, Walter Lippman wrote this insightful but disturbing remark back in 1920, "There can be no liberty for a community which lacks the means to detect lies."[23]

If all truth is God's truth, then Christianity presents the truth about the whole of reality and not just about religious values. This gives Christians a perspective for interpreting every subject matter, both public and private. Genesis tells us that God spoke the entire universe into being with His word, what John 1:1 calls *Logos*. The Greek word *Logos* translates into English as *Word* but also can mean *reason* or *rationality*. God's word is meant to be the *truth filter* by which all human reason and experiences must pass.[24]

The existence of an all-powerful God Who creates law means that any society that ignores His laws will be out of step with reality. A society or person that has lost sight of the transcendent God will promote ever-changing laws, which will cause people to lose respect for or even ignore legal morality. When that happens, truth is lost and every person is free to do *what is right in their own eyes*.[25]

## When Truth is Missing

Each year the Oxford Dictionary selects a Word of the Year. The idea is to find a word that best represents the mood of the culture. In 2016, the Oxford Dictionary selection committee picked the word *post-truth*, defined as, "Relating to or denoting circumstances in which objective facts are less influential in shaping public opinion than appeals to emotion and personal belief." The use of the word had increased by 2,000 percent that year.

Arguably, what is driving a lot of the cultural confusion is peoples' selfish desire for personal autonomy. Murray goes on to explain, "In a post-truth age, if the evidence fits our preferences and opinions, all is well and good. If it doesn't, then the evidence is deemed inadmissible or offensive."[26] When human emotion and personal preference replaces objective facts, the world becomes a very scary place to live in.

Dallas Willard once wrote, "Truth is the handle of reality by which we negotiate life." To live one's life correctly, truth is an essential item to understand and obey.[27] When your thoughts correspond with the reality they describe, this is known as *the correspondence view of truth*. Philosopher J. P. Moreland describes the correspondence view of truth in this way, "A theory is true if and only if what it says about the world does accurately describe the world."[28] Truth matches with objective reality and to that extent, it is not subjective. When truth corresponds with reality, as already mentioned, truth also allows us to cooperate with and to function properly with the real world. Objective truth exists, even when it may be the reality we don't want it to be or is not what we think it ought to be.

Recently, my wife Renee and I were traveling when we received a call from our daughters back home in Orlando. They started talking to us and said, "Mom and Dad, you're not going to believe this, but a black bear is sitting in our backyard!" At first, we responded to what we perceived as their joke. "You girls are kidding us, right?" They were all on the speakerphone, so we could hear all of the voices in the background saying, "No! We are serious." There is a bear in our backyard."

Thankfully, they were safely inside the living room looking out through both the glass doors and the screened-in patio. They videoed this encounter with the bear and sent the video to us to view. Sure enough, a black bear was sitting in our backyard just as they had said. They even put the video on Facebook and got hundreds of hits that day.

When I heard our daughters describe the event, certain images came to my mind. Their words painted a vivid picture in my mind, even though they were talking to us over the phone from hundreds of miles away. I did not think of a white polar bear or a brown grizzly bear. I envisioned *a black bear*. I believed there was a black bear in our yard.

My belief, like beliefs in general, consists of a mental act by which something is *held to be so!* As the girls sent us the link to the footage of the black bear in our backyard, we were able to confirm the truth of our belief. There was indeed a young black bear sitting in our backyard. The *correspondence view of truth* validates our expectations, allowing people to have faith in the real world as they conduct their everyday lives. Truth, in this case concerning the bear, described the actual state of affairs. There was a matching up or connection between the statement and the reality it pointed to. Like in the case of the bear sighting, the final truth of ideas or events are discovered by people, not created by them.[29] Truth is not determined by feelings, preferences, or sincerity. It is an objective statement of what is *really* there.

Now as I write this chapter, it's been well over a month, and there have been no more bear sightings. The bear is no longer sitting in our backyard, thank God. What remains true is that when thoughts and words match objective reality, then truth is established! Conversely, when people have thoughts or speak words that do not accurately correspond with reality, we call them mistaken, deceived, delusional, or in some cases even insane. When people claim certain things to be true that they know do not match the facts of reality, we call them dishonest. Truth demands a set of beliefs that must be coherent within themselves to be held as objectively real.

## When Sincerity is Not Enough

Many people believe that certain ideas must be true because they are sincerely held by an individual. Unfortunately, sincerity does not qualify any idea, belief, or thought to be true. Thoughts must represent an *accurate conception of the real world* in order to be true. Before we address all the objections being hurled at Christian truth claims let's talk about *propositional truth*. If a proposition or statement is true, then we say it has a *truth value* or it is "true." If a proposition is false, its *truth value* is "false." For example, "Grass is green," and "2 + 7 = 5" are propositions. The first claim has the truth value of "true" and the second claim is "false" because we all know "2 + 7 = 9" not "5."

All statements of truth, by their definition, are exclusive and universal. For example, 2 + 2 = 4. This mathematical statement is logically true everywhere in all cultures, for all people. That means that all other possible numbers are excluded from being the correct answer. You may adore the number "33," but "33" is not the correct answer. Let's imagine you depart from Atlanta, driving north toward New York City in your car. It is not physically possible to simultaneously be driving south toward Miami. You may desire to go to Miami but, by going north, you have excluded Miami from your travel plans, at least for now. One cannot be headed to New York City while at the same time traveling toward Miami. This demonstrates how truth claims, by definition, must be exclusive.

Just consider a person whose biological age is actually 22 years old, yet they sincerely believe and self-identify as being 65 years old. That claim would be regarded as delusional no matter how sincerely it is held by the individual. The IRS would quickly reject such a claim as false, denying the request for retirement benefits. One's sincerity or age preferences do not alter the truth of their chronological age.

This is exactly how propositional truths work in reality. If a truth assertion fits objective reality, then other conflicting assertions must be false and therefore excluded as a possible answer. Things cannot be right just because we prefer them that way or feel like they should be right. Facts must override our feelings even when sincerely felt. If the propositions put forth by the tenets of Christian doctrine are true, logically those truth propositions are valid even if, by the nature of being true, they eliminate other popular positions.

Among Millennials, forty-seven percent agree that it is wrong to share one's personal beliefs with someone of a different faith in hopes that they will one day share the same faith. Forty percent agree that if someone disagrees with your religious position, they are judging you! And the same number feel forced to choose between their faith and their friends.[30]

Our postmodern environment has given rise to the, *you* be *you*, and *don't criticize anyone's lifestyle* sentiment. Amid this *judgment-free* and *live-and-let-live environment*, we are confronted with some challenging and exclusive statements made by Jesus to His followers. Most secularists and a growing number of church-going Millennials and Generation Z-ers (those born between 1981 - 2015) are very troubled by what they perceive as the *exclusivity of Christianity*. This is one of the negative effects of pluralistic thinking, which wants to reject any hint of an exclusive truth claim. Unfortunately, many contemporary Christians now view biblical assertions of absolute truth as being "mean-spirited" and out-of-step with "love and tolerance."

The Book of Acts records, "And there is salvation in no one else; for there is no other name under heaven that has been given among men by which we must be saved (Acts 4:12). The Bible identifies Jesus exclusively as the only way to God. If one accepts these claims, does that make Christianity intolerant and bigoted?

C.S. Lewis wrote on the subject of morality and justice and how one could rightly by contrast discern the difference between right and wrong:

My argument against God was that the universe seemed so cruel and unjust. But how had I gotten this idea of just and unjust? A man does not call a line crooked unless he has some idea of a straight line. What was I comparing this universe with when I called it unjust?[31]

The Prophet Hosea reminded the nation of Israel that knowledge provides essential truth which is crucial for life. "My people are destroyed for a lack of knowledge. Because you have rejected knowledge, I will also reject you from being My priest. Since you have forgotten the law of your God, I also will forget your children" (Hosea 4:6).

The problem with atheism is that, with its denial of God's existence, there is a loss of any timeless, transcendent point of reference to guide us. Augustine, Bishop of Hippo (354-430), was known as the apostolic Father of the Western church and became one of the most influential theologians and apologists of the Christian faith. Augustine was a prolific writer. One of his works, *The Free Choice of the Will*, contains a theistic argument from the truth. Augustine claims absolute truths exist outside of and independent of personal perception:

We cannot doubt the proposition that affirms our existence or our thoughts. Nor can we doubt the facts of mathematics ($2+2 = 4$). These truths are held in common by all people and yet are not caused by finite minds. Our minds acknowledge these truths, but we did not cause them. These truths are not caused by changing contingent circumstances, since dependent things cannot cause independent realities. Truths are ideas, and ideas come from minds; therefore, there must be an absolute Mind - God. Whenever anyone affirms truth, that person is implicitly affirming the existence of Truth (God).[32]

Absolute truth exists only outside of our finite understanding and is established by an infinite, absolute mind. Remember Jesus' words, "I have come into the world to testify of the truth. Everyone who is of the truth hears my voice" (John 18:37). The Bible clearly states that the natural mind is hostile toward God, unwilling to subject itself to God's laws (Romans 8:7). Jesus strongly encouraged His followers that they were to take great care in negotiating the tension of being *in* the world without being of the world's system. In other words, the intentional Christian does not allow worldly trends or social fads to dictate his or her identity, message (proclamation of truth), or sense of mission.

## Bumping Up Against Reality

The majority of U.S. adults claim that truth is subjective and bound to the individual's taste. More than half of respondents participating in the State of Theology survey said that religious belief is not about objective reality. Over fifty-four percent of the people surveyed agreed that religious belief is a matter of *personal opinion*, not about objective truth.[33] Shocking as it may sound, more and more Americans are denying the existence of absolute values and truth claims.

Life has a way of placing boundaries on us that are physically real and objectively limiting. Reality is the nature of the world or the state of things as they actually exist, regardless of one's preferences or personal opinions. As Abraham Kuyper, former Prime Minister of Holland, wrote, "All created life necessarily bears in itself a law for its existence, instituted by God Himself.[34]

A baby finds out very quickly that the bars in their cribs are very real when they bump their head up against them while trying to climb out of the enclosure. And as teenagers quickly discover, crashing your dad's car into a tree or telephone pole can hurt very much, including increasing the insurance premium and shutting down one's driving privileges. Sooner or later the hard realities of the truths that govern our physical world come tumbling down on us if we violate them.

Bumping up against God's established physical and moral boundaries is unavoidable. Truth does not diminish when challenged, it is strengthened and becomes more evident.[35] This statement made by a professional writer sums it up, "Truth is eternal, and its conflict with error will only manifest its strength." It has been said that God's truth serves like the *concrete curbs* placed along streets to restrain automobiles from running off the road. We all can imagine what happens when moving vehicles leave the road and speed along city sidewalks bringing physical harm to people walking there. That is exactly what happens when people violate God's truth: there are dangerous effects and damaged lives. These examples all illustrate the critical lessons people must learn if they expect to live responsibly in God's world. The reason the scientific method is so reliable is that we live in a law-governed universe, not a universe that operates on random and changing laws.

A biblical view of truth gives us two important principles:

1. The intelligible order of the universe reflects a supreme intellect (God).

2. Our minds, made in the image of God, are specifically designed to study and understand the world that God has made.[36]

Theologian Alvin Plantinga wrote, "God created both us and our world in such a way that there is a certain fit or match between the world and our cognitive faculties."[37] This is what the majority of average people would consider "common sense." In a post-truth world, a person's sincerity or feelings can be deemed more important than factual content. It is mind-numbing to witness how so many skeptics and post-moderns claim to have found their own truth... and exhort others to discover *their own truth* as well.

Oprah Winfrey is a modern-day example of this phenomenon. In her 2018 Golden Globe Award acceptance speech, Oprah said, *"What I know for sure is that speaking your truth is the most powerful tool we all have."* Oprah's expression of *your truth* means that one's personal perception of reality can be fluid and change from one person's perspective to the next.[38] The message is clear... you can discover and craft your own truth to suit yourself. For the autonomous person, any random philosophy or ideology that liberates the person from accountability or moral obligation will do just fine. You cannot live in God's world and continually violate God's reality. Moral absolutes are binding regardless of a person's heartfelt sincerity to the contrary.

CHAPTER ONE

**Tripping Over Truth**

  Winston Churchill spoke of the immutable nature that truth possesses and the fact that we have to deal with it, "The truth is incontrovertible, malice may attack it, ignorance may deride it, but in the end; there it is." Truth is like that incessant ringing phone that declares, "Someone is trying to get your attention!" However, if secular educators and political progressives have their say in the matter, moral relativism, and post-truthism will maintain a stranglehold on absolute truth claims. These politically correct words, *choice, tolerance, and diversity,* have been weaponized by our secular culture to cancel out, or to whip into submission all competing opinions. The demonization of anybody labeled as *being intolerant* has worked well to silence most dissenting voices.

  The Apostle Paul taught that God's law is written on our hearts and our consciences bear witness to the law (Romans 2:14-15). Many people are convicted by their own conscience but are good at suppressing the truth by their unrighteous behavior (Romans 1:18). The problem is not the lack of evidence about the truth, it is the willful suppression of that truth.

  The majority of the people you meet are not on a *truth* quest, they are on a *happiness* quest. That is the reason why people try to suppress the truth, in most cases it interrupts their pursuit of pleasure. True fulfillment and happiness are not found in possessions and achievements but in knowing God and knowing the purpose for which He has made us. When we fail to see reality accurately, we begin to wander around in a wilderness of our illusions, trying to hide from ourselves and God.

  William Blackstone, a renowned eighteenth-century English jurist, who also served as an Oxford legal scholar, greatly influenced the legal framework of the American colonies and the writing of the Declaration of Independence. Blackstone asserted that there is a *higher law* than man's law. Therefore, human rights, laws, and freedoms are meaningless without their divine origin. Blackstone believed in a personal omnipotent God who is active in the affairs of men and human government. Consequently, men are bound by these common laws which are based on a system of absolutes being derived from God.[39]

25

Fallen human nature is well suited for making excuses and living in denial. The Postmodernist who tries to escape from the domain of natural law (written on their hearts) find themselves in a dilemma. In one instance they want to be free from God and moral law; and on the other, they still project moral obligations to others around them. By wanting autonomy from God, they realize objective morals are impossible. As people made in God's image and living in a fallen world, we realize objective moral truths are inescapable.[40]

## Rationalizing Immorality

I once heard a Bible teacher speaking about the issues that produce a person's theological and moral worldview. He said, "A man's morality will dictate *his philosophy*, and *his theology* of life, not the other way around." In other words, people will strongly resist arguments that unsettle their personal beliefs or demand a change in their values or lifestyle. For instance, an alcoholic who enjoys getting drunk may hate the homosexual and the thief, but his god doesn't mind if he has a few drinks to cheer up the boys down at the club. The homosexual may disdain drunkenness and abhor stealing, but since he is convinced that he *was born gay*, certainly his God understands and condones his lifestyle choice as being biologically determined and therefore natural.

Meanwhile, the thief may condemn the alcoholic and the homosexual both for their sinful, destructive behavior. However, the god he believes in is forgiving and understands that he got fired from his job for no fault of his own. He's a victim of circumstances, times are tough right now. Besides, the person whom he stole from is wealthy and won't even miss the money. Finally, in their own subjective cases, all three people can be exempted from their offenses and rationalize their sins away. After all, the alcoholic, the homosexual, and the thief are just complex bio-chemical machines that are the products of a random, mindless universe. As Richard Dawkins would remind us, they are just "dancing to the beat of their DNA" and consequently, are not responsible for their dysfunctional, antisocial behavior.[41] An individual's morality will always inform and shape their theology!

Equally enticing to the secular mind, Darwinian evolution provides the perfect worldview to justify any sin or deviant activity. Like finding a pair of comfortable gloves to fit one's hands, people look at their own ethical situation, rather than change their deviant behavior. They select a particular worldview that best fits, and excuse their moral failures. According to Alex McLellan of CRU Ministries, "When moral obstacles stand in the way of believing in Jesus, no reason to believe will ever be good enough." Sometimes people tailor their beliefs and behavior to fit the evidence. Other times people tailor the evidence to fit their beliefs and behavior.[42] Paul's warning to the church at Ephesus is relevant for us today:

> So this I say, and affirm together with the Lord, that you walk no longer just as the Gentiles also walk, in the futility of their mind, being darkened in their understanding, excluded from the life of God because of the ignorance that is in them, because of the hardness of their heart; and they, having become callous, have given themselves over to sensuality (Ephesians 4:17-19).

Nancy Pearcey describes in her book, *Love Thy Body*, the severe damage being done to those who deny their biologically determined sex. Pearcey points out, this sense of mismatching between physical sex and psychological gender is called *gender dysphoria*. Many people assume that there must be some hormonal malfunction or psychological trauma that is responsible for this gender confusion. As of yet, there is no clear medical evidence to support that assumption. Oddly enough, the advocates of transgender rights argue the exact opposite. They deny that gender identity is rooted in or determined by biology. "The implication is that the physical body does not matter. Their argument is that gender is completely independent of the body and based on feelings alone."[43]

Lesslie Newbigin accurately identifies this moral disconnect as a perversion of biological truth and destructive to the individual. *"We are by nature idolaters constructing images of truth shaped by our own desires."* In the heart of every secular person, there is an absolute commitment to self-justification. It is as though making excuses is the default position of the human soul. No matter how arrogant and self-sufficient humanity can get, most people, when they get honest with themselves, have some sense of their own inadequacies and lack of ethical behavior. According to Blaise Pascal, *"Humans are a strange and freakish mixture of greatness and wretchedness."*[44]

Nazi military leader Reinhard Heydrich is a prime example of this moral dissonance. Heydrich was the mastermind behind the *Final Solution* (the Third Reich's planned extermination of the Jews from Europe). Heydrich was highly educated and cultured. He loved the classical music of Bach, Wagner, and Beethoven. Yet, Reinhard Heydrich demonstrated the capacity for both sophisticated brilliance and unspeakable evil by advocating the systematic killing of millions of people just because of their race.[45]

The average person at the coffee shop or the college campus usually dismisses his or her ethical flaws by comparing themselves to more heinous figures of history like Adolf Hitler, Charles Manson, or Osama bin Laden. In comparison, most people appear angelic compared to these notoriously wicked figures of history. Secular man tries to rationalize his sin by reducing it to just another harmless blemish of *human nature.* God's truth is what ultimately convicts humanity, exposing our depraved nature and sinfulness, "Every man's way is right in his own eyes, but the LORD weighs the hearts" (Proverbs 21:2). The Scriptures and Christian history acknowledge that all people are made in the image of God and innately have a basic sense of right and wrong.

## Moving the Goal Posts

What eventually happens to any society that refuses to accept fixed moral anchors? G. K. Chesterton nailed it when he commented about an ever-changing moral standard, "The terrible danger in the heart of our society is that the tests are giving way. We are altering, not the evils, but the standards of good by which alone evils can be detected and defined."[46]

Centuries before Chesterton's moral analysis, the Bible foretold the same development. "Woe to those who call evil good, and good evil;

who substitute darkness for light and light for darkness; who substitute bitter for sweet and sweet for bitter" (Isaiah 5:20). Without understanding our need for a transcendent fixed point, and acknowledging our true moral condition, our world will continue to grope hopelessly in search of stability, healing, and purpose.

Scripture reminds us that sin, by its nature, poses self-justifying excuses that try to appease our guilt, "This is the way of an adulterous woman: She eats and wipes her mouth and says, 'I have done no wrong'" (Proverbs 30:20). Just like the adulteress, the relativists reasons, if there are no objective moral duties, I have done nothing wrong! No law, no violation, no guilt! Relativism is a convenient way of acquitting ourselves of guilt and shame. Our natural moral sense, the human conscience, along with the Holy Spirit tell us we fall short in our attempts to live morally. Rather than accepting our bent towards sin and finding our way to the foot of the cross to seek repentance and forgiveness, many times we try to rationalize our fallen behavior. The reason people avoid the truth is that they want to ultimately avoid any accountability to God.

In his book, *Degenerate Moderns*, E. Michael Jones analyzes many of the deviant sexual activities studied and promoted by such secular academics as Sigmund Freud, Margret Mead, and Alfred Kinsey. All three were looking specifically for a psychological rationale to accept and normalize sexual deviance. Jones concluded, "Relativism in this context is very appealing to secular society because it allows embracing certain sexual practices that Judeo-Christian ethics find evil and morally wrong. Relativism gives license to people to accept deviant sexual behavior while rejecting Christian moral standards as passe."[47]

## Self-Defeating Statements

Several years ago, a church in Hawaii had invited me to speak and to do some evangelism training on the campus with a group of students. The University of Hawaii is a notorious "party school" located just minutes away from the world-famous Waikiki Beach and downtown Honolulu.

Standing on a park bench, the campus leader handed me the microphone and I began speaking to a group of students who had gathered around eating their lunches and chatting with one another. I addressed the crowd about living under God's moral standard as recorded in the Ten Commandments. I then spoke of my personal testimony of how God delivered me out of my sinful and selfish lifestyle. As I spoke about God's absolute standard of right and wrong found in the Bible, immediately a student stood up and shouted at the top of his lungs, "There is no such thing as absolute truth!" He was so loud that his voice reverberated throughout the entire quad. This got the attention of everyone within earshot. After an awkward moment of complete silence, all eyes turned toward me to see how I would respond to this thunderous objection. I then directed a question back at the student, "Is your assertion... 'There is no such thing as truth,' a true statement?" The guy, whom I later discovered was a graduate student in philosophy, said confidently, "Yes, *I believe it is true.*"

I then pointed out to this philosophy student that because he was asserting a *truth proposition* that he had just contradicted himself. He looked at me and said, "What do you mean?" I explained to him, "It is like a person saying, 'A circle has three sides' or 'I can't speak a word of English.'" Strangely enough, they had just spoken seven words of English... while trying to assert that they *can't speak any English.* Such statements are nonsensical and logically absurd. Whenever people say things like, "You can't know the truth." I ask them, *"How do you know that?"* To make an absolute negative statement... you are admitting that you possess some *knowledge* about the subject you are negating.

These kinds of statements violate the rules of logic and rational thought and therefore cannot be true. Today objective truth is under siege by relativistic, postmodern culture. Rather than being a fixed constant, truth has been subjected to the individuals' feelings and whims. In some cases, truth has been rendered fluid and unknowable!

## If It's Legal... It Must Be Moral

After the Second World War, at the Nuremberg War Crimes Trial in 1945, some 200 German war crime defendants were tried for *crimes against humanity.* All of the Nazi officers accused of crimes argued that they had broken no laws. Germany's own legal system, they argued, allowed the elimination of those who resisted the progress of the Third Reich. Adolph Eichmann, charged with managing and facilitating the mass deportation of Jews to ghettos and killing centers in the German-occupied East, was among the major organizers of the Jewish Holocaust.

Eichmann protested before the court, "I had to obey the laws of war and of my flag." Robert H. Jackson, chief counsel for the United States in the Nuremberg Trials, appealed to a transcendent, permanent law that supersedes all man-made societal laws. Jackson rightly argued that there is a "law above the law" that stood in judgment of the arbitrary changing opinions of men.[48] Accordingly, all the German officers were found guilty of human rights violations. If there is no absolute moral standard beyond human ideas, then there is no final appeal to judge between individuals or cultures whose values and actions conflict. Absolutes provide humanity with a final and ultimate standard providing a fixed point from which to judge right from wrong and justice from injustice.

The prophet Samuel records Israel's moral confusion, "In those days there was no king in Israel; everyone did what was right in his own eyes" (Judges 21:25). Sadly, our society is quickly approaching ancient Israel's immoral, chaotic condition. The exact same day I sat down to work on this chapter, a Twitter notice popped up on my smartphone. The timing of this interruption was ironic. I hit the notice that linked me to a story. In Ottawa, Canada, the parents of a six-year-old girl who was upset after her teacher told her class, "There is no such thing as boys and girls," have filed a human rights complaint against the Ottawa-Carleton District School Board, alleging the teacher discriminated by creating a "poisoned environment."

The child's mother, Pamela Buffone, told a reporter in the story published in the _Post Millennial_ that her daughter became increasingly distressed after her teacher showed the class a video, "He, She and They?!? - Gender Queer Kid Stuff #2" to her six-year-old daughter in Jan. 2018.[49] Ms. Buffone should be disturbed with this kind of convoluted indoctrination being pushed onto small children by public school boards and teachers' unions.

The Book of Proverbs offers us some simple yet profound wisdom for our situation, "There is a way that seems right to a man, but its end is the way of death" (Proverbs 14:12). Contemporary society must decide to recognize truth claims. It must decide if reality is contingent on a person's preferences... or if truth exists outside of and independent of one's particular wishes. We have two paths set before us:

1. Conform our soul to objective reality or...

2. Attempt to subdue reality to meet our subjective desires.[50]

Jesus announced to Pilate that He came specifically to bear witness of the truth (John 18:37). The writer of the Psalms declared, "The entirety of your word is truth, and every one of your righteous judgements is everlasting" (Psalm 119:160 NKJV).

# CHAPTER TWO

# Secularizing Knowledge

"I think religion should be treated with ridicule, hatred, and contempt."

-Christopher Hitchens

The Cambridge English Dictionary defines secularism as (1) the belief that religion should not be involved with the ordinary social and political activities of a country. The term has also been used since the 1850s in a pragmatic and philosophical sense to refer to (2) a self-reliant humanism invoking the exclusion of belief in God from matters of ethics and morality.[51] Secularism puts its trust in this life, setting happiness, worldly status, and pleasure as its primary concerns. In ancient times, the Greek philosopher Protagoras (485-410 B.C.) taught that "Man is the measure of all things." Unfortunately, Protagoras never told us which particular man he was referring to.

## Public and Private Matters

Why is this understanding of the word *secular* so important? Secularism is an attempt to shift the traditional role of religion away from the jurisdiction and place in government it has long occupied. D.A. Carson describes *secularization* as follows:

> The process progressively removes religion from the public arena and reduces it to the private realm; secularism is the stance that endorses and promotes such a process. Religion may be ever so important to the individual, and few secular persons will object. But if religion makes any claims regarding policy in the public arena, it is viewed as a threat, and intolerant as well.[52]

Richard Dawkins holds the distinction of being one of the world's most famous atheists and also one of the world's most renowned evolutionists. His stated goal is to "kill religion."[53] He claims that "Faith is one of the world's greatest evils, comparable to the smallpox virus but harder to eradicate."[54] Make no mistake about it, Christianity is under real assault by secularists who label Christian beliefs as delusional and even dangerous.

Today's secular progressives and social media pundits have labeled individuals and organizations that champion their secular narratives as compassionate, tolerant, and inclusive. Who wouldn't appreciate such titles associated with their name? The flip side of that coin is that if you dare to voice a different opinion from the secular consensus, you will be immediately stigmatized as bigoted, hateful, and narrow-minded. So much for being tolerant of alternate opinions! The Apostle Paul wrote to the church at Rome, "And do not be conformed to this world, but be transformed by the renewing of your mind, so that you may prove what the will of God is, that which is good and acceptable and perfect" (Romans 12:2).

Many historic Christian beliefs and practices, that were once commonplace in society, are considered extreme by a growing number of Americans. For example, among non-Christians, two out of five adults believe it is extreme to try and convert others to their faith. Sixty percent of all adults in America and eighty-three percent of agnostics and atheists believe that evangelism, one of the central commands of Christian activity, is an extremist activity.[55]

## The Secular Assault

With secularism and pluralism growing steadily in America, there seems to be no reversal of this trend in sight. According to social researchers David Kinnaman and Gabe Lyons, four out of five Americans agree with this statement, "US society is becoming more secular, meaning more likely to exclude faith and religion from public life."[56] To help clarify this secular drift it is important to recognize that Millennials, (people born between 1981-1996), and Gen Z-ers, (people born between 1995-2015), are increasingly rejecting religious faith. This has opened up a whole new demographic category, Americans without a religious affiliation (which includes "nothing particular," agnostic, and atheist), sometimes referred to as "Nones."[57]

Not only is Christianity facing challenges from within its walls, but it is also facing threats from the public arena as well. Writing for the liberal magazine *The American Prospect*, former U.S. Secretary of Labor Robert Reich expressed what he saw as the greatest conflict facing Americans in the twenty-first century. Reich did not say this great conflict would be racially based, like white versus brown or black. He did not say it would be politically based, like Democrat versus Republican. Reich did not think it would be gender-based, like male versus female either. Reich stated that the greatest conflict facing America in the twenty-first century is between those who believe in *science and reason* versus those who believe in *truth revealed through Scripture*. Secretary Reich went on to state specifically:

> The great conflict of the 21st century will not be between the West and terrorism. Terrorism is a tactic, not a belief. The true battle will be between modern civilization and anti-modernists; between those who believe in the primacy of the individual and those who believe that human beings owe their allegiance and identity to a higher authority; between those who give priority to life in this world and those who believe that human life is mere preparation for an existence beyond life; between those who believe in science, reason, and logic and those who believe that truth is revealed through Scripture and religious dogma. Terrorism will disrupt and destroy lives. But terrorism itself is not the greatest danger we face.[58]

Without question, there is a dangerous conflict going on between secular ideology and the Christian religion. Where I would disagree with former Secretary Reich, is on which side he consideres to be more dangerous. Reich's attempt at name-calling and labeling sincere Bible believers as being duped by religious dogma is highly insulting and false. Christians cannot idly sit back and allow the world system to bully them into silence.

What happens when there is a conflict between an individual's secular reasoning and another person's moral convictions? When my truth clashes with your truth, whose truth wins? In ecclesiastical writing, the word *secular* is used in much the same way as the Greek word *aion*, or *kosmos*, meaning "of this world." As we reference the book of Romans again, we see Paul exhorting believers "not to be conformed to this world" (Romans 12:1). The Christian worldview acknowledges that this mortal life is temporal, that the pursuit of truth and bringing glory to God, are man's highest and noblest endeavors in this life. Every person will be held accountable for his or her decisions made in this life, facing the consequences of their choices eternally. John's writing in Scripture bears this out:

> Do not love the world nor the things in the world. If anyone loves the world, the love of the Father is not in him. For all that is in the world, the lust of the flesh and the lust of the eyes and the boastful pride of life is not from the Father but is from the world. The world is passing away, and also its lusts; but the one who does the will of God continues to live forever (1 John 2:15-17).

The Church frequently fails to teach people the reasons why we believe the Christian faith is valid. Laying the foundation for supporting truth claims is essential for every serious Christian believer. Many times, ministry leaders don't prepare their young people to intellectually engage with secular ideas at school or in society. The current need for Christians to become conversant with culture is urgent.

## Secularism and the Enlightenment

Liberal theologians early in the twentieth century began accommodating a man-centered worldview that drifted from its Christian heritage. This shift has often been traced back to the Enlightenment period, beginning in the 1700s, when rational thought was pitted against external authorities, primarily the Bible. Enlightenment thinkers tried to elevate human reason to the same level as Holy Scripture.

Enlightenment philosophy eventually anointed human rationality as being the supreme arbiter determining what is objectively true. Religious faith has been slowly locked away into the private domain of an individual's personal life. Empirical testing became the preferred vehicle to elevate human reason and science above religious faith. Eventually, it was believed that human reason, with the aid of science, would triumph over antiquated religious superstitions and myths.[59]

The fundamental question of ethics is, who gets to make the rules? This question can be reduced down to the answer: either God or the state. "The Enlightenment enthroned science, along with rationalistic man, as the sole source of genuine knowledge."[60] This shift tended to the acceptance and endorsement of the power of human reasoning as man's rationale, and not the Bible as the primary source of truth about life, morals, and the physical world. People sought to understand the natural world and humanity's place in it exclusively based on human reason, without consulting religious belief.

Before the Enlightenment, for fifteen hundred years much of the educated western world had looked to Scripture to answer life's questions about origins, meaning, ethics, and the afterlife. Then came along French mathematician and philosopher René Descartes (1596-1650). Descartes wanted to prove that all human knowledge could be placed on a secure foundation. Descartes realized that many of his beliefs were based on sense knowledge or perception. He acknowledged that his senses could often mislead him. Reviewing his own beliefs, he found them jumbled and unable to justify them as objectively real. So, Descartes began to reject all perceptual knowledge (empirical data). He adopted a radical skepticism, calling into question everything he could not prove beyond any doubt.[61] Suddenly, each person believed they could become their own judge, free to determine what was true or false or what was real or unreal based on their subjective perception.

## Education: The Secular Savior

As we continue our quest for truth and certainty, we need to remind ourselves why America's constitution and laws are exceptional among all the nations of the world. We will begin by looking at how secular ideas deteriorate Judeo-Christian values and freedoms. Our Founding Fathers designed the U.S. Constitution to protect the right of all American citizens to exercise religious freedom and pursue religious expression. As the First Amendment clearly states, "Congress shall make no law respecting an establishment of religion, or prohibiting the free exercise thereof."[62] Unfortunately, in the name of separation of Church and State, the courts have ruled in favor of restricting religious expression in public.

In the past sixty years, the Supreme Court has issued a host of decisions pressing for the secularization of America's public schools. The Supreme Court's rulings banned school prayer in 1962. One year later, the public reading of the Bible was also banned from U.S. public schools. In 1980, it became unconstitutional for students to even "see" the Ten Commandments at school since they might read, meditate upon, or perhaps venerate and obey them.[63]

Princeton professor and political philosopher, Robert George argues that over the last several years, secular progressivism has become the dominant state religion. According to George, "The underlying faith of this secularism is the sexual revolution, and its first commandment is that no sexual act between consenting adults is wrong." One needs to look no further than the public attack being leveled against traditional Christian values. "A fire chief in Atlanta was fired for self-publishing a Bible study book for men which included his belief that marriage should be between one man and one woman."

- The City of Houston issued subpoenas ordering specific pastors to turn over any sermons mentioning homosexuality or gender identity.

- Military chaplains have been forced out of the U.S. Department of Veterans Affairs for quoting Scripture and praying in Jesus' name.

- Intervarsity Christian Fellowship was banned from Wayne State University for requiring its leaders to be professing Christians.[64]

The framers of the Declaration of Independence wrote its preamble to unequivocally declare the origin of all human rights, "We hold these truths to be self-evident, that all men are created equal, that they are endowed by their Creator with certain unalienable rights, that among these are Life, Liberty and the pursuit of Happiness." Human rights come from God alone and are not derived originally from the state. In contrast, in the modern humanistic understanding, a citizen is reduced to being a "ward of the state." The right of citizenship is taken away from the individual and given to the state as if it were all-powerful. Consequently, if the state is the one who gives citizens their rights, then it can arbitrarily take away their rights, should it so desire.

The Supreme Court, with the appearance of *judicial neutrality*, greatly reduced Christianity's moral influence in America's public schools. Expelling God and the Bible from the public school created a vacuum that humanistic educators and social progressives quickly filled.

To arrive at this secular consensus, two things would be necessary:

1. Use public education to indoctrinate future generations of youth with a secular worldview.

2. Get rid of all competing ideologies by eliminating any dissenting voices.

To accomplish this, social engineers, academic progressives, and teachers' unions would need to *silence or marginalize* any detractors. Secular educators quickly identified Christianity, with its absolute moral standards, as the main obstacle preventing them from achieving their educational goals.

## The Christian Roots of Higher Education

Since the nineteenth and into the twentieth century, the *McGuffey Readers* were some of America's most popular textbooks. The McGuffey Readers were originally published in 1836. In the foreword it reads:

> The Christian religion is the religion of our country. From it or derived are prevalent notions of the character of God, the great moral governor of the universe. On its doctrines are founded the peculiarities of our free institutions. The Ten Commandments and the teachings of Jesus are not only basic but plenary.[65]

The 1636 rules of Harvard University stated:

Let every student be plainly instructed and earnestly pressed to consider the main end-of-life studies to know God and Jesus Christ which is eternal life (John 17:3) and therefore to lay Christ at the bottom as the only foundation of all sound knowledge and learning.[66]

Placing Christ as the base of education ensures that all learning is founded on the transcendent, eternal God who is the source of truth established in His creation. John Gresham Machen, Princeton Seminary Professor and founder of Westminster Seminary in Philadelphia, stated it clearly, "If liberty is not maintained regarding education, there is no use in trying to maintain it in any other sphere. If you give the bureaucrats the children, you might as well give them everything else."[67] How prophetic Machen proved to be by predicting what would be happening in modern-day America.

The idea of secularization was enacted in the name of improving higher education and exposing students to a "values-free" education that would promote dignity and awareness of other societies. John Dewey, one of the reformers of education in the twentieth century, has been called the Father of Progressive Education. Without question, his liberal ideology has affected every aspect of American public education. Dewey was firmly set against any form of supernaturalism in religion.

Dewey had turned away from the evangelical Christianity of his childhood and embraced Darwinian evolution. Since most religions pay homage to the supernatural, he was opposed to religion in general. Dewey proved to be a key figure in the Humanist movement. Dewey saw secularism as coming of age in the twentieth century. He went on to write, "The hold of these secular interests upon the thoughts and desires of men, will eventually crowd out the social importance of organized religion, driving religion to an ever-decreasing corner."[68] In other words, with the indoctrination of our youth through secular education, humanism would successfully diminish religious influences in public schools and push organized religion to the outskirts of society.

However, "American Christians exist in a republic in which the free exercise of religious convictions is *guaranteed* [emphasis added] by the Constitution, not as a government grant, but as a natural right."[69] Americans have the full freedom to express and publicly practice their religious beliefs. The first amendment was not put in place to prevent state support for religious adherents, but "to ensure that there would never be a state-sanctioned religion [in America] like the Church of England back in Great Britain."

Historian Christopher Dawson also warned of the growing segregation between secularized civilization and Christianity:

> Religion gradually retreated into man's inner life and left social and economic life to a civilization that grew steadily more secularized. A man's debt to religion was paid by an hour or two in church on Sundays, and the rest of the week was devoted to the real business of life... The new secularized civilization is not content to dominate the outer world and leave man's inner life to religion; it claims the whole man. Once more Christianity is faced, as it was at the beginning, with the challenge of a world which will accept no appeal from its judgment and recognizes no higher power than its own will.[70]

Even though Dawson wrote this article almost 90 years ago, this should be a major concern for present-day Christians. Such a dualism between the physical and the spiritual has produced compartmentalization in western thinking. The secular and sacred came to be seen as divided, distorting the understanding of one's worldly vocation as being strictly public.[71]

Coupled with the acceptance of Darwinian Evolution, this secular dichotomy gained the upper hand in public schools and institutions of higher learning. Secular ideology appeared to eliminate any need for an overarching moral lawgiver (God), who should be revered and obeyed in public life. People who were weary of religious dogma perceived as socially restrictive, now served a new savior, the savior of human reasoning and personal autonomy. They declared humanity emancipated from the laws of God. People could now stop feeling guilty and set a new course, using secular education as their springboard. Finally, autonomous man could be truly liberated to become the master of his own destiny. The resulting secular worldview left little place for the supernatural. Just as John Dewey had predicted, humanistic ideology began to undercut the significance of religion and belief in God, reducing the role of each in public life. The tendency has been to reduce Christian morals to the realm of personal feelings.[72]

Dr. Mary Polin, professor, and speaker with the Veritas Forum describes the ideology of secular humanism. "The defining tenet of secular humanism is the belief that human reason is sufficiently reliable and just to guide the course of our lives, individually and collectively, without any consideration of the divine authority."[73]

While many Christians are unaware of the secular revolution taking place in public schools, an organized group of secularists are strategically infiltrating schools across America. *The Humanist Magazine* boldly proclaimed its intentions, "The battle for humanity's future must be waged and won in the public school classroom by teachers who correctly perceive their role as proselytizers of a new faith: a religion of humanity."[74] Woe to anyone who expresses an opposing view to this secular narrative. They will be quickly categorized as narrow-minded fundamentalists whose ideas are dangerous and should be censored from the public.

Two students at a high school in Virginia were forbidden from singing a Celine Dion song that mentions "God" at their graduation ceremony. Besides mentioning the "G-word" once, the song contains the phrase, "Lead us to a place, guide us with your grace. Give us your grace and we'll be safe." According to the attorney at the school district, mentioning God and the offending phrase, breaches the separation of church and state clause.[75]

**Ideas Have Consequences**

The Pew Research Center in 2016 reported approximately half (49%) of the current *Nones* (people who identify as atheist, agnostic, or no religion at all) who were raised in religious homes, indicated that a lack of belief led them away from religion. Many respondents mentioned "science" as a reason they no longer believe in religious teachings.[76] Fredrich Nietzsche was a German philosopher and a strong advocate for Darwin's Theory of Evolution. He became infamous for coining the phrase, "God is Dead." Nietzsche also wrote, *Beyond Good and Evil*, a work that supported classic atheism while validating the survival of the fittest mentality in society. According to Nietzsche's worldview, all Christian virtues like charity, self-denial, and self-sacrifices, were seen as *signs of weakness*. He continued to support his belief in the base animalistic impulses of a man like the use of force, slavery, tyranny, and murder.

Nietzsche's infamous theory of "The Will to Power" regarded the drive for self-preservation and domination as the cardinal instinct of all organic beings. Nietzsche also believed that human evolution and selective breeding (eugenics) would eventually produce a race of *Übermensch* (supermen). Nietzsche's writings strongly influenced Adolf Hitler and Nazi Germany to push for a "Master Race." During World War II, Hitler popularized his belief in racial purity, by promoting the superiority of the Germanic race. Accordingly, this Aryan breed "master race" must be genetically pure to achieve domination over the inferior races. Hitler's quest to develop a master race demanded that he had to eliminate the weak, feeble-minded, physically disabled, and the genetically inferior.

Nietzsche accurately explains the atheist's dilemma this way:

> When one gives up Christian faith, one pulls the right to Christian morality out from under one's feet. This morality is by no means self-evident. Christianity is a system, a whole view of things thought out together. By breaking one main concept out of it, the faith in God, one breaks the whole. It stands or falls with faith in God.[77]

Nietzsche believed that because morality was an illusion, man needed to look past concepts like good and evil.[78] Nietzsche's claim that "God is Dead" was more figurative than literal. The famous "death of God" is simply the modern assertion that Naturalism is true and that human beings must create their moral standards rather than take them from some antiquated mythical revelation.[79] The main points that Nietzsche's naturalism makes are:

1. The idea of a God interferes with human autonomy.

2. Any concept of a God who judges humanity is offensive and frustrates human progress and happiness.

These are extremely important concepts to understand. As Christians, we need to expose the enemy's schemes (2 Corinthians 2:11). Individual autonomy frees humanity from any accountability or judgment. Naturalism has no one higher to whom to answer. Self-expression becomes the primary aim of human existence. Right and wrong become *whatever* a person feels they are. Individual autonomy and self-deification are the main attractions that draw multitudes to embrace secular worldviews.[80]

## Freedom of Religion

There is one problem with the secular progressive agenda, which is well-known by legal experts and students of constitutional law. The constitution guarantees Americans' freedom of religion, *not freedom from it!* This foundation of religious freedom is unique to the nation of the United States of America. The secular progressive ideal might have been that public institutions should not mix private faith with public life, however, virtuous, God-fearing people, while involved in public education and civic functions, have made great contributions to society throughout history.

Unfortunately, via the public education system today, young Americans are being indoctrinated that it is their personal right to pursue life and happiness based on and defined by their autonomy. Children in public schools and institutions are now taught that all ideas and morals, from gender dysphoria to satanism, are equal if they are *sincerely* held.

The secular agenda is to silence and replace any Christian voice. You may keep your private faith and your Sunday morning meetings, but don't you dare venture into the public square with your beliefs. Philosopher J.P. Moreland describes the secular sentiment directed at Christian beliefs:

The church is safe from vicious persecution at the hands of the secularist, as educated people have finished with stake-burning circuses and torture racks. No martyr's blood is shed in the secular west. So long as the church knows her place and remains quietly at peace on her modern reservation. Let the babes pray and sing and read their Bibles, continuing steadfastly in their intellectual retardation; the church's extinction will not come by sword or pillory, but by the quiet death of irrelevance. But let the church step off the reservation, let her penetrate once more the culture of the day, and the… face of secularism will change from a benign smile to a savage snarl.[81]

Contrary to Scripture, most secularists believe that *human reason alone* is the key element in determining right or wrong. *The Humanist Manifesto II* defines ethical relativism as, "The belief that no absolute moral code exists, and therefore man must adjust his ethical standards in each situation according to his judgment."[82] Unfortunately, we see this dismissal of decency and moral responsibility destroying our nation and ravaging people's lives under the guise of personal freedom and individual choice.

Those who choose not to believe in God no longer want to be reminded that others still do. If only getting rid of moral obligations would be that simple! This clash between autonomous man and God's transcendent moral truth shows up everywhere. Whether the culture acknowledges it or not, without a transcendent anchor (fixed point) there cannot be an absolute standard available for people from which to establish immutable rights such as liberty and human freedom. If we are going to preserve a future for religious liberty, or for that matter for individual liberty at all, we must remember why many of the first European immigrants came to America, and why this country's citizenship was established on certain *inalienable rights* (unchanging truths).

Secularism asserts the *autonomous self* as the only judge of truth.[83] Conversely, secularism rejects God's moral laws like the Ten Commandments for two primary reasons:

1. If they are adhered to: individuals must place themselves in obedience to an objective outside authority.

2. They are repressive to basic desires and suppress a person's individualism and human liberties.[84]

Perhaps no one has given a better explanation for their reasons to reject Judeo-Christian morality than the grandson of the famous Thomas Huxley. The elder Huxley is probably best known today for his debate with the Anglican Bishop of Oxford, Samuel Wilberforce. Thomas Huxley became known as "Darwin's Bulldog." His grandson, Aldous Huxley was an author, philosopher, and social critic. He voiced his reasons for wanting God out of the picture. Huxley explains it was for *personal reasons* that he was at war with conventional morality:

> For myself, as, no doubt, for most of my contemporaries, the philosophy of meaninglessness was essentially an instrument of liberation. The liberation we desired was simultaneously liberation from a certain political and economic system and liberation from a certain system of morality. We objected to morality because it interfered with our sexual freedom... There was one admirably simple method of confuting these people and justifying ourselves in our erotic revolt: we would deny that the world had any meaning whatever.[85]

The message is crystal clear. "We don't want a God interfering with our sexual behavior or moral decisions!" Humanism declared the Ten Commandments to be obsolete and part of a religion for losers.[86]

## Exposing Our True Nature

When looking at the facts of life, we all have *filters* that we use to process information. These so-called filters or lenses are how we see, analyze and make sense of things in our world. This filter informs our *worldview*. There are four vital questions that every worldview must

46

answer. These questions point to four categories that all people have to grapple with: *Creation, Meaning, Morality*, and *Destiny*:

- Creation: Where did I come from?
- The Fall: What has gone wrong with the world?
- Redemption: How do I fix it?
- Destiny: What happens to me when I die?

The answers to these four questions vary significantly depending upon which worldview one holds. However, for the Christian, his worldview is the most satisfying and rational because it accurately answers all these questions based on Scripture and human experience. It provides the best structure that fits objective reality and enables people to live in harmony with that reality.[87] All human beings have got to live in God's created world. To do that we must affirm God's created reality.

**The Secular Humanist's Answer:** People and societies are *depraved* (morally corrupt) only because they have been *deprived* (missing education, nurturing, security, and opportunity). Accordingly, Man is viewed as being basically good and can be conditioned by his social environment. Once basic human physical and psychological needs are met, people will automatically become more noble, selfless, and civilized.

Accordingly, humanity will evolve and adapt to become more sophisticated and enlightened beings with the help of educational enlightenment and social engineering. Trusting in science and technology, humanity will eventually build its own utopian society, eliminating all poverty, disease, and war. Socio-biology will help humanity create a just society. Secular men won't need God-given morals to bring about justice, peace, and human flourishing. In this future utopia, people can be free to live their lives without any religious allegiance or interference.

Jean Meslier, a seventeenth-century French priest turned philosopher, also shifted the source of man's problems, blaming external social issues as the primary reason for humanity's condition: "Men are unhappy only because they are ignorant; they are ignorant only because everything conspires to prevent them from being enlightened, and they are wicked only because their reason is not sufficient."[88]

**The Biblical Answer:** The Bible teaches, that mankind was created in the image of God and was morally innocent but chose to disobey God and fell into a nature of depravity. "Therefore, just as sin entered the world through one man, and death through sin, and in this way, death came to all men, because all sinned" (Romans 5:12 NIV). After the fall of Adam and Eve into sin, humanity's true spiritual condition became one of moral corruption and wickedness (Genesis 3). Why did Adam disobey God? Simple, the reason is found in Genesis when the serpent was tempting Eve with the fruit, "your eyes will be opened, and you will be like God, knowing good and evil" (Genesis 3:5).

The Genesis account shows how defiance toward God has spawned selfishness and human depravity:

> The woman said to the serpent, "From the fruit of the trees of the garden we may eat; but from the fruit of the tree which is in the middle of the garden, God has said, 'You shall not eat from it or touch it, or you will die.'" The serpent said to the woman, "You surely will not die! For God knows that in the day you eat from it your eyes will be opened, and you will be like God, [emphasis added] knowing good and evil"(Genesis 3:2-5).

Because of the effects of Adam and Eve's sin, the original relationship with God was broken and man's entire nature was polluted by sin. Total Depravity and The Fall are theological terms that characterize our true moral status before a holy God. Total Depravity does not mean that an individual or humanity is generally as bad as it could be, but that every aspect of existence is affected by sin. As Scripture teaches, "... By the transgression of the one, death reigned through the one" (Romans 5:17). Because mankind fell into moral depravity, God had to destroy all of humanity, sparing only Noah and his immediate family, because of the spread of immorality, "Then the Lord saw that the wickedness of man was great on the earth and that every intent of the thoughts of his heart was only evil continually" (Genesis 6:5).

## Diagnosing the Root of the Problem

According to the secular worldview, mankind's problems are all *external*. If we can manipulate the environment, provide education, eliminate disease and poverty, with time humanity will adapt to overcome all societal problems. Following this line of reasoning, secular education along with social evolution will produce benevolent, self-actualized, civilized people.

According to the Christian worldview, mankind's problems are *internal.* Because of the Fall, man's primary nature has a propensity toward selfishness, sin, and depravity. The Book of Judges demonstrates what happens when a society's moral compass is broken, "In those days there was no king in Israel; everyone did what was right in his own eyes" (Judges 21:25). Both Scripture and world history confirm mankind's fallen nature. Left unchecked, human nature has a frightening tendency towards selfishness, oppression, evil, and mass destruction. As Malcolm Muggeridge observed, "The depravity of man is at once the most empirically verifiable reality but at the same time the most intellectually resisted fact."[89]

The Apostle Paul writing to the church at Ephesus records man's true condition apart from God:

> And you were dead in your trespasses and sins, in which you formerly walked according to the course of this world, according to the prince of the power of the air, of the spirit that is now working in the sons of disobedience. Among them we too all formerly lived in the lusts of our flesh, indulging the desires of the flesh and of the mind, and were by nature children of wrath, even as the rest (Ephesians 2:1-4).

I remember speaking at the University of Houston some years ago. About a dozen students from a Christian club were preparing to give their public testimonies at the campus free-speech area. After a few students took the microphone and told of their personal encounters with Jesus, it was not long before a large crowd started to gather and began to ask questions. The club leader asked me to field all questions having to do with theological objections to the Christian faith. After a few questions and answers with various students, a university professor walked up and began to shout, "People are good and don't need a god to help improve them!" She definitely got the crowd's attention.

I asked the professor why she thought people were basically good? She went on a long diatribe explaining how individuals are all born innocent and naturally good. She went on to say, "It is their environment that makes them bad. Give them a good education, housing, and jobs, and people will turn out good."

She explained, "If we can manipulate the environment, we can successfully fashion humanity." This is the standard sociological explanation used by most humanistic educators. I then asked this lady if she drove her car to campus. She said, "Yes." I asked her if she locked her car or not. She answered, "Of course, I locked it." I then asked, "Why would you lock your car with all these educated, basically good college students around?" I then asked the professor if she left her house unlocked when she drove to work that day. She again replied, "No, I locked it." I asked her why wouldn't she just leave her home unlocked, situated inside an upper-class, gated community with all her good neighbors. After a prolonged silence, with a blank look on her face, the university professor turned and walked away. At that point, students in the crowd started to giggle and snicker, seeing that real-life experiences in no way bear out that humanity is basically good.

This professor's statements about man's nature did not match reality. History and psychology give irrefutable proof of man's corrupt nature. Parent don't need to teach their children to lie, steal, cheat, or be selfish. They behave that way instinctively. Put two toddlers in a room with one toy and you will quickly see fallen human nature at work. Ironically, Hitler's Germany, which murdered over six million Jews, along with many handicapped and mentally impaired people, was the most highly educated country in the world during the 1940s. Education, if it does not instruct regarding what is true, is not the answer. If there is mass ignorance or denial of objective truth and absolute morality, then it becomes very difficult to navigate reality. Much of our world seems to be adrift in a sea of choices, openly embracing postmodernism and relativism. Because the current culture is either unable or unwilling to acknowledge transcendent truth, many have lost their moral compass and are unsure where to turn or how to behave.

James Madison, one of America's founding fathers, composed the first drafts of the U.S. Constitution and the Bill of Rights. Madison declared that human nature reflected by the government is "sinful." He did not view people as being inherently good and socially perfectible:

> If men were angels, no government would be necessary. If angels were to govern men, neither external nor internal controls on government would be necessary. In framing a government, which is to be administered by men over men, the great difficulty lies in this: You must first enable the government to control the governed, and in the next place oblige it to control itself.[90]

America's founding fathers believed basic human nature was sinful. This theological understanding helped them set up a government that had appropriate checks and balances to ensure freedom and liberty for all its citizens.

This secular/sacred divide has now become a convenient category, serving the skeptic and the atheist quite well. This divide limits religious teachings to the private realm of personal preference and religious values while the public domain is for science and empirical facts. "That is because it allows secularists to claim a monopoly on *the truth*. They do not need to outlaw ideas or use coercive measures. All they have to say is, '*Our secular* views are based on objective science and facts, but *your theologically* based views are personal and private. And while we certainly respect them, you have no right to impose your personal preferences on others in the public square.'"[91] As we should begin to see, this statement is an attempt to reconfigure what is *religious* as less factual than what is *secular*.

If we follow this line of reasoning, a person's religious beliefs should never be considered on the same level as objective truth. This secular/sacred dichotomy is further reinforced when noted philosophers and scientists throw their weight behind it. One of the world's leading paleontologists and a devout evolutionist, Stephen Gould once said:

It is easy to harmonize evolution and religious belief. All you have to do is put religion in a little compartment over there, where you care about things such as ethics and the meaning of life, and leave the rest to us, scientists.[92]

Gould's dualistic view is a convenient arrangement for secular scientists and post-moderns, but it does nothing to answer the hard questions about morals, human consciousness, and the ultimate meaning of life. Oxford Professor Richard Dawkins confidently claimed, "Darwin made it possible to be an intellectually fulfilled atheist."[93] Secularists and atheists are delighted by evolution's new public appeal. Keep your religious belief to yourself, and let science and secular ideology shape and inform public consensus. This cultural erosion has had a major impact on our spiritual welfare. Presently, forty-three percent of all adults, and fifty-seven percent of practicing Christians, believe that America is increasingly becoming a secular nation.[94]

## Christian in Name Only

Interestingly, people surveyed in the US reveal that almost ninety percent believe:

1. God Exists

2. Jesus is the Son of God

3. Christ Rose from the Dead.

However, many of these very same people deny the existence of absolute truths. Within the church, we see an erosion of confidence in the nature of truth. Nearly half of those who call themselves "born again" also say they do not believe in absolutes.[95] These statistics reveal a glaring contradiction in the Christian community. The word that best describes this is nominalism. *Nominalism*, literally means "in name only."

The Anglican theologian Lesslie Newbegin spent many years on the mission field in India. When he returned home to England and saw the condition of the church, he wrote in his book, *Truth to Tell:*

... a serious commitment to evangelism, the telling of the story which the Church is sent to tell, means the radical questioning of the reigning assumption of public life. It is to affirm the Gospel not only as an invitation to a private and personal decision but as public truth which ought to be acknowledged as true for the whole of the life of the society.[96]

Nominal believers have little or no influence on their surroundings. To claim to have the truth, then to keep it private, never presenting it for the public view, is very troubling and contrary to Christian values. Jesus specifically warned against this kind of silence:

You are the salt of the earth; but if the salt has become tasteless, how can it be made salty again? It is no longer good for anything, except to be thrown out and trampled underfoot by men. "You are the light of the world. A city set on a hill cannot be hidden; nor does anyone light a lamp and put it under a basket, but on the lampstand, and it gives light to all who are in the house. Let your light shine before men in such a way that they may see your good works, and glorify your Father who is in heaven (Matthew 5:13-16).

The U.S. Supreme Court has declared several times, as in 1892, that "Our laws and our institutions must necessarily be based upon and embody the teachings of the Redeemer of mankind. It is impossible that it would be otherwise, and in this sense and to this extent our civilization and our institutions are emphatically Christian... this is a Christian nation."[97] Personal morality plays a noteworthy part in our public actions, as it should. Judeo-Christian morals undergird and protect us, our neighbors, and our civil liberties.

**Fracturing the Truth**

The prophet Isaiah witnessed a similar kind of onslaught against truth in his day:

Justice is turned back, and righteousness stands far away; for truth has stumbled in the street, and uprightness cannot enter. Yes, truth is lacking; and he who turns aside from evil makes himself a prey. Now the Lord saw, and it was displeasing in His sight that there was no justice (Isaiah 59:14-15).

The blurring of truth has opened the door for other human factors like individual preferences and personal feelings to replace transcendent absolutes. Noted Christian scholar Harry Blamires identifies the problem with trying to separate one's innermost convictions from the arena of the secular. Blamires writes:

We twentieth-century Christians, have chosen the way of compromise. We withdraw our Christian consciousness from the fields of public, commercial, and social life. When we enter these fields, we are compelled to accept for purposes of discussion the secular frame of reference established there.[98]

Christians must regain their balance and address the onslaught against the confusion raging in our present culture. This reestablishing of transcendent truth must be done before we can make a case for Christianity's truth claims like the Virgin Birth, the incarnation, the crucifixion, and the resurrection. As Francis Schaeffer insisted, "The *fracturing of truth* is the most crucial problem facing Christianity today."[99]

## Scientific Naturalism

Ironically, the worldview that is openly tolerated and even endorsed as acceptable for all public consumption is *scientific naturalism*. Naturalism is a view that denies the supernatural; it assumes that scientific laws are adequate to account for all phenomena.[100] Accordingly, only the things that can be observed, tested, or measured in a lab are to be *considered real*. The majority of atheists and skeptics hold to this worldview of scientific *naturalism*, which asserts that all life evolved through undirected forces and blind chemistry over millions and millions of years.[101]

Naturalism is in sharp contrast to the biblical view of theistic *creationism*, which claims that the universe and all life were created as a response to the voice of God. God spoke and the entire cosmos came into existence along with all the diverse, complex animal life, as well as the finely tuned, life-sustaining biological systems found on planet earth. Creationism credits God, the eternal, supernatural agent, as *the uncaused*, first cause (Genesis 1:1-3).

## The Religion of Naturalism

In his book "Man, Myth or Messiah," Dr. Rice Broocks states that there is a pervasive secular religion sweeping the nation. Broocks refers to atheism as a legitimate, creedal religion. It is not less religious or less dogmatic for all its anti-supernaturalism. The origin of the universe, its development, and facilitation of life are tenets of atheistic evolution that are as many products of faith as those of the most vehement Christian creationists. The assumptions and assertions of atheism are doctrinaire if not doctrinal. Broocks explains:

> And make no mistake: atheism is a religion. It is a set of beliefs about the nature of the world and us as humans, and those beliefs have dramatic implications for how we should live and how society should function. At the heart of this anti-theistic system is the necessity to dismiss the supernatural, especially the supernatural birth, life, death, and resurrection of Jesus Christ.[102]

Interestingly enough the Supreme Court's ruling considered *secular humanism* to be not so much atheistic as *religious*, in the same sense that Buddhism and Taoism are considered to be religions, without regard to their belief in God. Secular Humanism, along with the atheism attached to it, was granted status as a worldview with its own theology.[103] If this ruling is to be accepted at face value, then atheism is indeed a religion. It is at least legally recognized as such. Atheism may attempt to parade around as if it is backed by science and logic but it is a statement of religious non-belief nonetheless.

This dogmatic, anti-religious rejection is evident in the following tongue-in-cheek statement by Francis Crick, "Christianity is alright between consenting adults, but should not be taught to children."[104] In other words, atheists and evolutionists have a moral duty to protect the young and impressionable, who otherwise may be influenced and damaged by believing in a supernatural deity. There are a host of atheists and skeptics who openly object to any belief in religion, particularly Christianity. For starters, preeminent scientist and the world's most prominent atheist Richard Dawkins openly expresses a part of his motivation in writing his book, *The God Delusion*, "If this book works as I intend, religious readers who open it *will be atheists* when they put it down."

Biologist P.Z. Meyers further supports the public eradication of religion, "I'm on the radical side of things. I think really the only way to resolve the debate between science and religion is for someday religion to be reduced to little more than a hobby, or a little eccentricity that some people practice."[105] According to Myers, "We need widespread social stigmatization of religion to eradicate a belief in God." Myers hopes for the day "when we achieve post-theism" and "the question concerning God is regarded as… a string of nonsense syllables."[106] If Myers is right, progressive secular education can eventually stamp out the need for any belief in God.

There are, however, a growing number of prominent academics, and scientists like; Arno Penzias, Noble Prize winner for discovering the micro-wave background radiation; Francis Collins, Director of the Human Genome Project that mapped the DNA molecule; and Professor John Polkinghorne, a theoretical physicist at Trinity College Cambridge, who are optimistic about the historical and archaeological evidence supporting God's existence.

**Truth Can Stand any Criticism**

If Christianity does not square with objective reality, then bright, astute minds should be able to discern the obvious and dismiss it as false. Surely these open-minded, enterprising students will figure it out for themselves, and deduce that religion is little more than a superstitious holdover from ancient, unenlightened times if indeed that is the case. Unfortunately, many atheists don't like a level playing field. Rather than mutual dialog and informed, rational debate, they prefer to silence all competing ideologies that don't support their materialistic, atheistic narrative. As we all know, the best way to win any argument is to only allow one side to present their case.

Naturalists will accommodate most theories… except theories that have a supernatural deity involved. My question is: What are the secularists and atheists afraid of? If they possess overwhelming evidence showing that there is no rational basis to believe in God, then this proof will become obvious to everybody. Let's follow the evidence wherever it leads! Biochemist and medical physician Dr. Michael Denton observed:

> The triumph of evolution meant the end of the traditional belief in the world as a purposefully created order, the so-called teleological outlook which had been predominant in the western world for two millennia. According to Darwin all the design, order, and complexity of life in the eerie purposefulness of living systems were the result of a simple blind random process - natural selection. Before Darwin, men had believed a providential intelligence had imposed its mysterious design upon nature, but now chance ruled supreme. God was replaced by the capriciousness of a roulette wheel.[107]

At least atheists like Dawkins, Hitchens, and Meyer are honest about their motives. They are not just atheistic; they are *anti-theists*. These vocal *non-theists* do uncover an even bigger problem. If God does not exist, no one, not even God-hating atheists have any rational grounds for blaming God for allowing human suffering or evil.

There is a section in Fyodor Dostoevsky's, *The Brothers Karamazov* in which Ivan Karamazov claims that if God does not exist, then everything is permitted, "Destroy a man's belief in immortality and not only will his ability to love wither away within him but… moreover, nothing would be immoral then, everything would be permitted." Dostoyevsky asserted that atheism doesn't get rid of the pain in this life… only the hope."[108]

If Christianity is taken out of the lives of children, it is intending to take it out of the lives of adults. Nowhere has atheistic secularism gained a stronger foothold than in our nation's schools and universities.

## The Rise of Relativism

*Relativism* is the belief that a worldview philosophy can be true for one person without being true for another.[109] Rather than considering truth as a matter of objective knowledge that can be identified and discussed, relativism reduces all beliefs down to the level of individual subjectivity. If there is no overarching lawgiver (God), it follows that there are no absolute laws that are binding for people to believe in, adhere to, or obey. And if we can assume that every person's opinion is equal, then we might as well accept the notion that God, as an idea, can be just as easily accepted or dismissed. If the truth can be stripped of any objective merits, the equality of all beliefs can be assumed. Truth becomes a matter of preference or feelings. Relativism leaves all options open, so that truth can change because it is subject to the culture, the particular situation, or the person's preference.

With moral relativism, objective truth becomes fluid and impossible to grasp. This assumes that truth is *passé* and exists only as a social construct used for a time and to be discarded for convenience's sake. If that is the case, how on earth are we to have a meaningful, civil conversation about objective reality? Relativists, on the one hand, deny that truth statements have any meaningful sense, and on the other hand, assert that all viewpoints are equally true. How crazy and bizarre can we get? Relativists end up sawing off the tree limb they are sitting on. They can't have it both ways. If everything is relative, by definition that statement is also relative and therefore cannot be true. Very confusing, isn't it?

Consider this story of a philosophy student writing an ethics paper arguing that there are no absolute truths. According to this student, as the argument goes, all laws are relative:

> Upon receiving the assignment, the university professor remarked, 'Judging by the research, documentation, and scholarship, the paper deserves an 'A.' The professor

however gave it an 'F' with a note explaining, "I do not like blue covers." Once he received his grade the student stormed into the professor's office to protest, outraged. "This is not fair! This is not just! I should be graded on the content of my work, not the color of my folder!" The professor looked at the student and asked, "Was this the paper which argued that there are no objective moral principles such as fairness and justice, and everything is relative to one's taste?" The student replied, "Yes, that's the paper." At that point, the professor answered, "Well then, the grade will remain an "F" as I do not like blue covers." Suddenly, the young man understood that moral absolutes of some sort are inescapable.[110]

It becomes obvious that the *relativist* can't be too careful, because he will always be bumping into objective reality. In practical terms, transcendent moral reference points *are* unavoidable. This story vividly illustrates the practical impossibility facing people who profess to avoid the existence of moral categories, yet demand statements of categorical truth or judgment in the real world in which we live. Again, truth is that which corresponds with objective reality.

Curiously, people never argue about the relativity of traffic signs, prescription medicine, or the numbers on their weekly paychecks. People intuitively know that these things accurately represent reality and identify truth claims. This is what we mean by truth. Relativism may appear to be sophisticated on the surface, but it is philosophically false, self-refuting and unlivable for all people, including the people who promote it. The reason the relativistic belief system is so attractive to our present culture is that it promotes all morals to be personal, subjective, and equal. Blaise Pascal, the great seventeenth-century philosopher/mathematician, brilliantly diagnosed human nature when he wrote, "People almost invariably arrive at their beliefs not based on proof, but based on what they find attractive."[111]

**Embracing Postmodernism.**

The postmodern worldview teaches that individual beliefs are merely constructs of social forces, that no truth can be known. *Postmodernism* is a rejection of anyone's worldview or explanation of reality, as well as a rejection of any truth claim.[112] According to postmodernism, all morals, all laws, all beliefs are the products of *human constructs* used to control or oppress others.

Chuck Colson wrote of postmodernism and relativism, observing that institutions of higher learning have embraced this philosophy so aggressively that they have adopted campus codes enforcing equity, tolerance, and inclusion. Intolerance has become so demonized that any counter-argument against political correctness or groupthink will not be tolerated. A Barna-Omni Poll was taken in August of 2015 measuring the correlation between experiencing tension and being a person of faith. Here is a summary of Barna's findings:

> When we look at the broadest segment of practicing Christians, a group that includes Catholics, evangelicals, and mainline churchgoers, a majority of these say they feel "misunderstood" (54%), and "persecuted" (52 %), while millions of others use terms like "marginalized" (44 %), "silenced" (38 %), "afraid to speak up" (31 %), and "afraid to look stupid" (23 %) in describing trying to live out their faith in today's society. According to this same survey, Evangelicals are even more likely to see their experience of faith in culture in negative terms.[113]

Postmodern ideas clash everywhere with the Christian faith in our society. The Christian message must be presented as truth to our skeptical and relativistic culture. The Psalmist David wrote during his quest for direction, "All your words are true; all your righteous laws are eternal" (Psalm 119:60). "Forever, Oh Lord, your word is settled in heaven" (Psalm 119:89).

Paul also instructed Timothy regarding the Church's sacred duty to establish and *uphold the truth*, "I write so that you will know how one ought to conduct himself in the household of God, which is the church of the living God, the pillar and support of the truth" (1Timothy 3:15).

From God's perspective, the truth of Scripture is well evidenced by His creation, as well as, established in and supported by the doctrines of the Christian church. It is not subject to human preferences, social norms, or changing whims and wishes.

Scripture provides examples, "And this is eternal life that they may know You the only true God, and Jesus Christ whom You have sent" (John 17:3), and "Sanctify them in the truth, Your word is truth" (John 17:17). Truth has been absolutely and forever settled by the Author of all truth. Consequently, all of God's creation is subject to and responsible for applying His truth to their lives. This is where the conflict arises. Fallen humanity does not like to submit its will or desires to any other sovereign except to the *almighty self*. The message of salvation is meant to glorify God and to reconcile all of fallen humanity back into a right relationship with God.

**Why Trust Your Own Thoughts?**

How can we know which man or woman's ideas are to be embraced and followed? If all ideas are relative, making truth subjective and ever-changing, how do we navigate life? One has to wonder why relativists and atheists call themselves free thinkers if they truly believe, as they claim, that all human thought is nothing more than random neurons firing in their brains. If human thoughts are random atoms colliding in our heads, why trust them at all? C.S Lewis explained the atheist's problem best:

> Supposing there was no intelligence behind the universe, no creative mind. In that case, nobody designed my brain for the purpose of thinking. It is merely that when the atoms inside my skull happen, for physical or chemical reasons, to arrange themselves in a certain way, this gives me, as a by-product, the sensation I call thought. But, if so, how can I trust my own thinking to be true?" It's like upsetting a milk jug and hoping that the way it splashes itself will give you a map to London. But if I can't trust my own thinking, of course, I can't trust the argument leading to Atheism, and therefore have no reason to be an Atheist, or anything else.[114]

In the twenty-first century, the most attacked positions in the western world are the ones that assert *absolute truth claims*. Christians who desire to sanitize the gospel's message have embraced a more *risk-averse Christianity* that tries to soften certain unpopular biblical truths because of their *so-called* exclusive claims. This mindset views Christianity as needing to be more loving and inclusive, thereby making it more attractive and agreeable to potential converts. But we must be careful when engaging with non-believers that we do not allow our desire to befriend them cause us to compromise the truth for the sake of winning some public approval.

British historian, Christopher Dawson accurately describes the conflict:

> For a secular civilization that has no end beyond its own satisfaction is a monstrosity, a cancerous growth that will ultimately destroy itself. The only power that can liberate man from this kingdom of darkness is the Christian faith. For in the modern Western world there are no alternative solutions, no choice of possible other religions. It is a choice between Christianity or nothing.[115]

No matter what context we find ourselves in, Christians are fundamentally different from the secular culture around us. The New Birth has transformed the believer to be light in the midst of darkness. Our presence is meant to bring change to the environment that we walk into, not accommodate or excuse them. Morphing our message to accommodate the secular culture, just for the sake of peace and mutual acceptance, is a dangerous compromise.

# CHAPTER THREE

## Has Science Buried God?

"A little science estranges a man from God; a lot of science brings him back."

**- Francis Bacon**

I still remember my freshman biology class in college, sitting in a lecture theatre with 300 other students. I was formally introduced by my biology professor to a theory about the origins of man called "Darwinian Evolution." I still remember, strangely enough, that the biology professor only ever discussed one possible theory for man's origins in that class. That's right, we only heard about evolution. As a nineteen-year-old kid, I was eager to learn the course material and make an "A" in my biology class. At the time, I had no idea that absorbing Darwin's naturalistic teaching about human origins, would drastically affect my perspective of life, my morals, and my view of human destiny.

Today, when one talks about "science," people don't always have a clear understanding of what is meant. In the Middle Ages, theology was known as the "Queen of the Sciences." People understood that God created the universe, and God made the universe rationally comprehensible for people to observe, study, and understand. Science comes from the Latin word *scientia*, which means "knowledge." The sciences once encompassed all intellectual disciplines, including theology, politics, and philosophy. Understanding God was integral to understanding the world which He created.

German mathematician and astronomer Johannes Kepler once said, "The chief aim of all investigation of the external world should be to discover the rational order and harmony which has been imposed on it by God." Therefore, studying God's creation leads to the discovery of knowledge pertaining to God. Science assumes causality. Sir Isaac Newton's first law of thermodynamics makes this observation: *Every event must have a cause.* Things do not happen in our physical universe without some outside agency acting upon them.

Both science and theology are committed to explaining the world and helping us make sense of things in creation. Science tends to ask the "how" questions and theology explains the "why" questions. Science seeks to understand mechanisms; theology offers meaning and purpose.[116] Theology and science are valid academic enterprises and offer a great benefit to humanity's development and understanding of the world. Both science and theology should strive for mutual respect and collaboration. There is no intellectual incompatibility between science and theology. As we will discuss later, many of the brightest scientific minds of history, including Bacon, Boyle, Newton, Faraday, Mendel, and Kepler were God-fearing, if not Christian.

Unfortunately, modern science in the twenty-first century is depicted as rigidly naturalistic, leaving no room for any supernatural explanation. Since the beginning of the nineteenth century, much of modern science has intentionally excluded God from the laboratory. With the so-called Age of Enlightenment, human reason divorced from sacred Scripture, was elevated above any theological consideration and became viewed as the cornerstone of all knowledge.[117]

With the scientific enterprise gaining still more momentum, there came more emphasis on a methodology that was empirical (known through the human senses) and rational. As scientific naturalism would have it, if something cannot be physically tested and verified in a laboratory, it cannot be true. Yet with the scientific method, there are necessarily presuppositions involved. All scientists must rely on the following logical premises as a basis for their scientific inquiry:

1. Nature is comprehensible.

2. Nature is predictable and acts in precise patterns.

3. Science presupposes observable patterns in nature.

These premises are not themselves proven by scientific testing; they must be pre-assumed by any scientist attempting to examine the natural world to perform his or her experiment and draw any conclusion.[118]

## Molecules to Man

Darwinian Evolution continues to try and explain mankind's origins, as a random bi-product of time, matter, and dead chemistry without consideration for a Creator God. This materialistic theory of man's origins speculates that human development happened over long periods of geologic time. Over 60 years ago, a Yale graduate named Rudolph Zalenger created an image that was to become part of America's visual vocabulary. Using his creative imagination, Zalenger drew a line of morphing apes representing the various transitional forms of human evolution. Of course, Zalenger had never seen any of these creatures; he used his *imagination* and *artistic license* to reconstruct how he imagined they might have appeared millions of years ago.

The alleged ascent of modern-man from ape-like ancestors.

The public slowly accepted Zalenger's idea as a form of scientific proof of how humans must have come about. This "March of Progress," as it later became known, appeared in Time-Life books in 1965. It was soon accepted by the public as a scientific fact and placed in a majority of biology textbooks across North America. Since then, the image has become a cultural icon. These artistic renditions were given scientific-sounding names like *Homo Habilis*, *Homo Erectus*, and *Homo Neanderthalensis*. Finally, after millions of years of natural selection and chance mutation, life had miraculously produced a fully evolved *Homo Sapien or modern man*.[119]

In my biology class, human evolution was neatly presented with a kind of scientific expertise and illustrated in my textbook with an artistic imagination which made it very easy for me, and multitudes of other students to swallow. We were being persuaded by "so-called" expert scientists and university professors who were endorsing evolution. My thinking was, "If this information is in my biology textbook and my professor is teaching it... it must be true! If I am going to pass this course, I must learn the material and accept this stuff as a fact."

As I continued my college education, I was exposed to more courses like psychology, anthropology, and sociology. All of these subjects were taught with a pre-assumed bias towards evolution. Scientific terms like *common descent, survival of the fittest, natural selection,* and *chance mutation* all seemed very convincing to me. I had accepted the idea that modern science had proven evolution to be a fact.

It was not until several years later that I began questioning some of these so-called scientific facts which I had so naively absorbed. I remember thinking, how can there possibly be a God if evolution is true? The biblical account found in Genesis is not believable. Or, is it? During my college years, I had falsely assumed that science had settled the issue about human origins. By the time I was a sophomore in college, I was convinced that science had buried any notion of a God!

In his popular book *Darwin's Dangerous Idea*, Daniel Dennett called evolution a "universal acid" that erodes traditional religious and moral beliefs.[120] Philosophers and Scientists like Daniel Dennett, Richard Dawkins, the late Christopher Hitchens, and Sam Harris have similarly endorsed evolution to liberate people from religion and encourage support for atheism. How are these ideas about evolution affecting others?

The Discovery Institute conducted a nationwide survey to ascertain the importance of evolutionary ideas on those who had lost their faith and now self-identify as atheist or agnostic. Here are some key findings from the survey results:

- Sixty-seven percent of atheists and Thirty-five percent of agnostics believe the findings of science make the existence of God less likely.

- Seven out of ten atheists and four out of ten agnostics say that unguided chemical evolution and Darwin's mutation/natural selection mechanism make the existence of God less likely.

- Forty-five percent of Americans, sixty-nine percent of atheists, and sixty percent of agnostics agree with the statement, "Evolution shows that human beings are not fundamentally different from other animals."

- Fifty-five percent of Americans, seventy-one percent of atheists, and sixty-eight percent of agnostics say that "Evolution shows that moral beliefs evolve over time based on their survival value."[121]

Many of these people once believed in God but were persuaded by evolutionary teaching to doubt and reject theism. What does evolution say about creation? Those who adhere to the theory believe the following:

1. The universe is the result of matter, time, chemistry, and chance formed by undirected natural forces.

2. All organisms: plants and animals have evolved over millions of years from a common ancestor by natural selection.

Evolution also subscribes to a belief in natural selection and random mutation. According to natural selection, also known as, survival of the fittest, certain advantageous traits are passed on from an animal to its offspring, causing it to better adapt and cope with the changing environment. *Random Mutation* holds that rare and sudden alterations in the gene code in an organism occur. The idea is that there are random mutations that can build on one another resulting in dramatic transmutation (physical change) over time. However, mutations, whenever they do occur, are mistakes. They are a loss of genetic information that causes defects or death in the offspring of the animal with the mutation. We now know, with the aid of powerful electron microscopes and discoveries in Molecular Biology, that gene mutations are mostly harmful to the organism and do not confer any evolutionary advantage

Decades ago, C. S. Lewis distinguished between scientific evolution and what he called *evolutionism*, a theological creed. Lewis reveals in his letters that he believed that evolution "is accepted by zoologists not because it has been observed to occur or... can be proved by logically coherent evidence." For example, Harvard paleontologist Stephen Jay Gould, without physical evidence, speculates about ancient events happening on the earth millions of years ago, to get humanity where it is today:

> We are here because one odd group of fishes had a peculiar fin anatomy that could transform into legs for terrestrial creatures; because the earth never froze entirely during an ice age; because a small and tenuous species, arising in Africa a quarter of a million years ago, has managed, so far, to survive by hook and by crook. We may yearn for a 'higher answer'– but none exists.[122]

If Gould is right, we are alive because of blind chance, existing as "lucky mud," with no ultimate meaning or purpose in life except to pass on our genes to the next generation. Richard Dawkins fully endorses Gould's fatalistic worldview, "The universe that we observe has... no design, no purpose, no evil and no good, nothing but blind pitiless indifference. DNA neither knows nor cares. DNA just is. And we dance to its music.[123]

It seems ironic to me now, but both of these world-renowned scientists felt it was meaningful and necessary to remind their readers that there is no such thing as meaning or purpose in the world. If there is no real meaning in this life, why bother telling anyone anything? If Dawkins is right, teaching science or any other subject in such a meaningless world serves no purpose at all!

## Darwin Loses Credibility

Later on in graduate school, I started looking at the evidence offered by critics of evolution. I was surprised and troubled by what I discovered. Why wasn't this information offered to me in my biology or anthropology class? Other theistic scientists were making very convincing arguments that evolution was not factual but instead a theory with several holes in it. The lights started to come on for me.

The more I studied, the more I realized that the idea of evolution was a bankrupt theory. The more I looked at the evidence, the more incredible Darwin's theory became to me. Dr. Lyall Watson, anthropologist and evolutionist, admits, "Modern apes, for instance, seem to have sprung out of nowhere. They have no yesterday, no fossil record. And the true origin of modern humans, of upright, naked, tool-making, big-brained beings... is, if we are to be honest with ourselves, an equally mysterious matter."[124] If we are descendants of apes or share with them a common ancestor, why is there little or no evidence for that alleged claim?

For decades there have been three main examples consistently used by evolutionists to promote their theory.

**First,** is the idea of the common descent of humans from *ape-like ancestors.* As previously mentioned, this is largely thanks to the artistic license and the imaginative drawings found in biology textbooks; pictures showing how humanity is allegedly linked from lower primates to modern man. These artistic images do not represent any extinct specimen found in any of the fossil records. Are these fossils really missing links to humans... or are they simply conjecture based on biased speculation?

**Second,** was the discovery by Charles Darwin of *the Galapagos Finches* isolated on the various islands of the Galapagos? These isolated birds demonstrated beak variation, which was assumed to be proof of natural selection in action and therefore evidence of evolution.

**Third,** the now-debunked example of the *Peppered Moth* found in Manchester, England. We will discuss these three examples of Darwinian Evolution to see if they offer reliable evidence for Darwin's theory.

According to biologists Dr. Ann Gauger and Dr. Douglas Axe, paleoanthropologists face several challenges in their quest to reconstruct any story of human evolution.[125] Here are two of those major obstacles:

**The First Challenge: Hominin fossils tend to be few and far between.** "It is not uncommon for long periods to exist from which few fossils are documenting the evolution that was supposedly taking place."[126] Paleontologists Donald Johansen and Blake Eager observed in 1996 that "about half the periods in the last 3 million years remain undocumented by any human fossils." From the earliest period of hominid evolution, more than 4 million years ago only a handful of largely unknown diagnostic fossils have been found. Upon careful study of these fossil remnants, Harvard zoologist Richard Lewontin concluded, "They are so fragmented and disconnected... no fossil hominid species can be established as our (mankind's) direct ancestor."[127]

**The Second Challenge: Most fossils we have now come in fragments.** Most fossil remnants are the remains of simple bone fragments. Paleoanthropologists find it difficult, if not impossible, to form any conclusion about the morphology, behavior, and relationship of many specimens.[128]

Evolutionary anthropologist Lyall Watson reported:

The entire hominid collection known today would barely cover a billiard table, but it has spawned a science because it is distinguished by two factors that inflate its apparent relevance far beyond its merit. First, the fossils hint at the ancestry of a supremely self-important animal - ourselves. Secondly, the collection is so tangibly incomplete in the specimens themselves. They are often so fragmented and inconclusive that more can be said about what is missing than about what is present.[129]

Bear in mind, not all scientists are neutral on the subject of human evolution. Many would welcome the academic notoriety, professional clout, and potential research grants available for someone landing a "big discovery" by finding the so-called *missing link*.

## Piltdown Man

The Piltdown Man was once thought to be an evolutionary link between apes and modern man. However, Piltdown Man turned out to be a hoax in which bone fragments were presented as fossilized remains of an unknown, early ape-like humanoid. In 1912, an archaeologist Sir Arthur Keith claimed he had found "the missing link" between ape and man after discovering a human-like skull in a gravel pit near East Sussex, England. Other bones were later found and conveniently connected to the same dig site.

A reconstructed skull was claimed to have belonged to a human ancestor from 500,000 years ago, but upon further investigation, Piltdown Man proved to be a combination of the jawbones from an orangutan mixed with the remains of a modern human. The fraud was exposed in 1953 as a forgery, forty-one years after its initial discovery. People, including hundreds of scientists, had readily swallowed this fabrication, not based upon scientific evidence, but because they had a pre-existing bias to believe it. According to several paleontologists, the Piltdown Man scandal remains arguably the greatest scientific fraud ever perpetrated in the United Kingdom.[130]

## Nebraska Man

Nebraska Man was touted as another supposedly human ancestor. This specimen was officially designated as *Hesperopithecus Heraldcooki*, a name given by geologist Harold J. Cook. At the time, leading evolutionist Henry F. Osborn publicly attested to the authenticity of the specimen as a *genuine missing link*. In 1925, the Nebraska Man fossil discovery was even put forth to be used as scientific evidence for teaching evolution in the famous "Scopes Monkey Trial" held in Dayton, Tennessee.[131]

Further study was conducted on the fossilized remains of Nebraska Man. It was found that the only item of evidence for this supposed evolutionary link to man was a *single tooth*. More excavation was done at the dig site. Examiners soon discovered that the tooth was not that of any ape-like anthropoid; it was the ancient tooth of a pig, now extinct in North America and only found in Paraguay.[132]

After this revelation, Nebraska Man was eventually discredited and renounced by the scientific community. Even up through the 1970s and 80s, Nebraska Man was still being used as an example in biology textbooks in North America as a missing link between modern man and apes. Unfortunately, for some scientists, facts only matter *when* and *if* they support their evolutionary narrative.

## Darwin's Finches

While traveling aboard the *HMS Beagle*, Charles Darwin visited the Galapagos Islands in 1835. There he discovered a species of finches with beak characteristics that varied from island to island. The Galapagos

Islands are isolated from the South American mainland, supposedly making them a natural laboratory for natural selection to work its magic. According to the story, the finches adapted or evolved different traits depending upon the environment of the particular island inhabited.

In 1977 biologists Peter and Rosemary Grant did extensive studies on the Galapagos Island, Daphne Major. Their study focused on a particular finch, the medium ground finch. In 1977, a severe drought reduced the food supply, leaving only rock-hard seeds for the finches to survive on. Eighty-five percent of the birds died. The only finches that survived were the ground finches with slightly thicker beaks. This enabled the bigger beaked finches to eat the hard-to-crack seeds. If these kinds of environmental changes kept on occurring, supposedly these ground finches would evolve into a brand-new species if the theory were correct.

After the drought ended on the island, Grant found that the birds with the smaller beaks flourished once again. There had been no evolutionary advantage conferred on the new finches. Grant went on to study the interbreeding of the different Galapagos finch species from various islands. The hybridization of finches of different species produced hearty offspring that possessed characteristics of both parents. These new offspring remain a sub-species of the ground finch.[133]

Were the finches changing? Yes, only in slight variation of beak sizes. The characteristic larger beaks of some finches gave them a survival advantage over the finches possessing smaller beaks. However, this advantage of larger beaks changed back when the drought was over. With normal rain, big beaks served no advantage for the finches. All that transpired were slight variations. Slight variations within a species are known as *micro-evolution also known as special evolution*. This is not even remotely close to the genetic emergence of a new species. Special evolution is not capable of producing the huge morphological changes necessary for an organism to evolve into a brand-new species!

Even though the finches on different islands have small physical variations, they are still of the *finch kind or species*. It is very much like breeding dogs. You can cross a Great Dane with a Dachshund and produce puppies that have characteristics of both parents. Great Danes and Dachshunds are morphologically different from one another but are both still of the dog *species*. A wide range of physical variations can be seen with breeding cats, sheep, cows, horses, guppies, etc. This is not an example of a precursor of evolution at work. Microevolution is simply a trait variation resident within the genome of that species. Different breeds of dogs that are mated together are still dogs! Genesis confirms this biological fact, that every living thing from birds to fish to whales to cattle will produce after their own kind (Genesis 1:21-25).

I can still remember the first time I saw a Shetland Pony standing next to a Clydesdale stallion. They are physically so different. It's hard to believe they are both horses, but they are! The Shetland Pony and the Clydesdale are good examples of microevolution brought on by selective breeding. To repeat, *microevolution* is a slight variation within a breed or a kind. This can be demonstrated with the selective breeding of pigeons, dogs, horses, and guppies.

*Macroevolution in contrast*, also known as *the Theory of Universal Common Descent*, is the alleged changing of one species into an entirely different species. Unlike microevolution, macroevolution *has never been observed* in the fossil record or proven through empirical evidence. It is still speculation at best.

In 2015, Dr. Peter Grant and a team of scientists confirmed that they had sequenced the genome with all the species of Darwin's finches. The hybridization of Darwin's finches, which produced the variation of physical features Darwin observed, did not prove that any new species of finch had emerged.[134] The finches on the Galapagos Islands are still finches. Despite the elapsing of even more time since Darwin's death. They are nothing more, nothing less than finches. As it turns out, Darwin's finches are not very compelling as an example of evolution.

**Common descent claims all living organisms have evolved from one common ancestor.**

**The Third Challenge:** **The Peppered Moth.** Another hopeful candidate promoted by naturalists to endorse Darwin's theory was the Peppered Moths of Manchester. The moths were believed to have evolved their coloration to blend in with the trees that were covered from soot from nearby factories across England. This color change would help camouflage the moths from being eaten by birds. Supposedly, the light-colored moths morphed into a darker form, thereby avoiding being eaten by predators. Certainly, it was argued this was proof of natural selection in action before our eyes. The peppered moth example was enthusiastically advanced by leading biologists as *proof of evolution at work.* So compelling was this example of evolution by natural selection that it became a staple in biology textbooks around the world.

In 1998, British biologist Michael Majerus published a book about the peppered moths found in the wild. Mejerus' study confirmed that peppered moths do not rest on tree trunks but instead in the upper foliage of the leaves. Therefore, any variation in moth coloration could not have been a result of the soot on the tree trunks, since the moths reside mostly in the leaf region of the tree. The so-called evolutionary cause-and-effect scenario and explanation simply were not valid. The locals soon confirmed that before the Industrial Revolution the moths could be found in both the speckled and black varieties. When the photos used were examined in more detail, biologists found that the photos had been staged by pinning dead moths to particular tree trunks that matched their wing coloration. The moths had been caught in traps at night, not during the day. Dead moths were then glued to the bark of trees for a television series about demonstrating "evolution in action." By this time the number of light-colored moths was back on the rise once the effects of pollution and soot-stained trees had diminished. Light-colored lichen had already begun to grow back on trees. "Due to the many holes in the experiments, Jerry Coyne had decided to dismiss the idea of peppered moths offering an example of natural selection in action."[135]

The moths had not evolved their coloration to blend in with the soot-covered trees, as erroneously claimed. They had existed in their different colors long before the industrialization of England.[136] The debunked natural selection of the peppered moth is now a major embarrassment for most Darwinists.

## The Cambrian Explosion

The geologic period known as the Cambrian Explosion shows a myriad of complex animals fossilized in the same stratum of rock alongside simpler organisms. All the organisms appear to have been alive at the same time and have been captured in the same fossil layer. Why did so many species suddenly appear in the Cambrian period without any fossil ancestors at all? Dr. Benjamin Wiker poses a critical question about the lack of evidence found by geologists and paleontologists regarding present-day animals. "If environmental conditions have changed so greatly over time and creatures are always changing under the pressure of natural selection, why are there 'living fossils,' creatures who have not changed significantly over hundreds of millions of years? Animals like the crocodile, alligator, cockroaches, and dragonflies have not changed over millennia."[137]

These species appear morphologically identical to our present-day specimens as they did millions of years ago. Why has natural selection been *conspicuously absent* without any change in these ancient species contrary to what evolutionists would expect? Why is it that with the passing of time, coupled with Darwin's natural selection, evolution has shown no effect on the majority of living species?

## Darwin's Doubt

When Charles Darwin asserted his theory of evolution, he believed the process of natural selection could explain the complexity of all animal life. Later Darwin expressed considerable doubt concerning the formation of the human eye by slow, gradual changes, as impossible. Darwin wrote, "To suppose that the eye... could have been formed by natural selection, seems I freely confess, absurd in the highest possible degree."[138]

"If it could be demonstrated that any complex organ existed, which could not possibly have been formed by numerous, successive, slight modifications, my theory would absolutely break down." Charles Darwin[139]

The unfruitful results from the fossil record have further dashed the hopes of many of the Darwinian faithful. To their dismay, paleontologists have found no discovery of any *intermediate* or *transitional* life forms indicating the evolution of one species to a more complex species. The lack of evidence is not an encouraging sign for evolutionists trying to scientifically validate their "pet theory."

Paleontologist Stephen Gould found it difficult to reconcile the fossil record found in the Cambrian rock strata. There appear to be highly developed, complex fossils showing up alongside very simple ones. At no place in this formation was there recorded any gradual progression from simple to more complex fossils. This is hardly what an evolutionary paleontologist would expect to see. As Gould stated, "There simply is not one reliable example for an intermediary form... *found in the fossil record [emphasis added]*."[140]

To compensate for the lack of evidence, Gould theorized the idea of *Punctuated Equilibrium*. Gould suggested via this phenomenon that there must have been huge transitional jumps in the evolutionary process that helped morph organisms much more rapidly than the exceedingly slow process required by natural selection.[141] Evolution would have had to occur, according to this theory, through sudden physical changes rather than gradual small variations over time.

To put forward this theory, little or no evidence of its scientific veracity was needed. Gould asserted that the absence of any intermediate fossils was the "trade secret" of paleontology. Wait just a minute, what does Gould mean, about missing fossils being *the trade secret* of his profession? I thought science was supposed to be based on observable, verifiable evidence, open for all inquiring minds to witness and empirically confirm! The still-missing intermediate life forms, completely absent from the fossil record demanded a new explanation. And Gould was quite happy to give one *without any empirical evidence*. The fragile theory of evolution could be safely protected by asserting Gould's theory of punctuated equilibrium as the needed explanation without any scientific proof to back it.[142] In an article written for *Discovery*, Dr. James Shreeve, an anthropologist, and noted atheist wrote, "Everybody knows fossils are fickle; bones will sing any song you want to hear."[143]

Distinguished scholar Dr. Jim Nelson Black, a fellow at the Wilberforce Forum, wrote this, "The secular science community has joined forces with the mainstream media, the educational establishment, and the universities, to make sure that the weaknesses of Darwinism are never exposed."[144]

Popular science fiction writer, G. Richard Bozarth, who is a self-proclaimed atheist, understands exactly why Christians must resist the indoctrination of falsehoods, such as evolution. Bozarth contends that if evolution is a fact, then the Bible narrative of creation along with the life and message of Jesus of Nazareth is false!

> Christianity has fought, still fights, and will continue to fight science to the desperate end over evolution, because evolution destroys utterly and finally the very reason Jesus' earthly life was supposedly made necessary.

Destroy Adam and Eve and the original sin, and in the rubble, you will find the sorry remains of the Son of God. If Jesus was not the redeemer who died for our sins, and this is what evolution means, then Christianity is nothing.[145]

Contrary to scientific naturalism, the so-called icons of evolution are turning out to be convincing evidence refuting evolution rather than supporting it. The missing links for evolution are still, well, missing! Through the course of studying other scientific material on the subject and growing in my Christian faith, I finally got to the point that I knew with certainty that belief in Darwin's theory was not trustworthy science. The theory is human speculation with a commitment to naturalism and a bias against anything related to the supernatural.

Modern science was itself birthed out of a Judeo-Christian worldview. This historic fact is mostly lost in the current academic landscape, which tries to focus on the supposed backwardness of the Middle Ages and religious dogma. Even now, some atheists and skeptics tend to highlight an alleged "warfare" between religion and science to bolster their case for their own brand of science. Today the mindset of secular culture and much of academia insists that naturalistic science is the only reliable recourse to the knowledge of the real world.[146]

## The Myth of Neutrality

Theologian Paul Weston is the Director of The Western Culture. Weston is critical of the increasingly secularized culture in the west and its alleged neutrality:

> We have to question the assumption that a secular state is neutral. It does not establish any of the world's religions, but it does establish a worldview that embodies truth claims that Christians cannot accept and must be brought into the open and challenged.[147]

This idea of neutrality is unanimously championed by the scientific community. There is a common assumption that science and scientists are "neutral" and "objective" with no personal prejudices or bias influencing them or their findings. Whenever the *science card* is played, it is intended to reinforce this claim to the exclusive ownership of objective facts. This is nothing short of the elevation of science as the final arbiter of truth.

Philosophers and scientists like Richard Dawkins, Aldous Huxley, and Thomas Nagel have openly admitted their bias towards scientific naturalism and evolution because they did not want to have to deal with the *God hypothesis*. Biologist Richard Lewontin is honest about his anti-supernatural bias:

> Our willingness to accept scientific claims that are against common sense is the key to an understanding of the real struggle between science and the supernatural. We take the side of science despite its failure to fulfill many of its extravagant promises of health and life, despite the tolerance of the scientific community for unsubstantiated just-so stories, because we have a prior commitment - a commitment to materialism. Moreover, that materialism is absolute, for we cannot allow a Divine foot in the door.[148]

Not to be left out, theoretical physicists and self-avowed evolutionist Steven Weinberg confidently declared one of the benefits which he saw as a result of modern science:

> The teaching of modern science is corrosive of religious belief, and I'm all for that! One of the things that have driven me in my life, is the feeling that this is one of the great social functions of science... to free people from superstition.[149]

## The Cosmic Authority Problem

According to physicist Steven Weinberg and other atheistic educators, science offers the key to liberating humanity from its oppressive religious teachings and rules. Philosopher John Locke once wrote, "The visible marks of extraordinary wisdom and power appear so plainly in all the works of creation that a rational creature, who will but seriously reflect on them, cannot miss the discovery of a Deity."[150] The average person can see that reason and faith are mutually affirming assets for studying science. The reason atheistic scientists don't want religious faith associated with their naturalistic worldview is because the idea of an omnipotent Creator brings with it two inescapable truths:

- The Admission of a Transcendent Law-Giver, and

- An Obligation to Venerate and Obey His Laws.

These two issues strike at the crux of the matter. The elephant in the room is... who gets to call the shots? God or man? New York University Law professor, Thomas Nagel believes the "cosmic authority problem" is widely shared among secular intellectuals. It accounts for the stubbornness with which they cling to materialism and for the hostility that greets an intellectual who starts to wander off from the herd. Materialism must be true because it "liberates us from religion."[151]

## When Evidence is Uncomfortable

Albert Einstein was uncomfortable with some of the theory of relativity implications. One of the biggest issues was that astronomy and physics proved the universe was not static but was expanding. This was unthinkable to Einstein, who believed the universe was eternal, existing in a "steady state." According to this belief, the universe is seen as eternal, with no beginning. So, Einstein added a fudge factor to his equations, a kind of energy associated with empty space. This manipulation of the cosmological constant allowed for a stable universe.

Sure enough, in 1929 Astronomer Edwin Hubble confirmed that the universe was expanding in all directions because of the redshift of celestial objects. Later confirmed by Robert Wilson and Arno Penzais' findings in 1965, in which they discovered the Cosmic Microwave Background (CMB) afterglow of what was believed to be the Big Bang. This CMB discovery, along with Hubble's redshift revelation, provided convincing evidence for the Big Bang.

This proved the universe was not eternal and had a definite beginning in time and space in the finite past. The law of causality already established that whatever begins to exist is caused! The question that remained was, what or who caused the universe? There are only two possible answers: either *nothing* caused the universe to come into existence, or something or someone caused the universe. Recognizing his lack of integrity on the matter, Einstein later called the cosmological constant the "greatest blunder" of his career.[152]

Why did Einstein feel the need to manipulate his equation? If the universe had a beginning, the logical conclusion is there had to be something or someone outside of time, space, and matter to bring the universe into being. A Creation necessarily points to a Creator! The Genesis account in the Bible declares that creation came into being from the words of God. Yet the western scientific tradition from Aristotle until 1940 viewed the universe as eternal and permanent.

Prior to the 1960s, the scientific community and academic elites viewed any talk of the universe having a chronological beginning as being totally absurd. Suggesting the universe had *a beginning in time* was grounds to be reprimanded or censured for not towing the popular narrative of a "steady-state theory." The scientists were wrong! Thanks to discoveries by other scientists like Edwin Hubble, Robert Wilson, and Arno Penzias, the vast majority of astronomers and cosmologists now agree the universe had a beginning in the finite past. Over the past 60 years, these discoveries gave rise to what is now known as the "standard cosmological model."[153]

Despite these admissions of human error and intentional deception, the scientific establishment still casts a big shadow and is quick to reprimand and censor anyone who upsets its materialistic ideology. Trying to enforce or manipulate scientific consensus is not necessarily good science, as we have seen with Einstein's now-debunked steady-state theory. Scientists and atheists are just human beings and, like regular people, they too are sometimes overcome by personal biases, peer pressure, and professional ambitions. Popular scientific consensus has many times been proven wrong. We may now be able to better understand what Einstein meant when he was quoted by *The London Observer* on April 5, 1964, as saying, "I cannot believe that God plays dice with the cosmos."

## No God... No Problem

Is Darwin's theory right about humans? Are people just highly evolved, cerebral apes that have figured out how to control our world and master our destiny? Many educated and influential people are convinced that this is the case. Rabbi Daniel Lapin writes, "On some subconscious level, humans find it convenient to view themselves not as very special beings touched by the finger of God, but rather as a very smart animal. The smart animal view of humanity is convenient because it frees people from complex moral analyses of their lives." As far as science knows, animals never experience emotional pain or shame.[154]

Cats don't feel remorse for killing and eating mice. Male grizzly bears have no moral guilt for killing the cubs of a female to induce estrus. Once in estrus, the male grizzly mates with the female to sire his offspring. Chimpanzee troops in central Africa have been recorded attacking and cannibalizing solitary chimps who were caught trespassing on the troop's territory. Biologists dismiss the behavior of chimpanzees as primal animal nature. If humans see themselves as sophisticated animals, what prevents them from behaving similarly and exempting themselves from guilt or shame? If humanity is a product of nature and genetically predisposed to behave a certain way, how could there be any sense of moral wrongdoing associated with human actions?[155]

Why do all civilized nations build prisons, correction centers, and rehabilitation facilities to help restrain and reform deviant, destructive behavior in people? Could it be that they deem certain actions to be wrong and deem other actions to be right? Evolutionary ideology conveniently sidesteps man's moral accountability. That is evolution's real attraction! No God, no guilt, no judgment, no problem! As Scripture informs us, "The fool has said in his heart, 'There is no God.' They are corrupt, and have committed abominable injustice; there is no one who does good" (Psalm 53:1).

## Christianity in the Crosshairs

In the state of California, the educational department has set guidelines for teaching evolution in public schools which are not to be challenged or questioned by students or faculty.

> At times, some students may insist that certain conclusions of science cannot be true because of certain religious or philosophical beliefs they hold. It is appropriate, if that happens, for teachers to express the following:

"I understand you may have personal reservations about accepting scientific evidence, but it is scientific knowledge about which there is no reasonable doubt among scientists in their field, and it is my responsibility to teach it because it is part of our common intellectual heritage.[156]

Notice the particular wording of the article, it is about how to discern and teach *real knowledge* versus *personal beliefs*. The document is accepting of *scientific evidence* and dismissive of personal *reservations*. Notice the descriptors used to emphasize science, "scientific evidence," "scientific knowledge," "no reasonable doubt," and "common intellectual heritage." Contrast these descriptors with the adjectives used in describing religious claims: "personal reservations" and "beliefs they hold."[157]

It is easy to see the difference between the way science is being portrayed as the source of real intellectual knowledge, while Christianity and religious claims are dismissed as subjective, personal feelings. This is simply another example of how the fact/value divide is being used to categorize empirical evidence as *public truth* versus personal ethics as one's *private values*. Make no mistake about it, Christian morality is under full assault by secular progressives. Personal life experience, societal norms, and our inner consciences demand that humans must be aware of and accountable for their actions. No legal system in the world would accept "it's only natural" or "am genetically pre-disposed" as a plausible defense for rape, child abuse, or murder.

Every person has an innate sense of right and wrong. God has written his moral code on our hearts (Romans 2:14-15). The majority of our civil laws are based directly on the ethical code provided by the Ten Commandments. All just societies have civil laws to protect the innocent, law-abiding citizen and to incarcerate and punish the deviant and criminal. Common moral courtesy along with civil respect is mutually acknowledged by all people and cultures.

## Faith and Science: Bridging the Gap

In identifying some of the criticism leveled at Christianity from some in the scientific community, it is important to understand the points of contention and to discern to what extent they are real and to what extent they are perceived. First, we must define our terms. Science, by its definition, has to do with methods of testing which can be repeated and thus empirically validated. The verification of an observation is based on sense knowledge and human experience. Notice the three components for verifying something scientifically:

1.  It must be observable (empirical: detectable by five senses).

2.  It must be repeatable (observable by multiple accounts).

3.  It must be testable (provides a necessary exam to prove validity).

Faith, on the other hand, is a belief that may or may not be proven empirically. Yet claims made by faith can be legitimate and reasonable to believe. Centuries earlier, Augustine called reason indispensable to faith. He acknowledged that "Faith must precede reason and purify the heart and make it fit to receive and endure the great light of reason."[158] It is for this reason that faith can be considered cooperative with reasonable use of science. Science properly understood and applied reinforces the Christian faith.

Historian Rodney Stark wrote the rise of science was not an extension of classical learning instead, it was the natural outgrowth of Christian doctrine. To appreciate and glorify God, people needed to examine and explore the wonders of nature through God's creation.[159] Three criticisms of religion and faith were identified as emerging from the scientific literature of the period. It was a period in the European intellectual movement of the late 17th and 18th centuries with an emphasis on reason and individualism rather than tradition. The three criticisms were:

• Religious faith cannot be validated by empirical scientific methods; therefore, it cannot be considered objectively true.

• Science represents reason while religious faith represents myth and superstition.

• Religious faith became viewed as one's subjective values occupying a private domain while science was viewed as objectively true and universally applicable, therefore occupying the public domain.

Richard Dawkins, a critic of faith and a vocal member of the New Atheists, argues that science proves things by appealing to evidence, whereas religion runs away from the evidence. Dawkins tells us, "Faith means blind trust in the absence of evidence, even in the teeth of evidence."[160] Many academics and scientists, who are believers, disagree with Dawkins. Their faith is a response to evidence, not blindly believing in something despite the evidence. It may be true that some of the tenets of faith cannot be quantified by scientific methods, however, that should not invalidate one's faith.

Faith is placing one's *trust* in a corresponding belief that matches objective reality. Scientists, whether they be Christian or atheist, all operate using this type of faith every day of their lives, whether they acknowledge it or not. They go out and put the key into their car ignition to drive to work. They believe their car will start and trust that the key they have will properly fit the ignition. They also believe in the location of their place of employment, that when they drive to it, it will still be there. They believe the freeway that connects their home to their workplace is still there, too. They assume a consistency of reality that their five senses cannot immediately prove. These realities are assumed and not empirically tested until they are acted on by one's faith.

For example, as of this moment, hundreds of millions of Christians believe in Christ's resurrection as described in the Bible. Yet, it is not scientifically possible to repeat that historical event. We cannot presently observe the resurrection to verify its objectivity. This is true with all the events of history, from Abraham Lincoln's assassination to the march of Martin Luther King, Jr., in Selma, Alabama. There are historical events that must be taken on face value, based on written evidence or on oral testimony from witnesses who were present at the event. This requires trust, but so does taking a scientist (a fallible person) at their word. While religious faith may not be testable in a laboratory, every scientist alive has also demonstrated faith in things he or she cannot prove or quantify empirically. The real question we should be asking is, who authorized science to set the naturalistic parameters dictating what determines objective truth? In this regard, the hubris from the scientific community can be nauseating.

An individual can embrace both faith and science as valid methods for studying the created order which God has made. Thomas Aquinas argued that faith and reason are *intertwined*. He asserted that faith uses reason and reason cannot succeed in finding the truth without faith. Reason can accompany faith but does not always cause faith.[161]

## Science: God's Truth Hidden in Creation

The development of the scientific enterprise emerged early on in the seventeenth century. With the advent of scientists like Isaac Newton, Johannes Kepler, and Galileo Galilei, the scientific enterprise began to gain momentum. The inductive view of science originated fairly recently from Sir Francis Bacon, who popularized inductive methodologies for scientific inquiry, often referred to as the "Baconian Method."[162]

Isaac Newton was able to demonstrate that a range of observational data could be used to explain universal principles that governed celestial bodies. Newton's successes in explaining terrestrial and celestial mechanics lead to the idea that nature and the universe could be likened to a great machine operating according to fixed laws.[163] It was not long afterward that the idea of the celestial clockmaker emerged. Newton's emphasis on the regularity of nature was believed by many scholars to be responsible for the rise of Deism.

During this period, the majority of scientists were functioning from a Christian basis. This basis included the belief in a God as the Creator and Lawgiver who has implanted laws in his creation that can be discovered. Faraday's posture regarding science was as follows, "Where Scripture speaks, we speak; where Scripture is silent, we are silent."[164] Of course, some truths about the created world may defy scientific examination because they elude observation, repeatability, and empirical verification. This is simply because science tends to answer mechanistic questions of *how* something works (function), but science can never comprehensively answer the *why* (purpose or design) some things work the way they do.

Human reason can examine physical reality and conclude that God exists and is trustworthy (Romans 1:18-20). If God is trustworthy, then that logically leads to acknowledging that God did indeed send his son Jesus Christ to be crucified for our sins to be raised from the dead to provide redemption for all who would believe and receive Him. We can trust what He has revealed to us in His Word, the Bible. The Holy Spirit can use human reasoning to supply the faith to trust in God even when a person's own reason does not understand (Hebrews 11:1-3). God has made both faith and reason.[165] Through *special revelation*, God reveals Himself to humanity.

Albert Einstein is credited with saying, "The most incomprehensible thing about the universe is that it is comprehensible."[166] Christians do play an active and enduring role in the scientific community. There has been a kind of conflict thesis that has become expected and advanced between science and faith. However, it is important to understand that from a historical perspective it is religious ideas and institutions that played a significant and positive role in motivating scientific inquiry. It has been established that religion was a *necessary condition* for the emergence of science in the West.[167]

According to the writings of George M. Trevelyan (1876-1962), the members of the Royal Society familiarized the minds of their countrymen with the idea of the laws of nature. By endorsing the scientific methods of inquiry, they believed they could discover God's truths hidden in creation. They held that discoveries would never contradict Bible history or the miracles found in Christianity. Trevelyan asserted, "The Christian base never hindered science. Rather, the Christian base made modern science possible."[168]

# CHAPTER FOUR

## Origins:
### How Did We Get Here?

Whenever the subject of the origins of *life* is discussed, there appear to be only two satisfactory explanations that best fit the evidence. We are either here because of a cosmic accident that did not have us in mind or… we are the purposeful, special creation of an omnipotent, supernatural deity. Make your choice.

1. Cosmic Accident: All biological life forms, including humans, are the accidental products of blind chemistry, time, and chance. All life evolved from the merging of random molecules in a primordial sea millions of years ago.

2. Special Creation: All plant, animal, and human life were specifically created by an Omnipotent, Super-intellect who finely tuned the physical universe making it hospitable for organic life to survive and flourish (known as the Anthropic Principle).

*The Anthropic Principle* is demonstrated by the fine-tuning of many physical properties we see on the earth. Without these features (and many more not listed) life would not be possible.

- The earth exists 93 million miles from the sun placing it within in the Goldilocks Zone: not too hot… not too cold. This "habitable zone" is necessary to keep the earth's water in liquid form which is essential for biological life. If too close to the sun, the earth's water would vaporize. If too far, the earth's oceans and lakes would freeze solid. Either scenario would be catastrophic for life.

- The force of gravity on the earth is accurately fine-tuned to one part in $10^{80}$. Gravity (precisely tuned) keeps our oceans and lakes from evaporating and flying off into space. Gravity also keeps the moon orbiting the earth at exactly 250,000 miles away, precisely the right distance, stabilizing the earth's axial tilt. Gravity is also crucial in keeping the earth's atmosphere enveloping the globe, preventing it from escaping into space.

- The earth's stratosphere has an ozone layer that blocks out the sun's dangerous ultraviolet radiation from reaching the earth's surface. Ultra-violent rays are extremely harmful to plant and animal life. Without the ozone layer, complex biological life could not survive on earth.

- The tilt of the earth on its axis is exactly 23.5 degrees. Due to this precise axial tilt, the sun shines on different latitudes at different angles throughout the year. This causes our planet to experience seasons, which help regulate earth's temperature along with aiding in biospheric hydration around the globe.

- If the earth took more than twenty-four hours to rotate, temperatures on the planet would become too extreme between sunrise and sunset for supporting plant and animal life. If the earth's rotation was slightly shorter, wind velocities and tidal surges on the planet's surface would be too severe for plant or animal life.[169]

## Biogenesis: Life Begets Life

There are serious problems with the theory of Darwinian Evolution. It exalts chance, blind chemistry, and materialism (via speculation) while denying the scientific means necessary to confirm any empirical facts. For example, when observing the Cambrian Explosion, we don't observe transitional forms evolving from one species to another species anywhere in the fossil record. Life only arrives from other living things. We see that dogs have puppies, cats have kittens, sheep give birth to lambs, and bacteria produce more bacteria. Life only comes from other living organisms, and that only after its kind. This is known as *biogenesis*. The theory of evolution never tackles the big question of life's origins. Darwin's theory only addressed the survival of the fittest, never the *arrival* of the fittest.

The notion of life magically arising from non-life (abiogenesis) still presents a major problem for naturalistic scientists. The early notion of *spontaneous generation*, once a hopeful explanation for naturalists, has long been debunked by the scientific community. Centuries before Darwin, the Greek philosopher Anaximander (610-546 B.C.) believed that living things originated by natural processes from moisture and were originally aquatic beings that later transferred to dry land.[170] The only problem is… we have no evidence of this ever occurring.

## The Recipe for Mice

We should not be surprised that scientists come up with crazy theories in the name of science. Flemish scientist Jan Baptista van Helmont (1580-1644) believed that mice would spontaneously appear when certain ingredients were mixed together. He wrote, "Place a dirty shirt or some rags in an open pot or barrel containing a few grains of wheat or some wheat bran, and in 21 days, mice will appear."[171] We all know that mice do not magically appear from rotting clothes and kernels of grains. They come from other mice. It took observation from others to verify the falsehood of the theory.

Dead matter has never been observed to produce anything close to a living cell, let alone complex living organisms like mice, rabbits, dogs, or humans. The attempt to produce life in a lab, even with the help of eager scientists manipulating chemicals and laboratory conditions to try and induce amino acids to form into a protein molecule, has been unsuccessful. These experiments have repeatedly failed to produce even the simplest chemical building blocks essential for life.

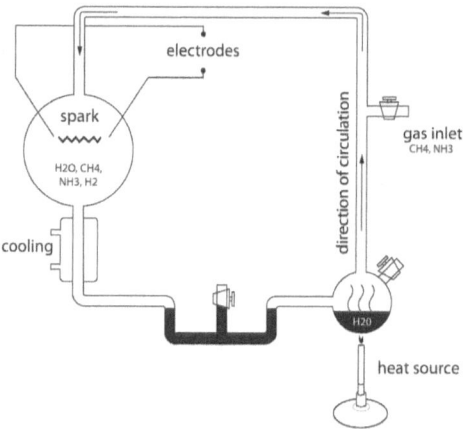

Stanley Miller, at the University of Chicago in 1953. Miller, along with his colleague Harold Urey, used a sparking device to mimic a lightning storm on early earth. Their experiment produced a brown broth rich in amino acids. Random amino acids left to themselves are not capable of producing a protein molecule. Miller and Urey understood that their methane-induced "prebiotic soup" of amino acids would be destroyed by oxidation if oxygen were present. Since oxygen was present on the early earth, and oxygen is essential for organic life, there is no way amino acids could have developed under these conditions. Stanley Miller himself admitted, "making compounds and making life are two different things." The Miller-Urey experiment failed in its quest of creating life in the laboratory.

## Life is Irreducibly Complex

To get life from inorganic chemicals requires huge amounts of ordered and specific information. There are twenty different types of amino acids that are responsible for protein molecule production, and there are approximately 20,000 different proteins found in the human body. Amino acids by themselves do not constitute life. They are building blocks for proteins which in turn are the building blocks for DNA, enzymes, and living cells.

Amino acids must be arranged in a precise way to form any protein molecules. In all replicating organisms, the DNA in those cells store information which cannot be read without the RNA molecule which carries messages from the DNA molecule to other parts of the cell for processing. Most often, this information is used to manufacture proteins. This leaves molecular biologists with a huge dilemma. Which came first, in other words: the chicken or the egg? You can't get enzymes and RNA without proteins, and you can't organize amino acids into proteins without RNA and enzymes! If there are no proteins, there can be no living cells. But if there are no living cells, there can be no living organisms! Physicist Gerald Schroeder writes, "Highly sophisticated attempts to get amino acids to join in any sort of complex molecule has been one long study in failure. The complexity of life is still one bewildering mystery."[172] We are back at square one. Where did life come from?

According to Hubert Yockey, an Information Theorist, "Granting that a primordial pond was teeming with amino acids over a billion years of trial and error, this would not be enough time to get even one protein molecule. A typical living cell requires at least 387 different proteins to survive and thrive in an environment."[173] Life simply could not originate undirected from a primordial soup in the ancient past. With the information revolution over the last 60 years, advances in molecular biology have shown that cells require both high information content and a means to pass this information on to the next generation.[174] Dr. Dean Kenyon, Professor Emeritus of Biology at San Francisco State University, co-authored a book in 1969 entitled *Biochemical Predestination*. In this book, he argued that the science of the origin of life left *no room for a Creator [emphasis added]*. However, a further study examining the molecular complexity of the cell forced Dr. Kenyon to change his mind:

> No longer is it a reasonable proposition to think that simple chemical events could have any chance at all to generate the kind of complexity that we see in the very simplest living organism. We have not the slightest chance of a chemical evolutionary origin for even the simplest cell with the new knowledge that has accumulated in this century.[175]

Dr. Kenyon and William Dembski both confirmed that the information-rich, complex specified information (CSI) found in all living organisms is very difficult for materialists to explain without invoking an *intelligent first cause*. The fact that specified complex patterns can be found in all living things, as well as, in the physics of the fine-tuning of the universe, indicates some kind of guidance in their formation, which is what points to intelligence.[176]

Can you get highly organized living cells from dead matter? This question still haunts naturalistic scientists, and it should! According to astrophysicist Fred Hoyle, the likelihood of the formation of single-cell life coming from inanimate matter is $1 \times 10^{40}$. The chance of life happening is an impossible number of one in ten with 40 zeros after it! According to Hoyle, the likelihood would be comparable to a tornado blowing through a junkyard, and in the aftermath of all the wind randomly blowing the metal and debris into the air, a fully assembled Boeing 747 jetliner being produced.[177] Life only comes from other living things.

Darwin's theory of evolution never addressed this huge problem of biogenesis. Where did life originate from? Instead, Darwin thrust his theory of natural selection and gene mutation onto already *living, reproducing animals*. Then, he speculated as to where all the various species of animals came from.[178] Evolution fails to account for the origin of life and it has not been able to demonstrate scientifically the diversification of life.

The second and more reasonable explanation for the origin of life is that all living creatures, including humans, are the product of an omniscient, omnipotent entity that supernaturally created life from inanimate matter. Only God could create self-aware, reasoning, living creatures like us. We have already established that life can only come from other living things. According to the Bible, God is the Creator and the source of all life.

Our choices are limited:

1. God exists and is the Creator of the cosmos and giver of all life, according to the Genesis account.

2. All life is the product of dead matter, undirected physics, and mindless chemistry.

If God exists, He is responsible for creating all matter, energy, and space out of nothing. We observe our planet full of complex biological organisms that fill the land and the sea with abundant and diverse life. Life had to get here from somewhere, somehow. We should not discount God's ability to work with and beyond natural laws and to create and call into existence that which did not exist. I am convinced that God and the laws of physics He created are the logical conclusions and that He is responsible for all biological life on earth.

## The Theory of Evolution

The debate over evolution has been somewhat confusing for many people because of the different definitions used for the term *evolution*. Micro-evolution in this sense simply means "change over time." This refers to minor changes in features of individual species, changes that can occur over a short period of time. Even skeptics of Darwin's theory agree that this type of "change over time" takes place.

Most scientists and academics commonly associate the word evolution with the idea that all biological organisms we witness today, have descended directly from a single common ancestor, known as Macro-evolution. This suggests a picture of the history of life on earth as a great tree, with all animal and plant species branching out from one common trunk/origin.

According to this assumption, evolution aided by chance mutation, and millions of years of survival of the fittest, produced all the amazing diversity of animal and plant life on the earth today. The idea of common descent, natural selection, and genetic mutation form the core of the *definition of evolution* that the vast majority of university and high school textbooks use in western/industrialized nations whenever teaching or discussing evolution.[179]

Macroevolution bears no serious scientific clout in light of the empirical evidence from the fossil record and is today being denounced by more and more credible scientists. If undirected natural laws, blind chemistry, and millions of years have not demonstrated how non-living matter could have changed into living organisms, there are no naturalistic explanations that are sufficient. The most reasonable explanation is that a supernatural, intelligent, first-cause agent, best fits the evidence we see of the physical universe. Astronomer Robert Jastrow once stated:

For the scientist who has lived by his faith in the power of reason, the story ends like a bad dream. He has scaled the mountain of ignorance; he is about to conquer the highest peak; as he pulls himself over the final rock, he is greeted by a band of theologians who have been sitting there for centuries.[180]

The rational comprehensibility of the natural world coupled with the laws of nature strongly point to a transcendent law-giver and Creator of the natural order. The consequences of this fact have profound philosophical and theological implications. Even as one studies the beauties of a painting and better understands the creativity and skill of the artist, human beings must believe that God has blessed us with rational faculties and believe that the Creator has purposely opened up the discovery of creation for the curious enquirer. God has given humans the capacity to reason and understand to some extent concerning the coherent makeup and function of the world around them. The discipline of science is a tool to help people along the way of inquiry, discovery, and understanding. Faith and science are meant to be companions in the great enterprise of the discovery of God's world according to the laws and principles by which He created and now sustains it. Both the Bible and science have a great deal to say about what it is to be a human being, but without recognizing their interdependence they can be used to say very different things.

For some time, faith has been misunderstood as a subjective hideout into which Christians could retreat from the onslaught of scientific knowledge and the secular assault. But this writer believes that Christians must make public and meaningful claims of truth. By coming forward, the Christian's faith is emboldened to stand in the light of criticism and rational scrutiny. Real truth welcomes examination and always prevails whenever challenged. Even though most people who reject Christianity treat it as a refuge for enemies of reason, "The truth is that there is no other worldview in the history of the human race that has a higher regard for the laws of logic."[181]

Humans have an innate capacity to apprehend God's existence and recognize God's handiwork in nature. If all truth is God's truth, then science and human reason combined with faith can accurately point the way to the reliability of God's word and God's way. When faith is exercised alongside scientific inquiry, it is an arrangement in which both can flourish. According to both William Provine and Richard Dawkins, to believe in evolution one would have to automatically adopt an atheistic worldview. Following this ultimatum, any belief in God is superstitious and unnecessary. Not only is the theory of evolution corrosive to the idea of a creator God, but it also destroys any foundation for human meaning or ethics. As William Provine points out:

> Let me summarize my views on what modern evolutionary biology tells us loud and clear... There are no gods, no purpose, no goal-directed forces of any kind. There is no life after death. When I die, I am absolutely certain that I am going to be dead. That's the end for me. There is no ultimate foundation for ethics, no ultimate meaning to life, and no free will for humans either.[182]

## Is Evolution a Religion?

A celebrity scientist, astrophysicist, and star of the PBS documentary series *Cosmos*, Carl Sagan became a household name back in the 1980s and '90s. Sagan began the series with his famous assertion, "The Cosmos is all there is, or ever was, or ever will be." Strangely, this sounds more like a creedal confession of faith than an observation of science. What is more, if we as the human race are a cosmic accident and the mindless product of evolution, how is the average person to behave? In this case, objective good or evil does not exist. Remember, according to Dawkins, we are "just dancing to our DNA." Humans are nothing more than biologically determined creatures guided by base animal instinct. If Dawkins and Provine are correct, free will is an illusion and there is really no meaning or purpose to this life.

Dr. Michael Ruse, formerly a professor of philosophy and zoologist at the University of Guelph, Canada openly expressed his trust in Darwinian religion.

Evolution is promoted by its practitioners as more than mere science. Evolution is promulgated as an ideology, a secular religion - a full-fledged alternative to Christianity, with meaning and morality. I am an ardent evolutionist and an ex-Christian, but I must admit that in this one complaint - and Mr. [sic] Gish is but one of many to make it - the literalists are absolutely right. Evolution is a religion. This was true of evolution in the beginning, and it is true of evolution still today. Evolution, therefore, came into being as a kind of secular ideology, an explicit substitute for Christianity.[183]

Thomas Nagel identifies the extreme polarization existing between Christianity and the evolutionary worldviews. "Darwin enabled modern secular culture to breathe a great collective sigh of relief, by apparently providing a way to eliminate purpose, meaning, and design as fundamental features of the world."[184] The atheist who subscribes to the naturalistic view of human origins, cannot logically appeal to any moral absolute or any transcendent meaning for his life. To live with any sense of meaning or morality in the secular world, the atheist must borrow his ethics from Christianity.

Socio-biologist Michael Ruse wrote along with Edward Wilson that, "Morality is merely an adaptation of our species to further our reproductive ends." They further explained: "Ethics as we understand it, is an illusion fobbed off on us by our genes to get us to cooperate." Through their convenient redefinition of terms, evolutionists hope to escape any ethical accountability by shoving values and morality into the category of being an illusion with no real-world application.[185]

Many former scientists and philosophers are now rejecting the evolutionary worldview strictly based on scientific evidence alone. World-renowned British journalist and philosopher Malcolm Muggeridge once wrote regarding the theory of evolution and its blind acceptance by modern man:

I am convinced that the theory of evolution, especially the extent to which it's been applied, will be one of the great jokes in the history books in the future. Posterity will marvel that so very flimsy and dubious a hypothesis could be accepted with the incredible credulity that it has.[186]

# CHAPTER FIVE

# Is the Bible Reliable?

"The Bible is the inexhaustible fountain of all truths. The existence of the Bible is the greatest blessing which humanity ever experienced."

**– Immanuel Kant**

One of the most common objections to Christianity concerns the reliability of the Bible. "How do we know that the Bible is true? Wasn't the Bible written by men? There have been so many translations passed down through the centuries… which one is authentic? Isn't the Bible full of contradictions, and literary mistakes?" Is the Bible really the Word of God? What makes the Bible more authoritative than the Koran, or The Sayings of Confucius, or the Hindu Vedas? Aren't these other religious writings believed, by their followers, to be divine?

These questions pose valid objections that deserve an answer. I intend to address these questions and to establish the historical, literary, and spiritual accuracy of the Bible. As we investigate the reliability of the Bible, it is important to note that the Bible, without exception, has been the most scrutinized and critiqued book in all of human history. Does this literary scrutiny reveal that the Bible is just another human product, or is it truly the inspired, infallible Word of God? The Bible itself claims two main characteristics that mark it as truly inspired by God:

1. Inerrancy: The Bible is perfect. In the original copies of each manuscript written by the particular Bible author, there were no mistakes or tinges of error.

2. Infallibility: The Bible is unfailing as a trustworthy guide for faith and practice, life, and behavior.[187]

101

There are 66 books contained in the canon of Scripture believed to be divinely inspired by God and infallible (without error). These 66 volumes that make up our Bible today were written over 1,500 years by 40 different authors, over three different continents: Asia, Africa, and Europe. The reality that the Bible can be read as a cohesive whole is supernatural enough given this context.

The Bible is divided into two parts, the Old Testament, written before Christ, which is made up of 39 books, and the New Testament, addressing Christ's life and the time after Christ consisting of 27 books. The earliest known complete list of the 27 books of the New Testament is found in a letter written by Athanasius, a fourth-century bishop of Alexandria, dated back to 367 A.D. Athanasius compiled this list to protect his congregation from the heretical writings circulating at the time. The 27 books of the New Testament were first formally canonized during the council of Hippo (393 A.D.) and Carthage (397 A.D.) in North Africa.[188]

The word canon comes from the Greek word *kanon*, which means "measuring rod" or "rule."[189] In essence, the canon of Scripture was meant to be the standard or measure to compare all other theological teachings or writings against. The early church used three criteria to determine the canonicity of New Testament books:

1. Apostolic Connection: Was each book written by an apostle, a prophet, or one closely associated with an apostle?

2. Orthodoxy: Were these books recognized as divinely inspired? Does the book agree doctrinally with the teachings of other canonical books? Did individual books gain acceptance by the Early Church Fathers as being theologically sound?

3. Universal Acceptance or Church-Wide Consensus. Were the letters recognized by the early Church Fathers and circulated for the benefit of other Christians?

The complete canon of the Old Testament was assembled after the destruction of Jerusalem in 70 A.D. but, a part of the canon had been recognized far earlier by the Jewish people. The books of the law (also known as the Torah or Pentateuch, Genesis to Deuteronomy) were acknowledged as being written as early as the Old Testament history found in the Book of 2 Kings, chapter 22 recorded around 500 B.C. When the 27 books of the New Testament were gathered into the canon at Hippo, the Holy Scriptures were considered complete.[190]

## A Self-Authenticating Book

**1) The Bible proclaims itself to be the inspired Word of God.** The canon of Scripture possesses certain qualities that authenticate it as true. There are two unique qualities that the Bible displays when read. First, reading the Bible has the power to change the reader.

> For the word of God is living and active and sharper than any two-edged sword, and piercing as far as the division of soul and spirit, of both joints and marrow, and able to judge the thoughts and intentions of the heart. And there is no creature hidden from His sight, but all things are open and laid bare to the eyes of Him with whom we have to do (Hebrews 4:12-13).

The Bible is self-authenticating because of its power to change people's lives. It is God's Word alone, not human reasoning, that is the source of liberating truth. Some people are afraid to seriously read the Bible because the Bible ends up reading them, exposing their carnal, selfish desires. How many testimonies have you heard of someone reading the Bible or reciting a scripture verse and their lives becoming immediately impacted by that encounter? I have personally met dozens of people who were instantly transformed and converted by quietly reading a Bible verse.

**2) The Bible is trustworthy based on its internal harmony and unity.** The stories, history, and prophecies recorded in the Bible beautifully fit together and confirm the overarching, coherent narrative of God's message of redemption to humanity. Like an amazing puzzle pieced together, the 66 books of the Bible weave a clear tapestry of humanity's origins, their fall, their redemption, and their restoration back to God.

King David wrote, "The sum of Your word is truth, and every one of Your righteous ordinances is everlasting" (Psalm 119:160). It is important to note that some of the writers of the New Testament were not apostles. How then can one explain their inspired authority? These writers used the apostolic message that they heard from and had confirmed by the Lord Himself (Hebrews 2:3). We know that the author of the Gospel of Mark worked very closely with the Apostle Peter (1 Peter 5:13). The author of the Gospel of Luke was a companion with the Apostle Paul (2 Timothy 4:11). We also know that Luke (the writer of the books of the Gospel of Luke and the Book of Acts), interviewed many witnesses to produce his accounts of historical events (Luke 1:1-4).

James and Jude, who authored the books in the Bible of the same name, were most likely the brothers of Jesus and were very familiar with the apostles in Jerusalem (Acts 15:13; 21:18; Galatians 1:19; 2:12). Lastly, Paul's epistles were given the same status and equated with Scripture by the Apostle Peter (2 Peter 3:15-16). With all the writers of the New Testament, there is a direct connection to the Lord Jesus or a direct link between the writer and one of the Apostles of Jesus who gave them the information firsthand.[191]

The process by which the Bible was written is called *inspiration*. That definition comes from 2 Timothy 3:16, which states, "All Scripture is inspired by God and profitable for teaching, for reproof, for correction, for training in righteousness." The word inspiration means God-breathed. God is the direct source of all that is revealed and recorded in the Scriptures. This implies that God Himself used human scribes as his divine instruments to record the precise message he intended.

It is important to clarify that these authors were not mere secretaries, taking down dictation. They had each received revelation from God and were giving the revelation expression by writing down their experiences with human hands. Likewise, 2 Peter 1:20-21 reads, "But know this first of all, that no prophecy of Scripture is a matter of someone's own interpretation, for no prophecy was ever made by an act of human will, but men moved by the Holy Spirit spoke from God." The word *moved* is translated from the Greek word *photo*, which means,

"To be carried along like a ship is carried by the wind." This implies that God carried each writer along as he wrote so that the message was kept intact.[192] Here it is easy to see both the divine and human dynamic working in conjunction to inspire, reveal, and record God's message, a message we now have in Scripture.

## Is the Bible Trustworthy?

Can we trust the claims of the Bible? We will look at three academic disciplines: History, Archeology, and Prophecy to address that question. Evidence from history *verifies* biblical claims, the discoveries from archeology support biblical writing, and the fulfillment of Bible prophecies *prove* the reliability of the Bible. These three areas of study supply very strong evidence for the authenticity and veracity of the Bible.

Christianity is a historical religion. Therefore, the first area of investigation deals with authenticating the *historical relevance* of events, people, and places recorded in the Bible. History can be defined as a knowledge of the past based upon written or oral testimony. The discipline of history answers the question concerning sufficient historical evidence to support the accuracy of the biblical record.

The second area is *Archaeology*. Archaeology is the science that investigates human history and prehistory through the excavation of sites and the analysis of artifacts to ascertain the truth regarding ancient civilizations and customs. When eye-witness accounts or physical artifacts are not available, forensic techniques can be used. Forensics studies evidence from the past in order to discern what sort of single cause would have created a certain effect. In the example of a crime scene, there might be fingerprints, bloodstains, a murder weapon, or muddy footprints found at the scene of a crime. Forensics uses these types of clues to piece together the logical cause of the effect surrounding an event. Are there recent archeological discoveries that confirm the historical events and geographical places recorded in the Bible? Yes! And more sites are being discovered yearly.

The third area of examination concerns Bible prophecy. *Prophecy* is the foretelling or the prediction of God's future message through human lips, to His people. The Old Testament prophet's ministry also included predictions and revelations identifying specific events in Christian history.[193] The Old Testament records 300 predictions regarding the Jewish Messiah. There are numerous prophecies about Jesus' virgin birth, the place of his birth, his death, the method of his death, and his physical resurrection. All these prophecies were fulfilled by Jesus of Nazareth. Remember, these things predicted about Jesus' life and death were written 700 to 1,000 years before Jesus' physical birth. They could not just have happened by coincidence.

## Bibliographical Evidence

In historical science, an ancient scroll, clay tablet, or papyrus must pass three tests: *the internal test, the external test, and the bibliographic test.* The bibliographic test includes three features: The document must contain *eyewitness accounts*, there must be a *short amount of time between copy and original, and several copies must have been made.*[194]

For the New Testament, we no longer have the original autograph copies written by the apostles, therefore we must rely solely on copies. There are thousands of documents made from those original manuscripts that make up our present Bible. The original New Testament texts have been dated to be within 30 to 300 years from the time that the autographs were written. By ancient manuscript standards, these copies appear amazingly close to the originals. No other ancient document has been copied and recopied over such a long period of time as the Bible.

According to research done by the President of the Christian Apologetics and Research Ministry (CARM), Matt Slick describes *Paleographers* as being specialized historians who study ancient texts including the 5800 manuscripts that make up the New Testament. According to these expert analysts, the surviving manuscripts of the New Testament are dated between the early second century and fifteenth centuries A.D. They are remarkably close to the autographs, considering that the original documents making up the New Testament were produced from 50 to 95 A.D.

The New Testament is unlike any other ancient manuscript when you consider the number of surviving copies (5,795) and their closeness to the original autographed manuscript. Compared to other ancient manuscripts like those written by Homer, Plato, Aristotle, or Caesar, only a very few copies of those secular works exist, and the surviving copies are separated by huge gaps of time. Remember, the closer a copy is to the original manuscript date, the more reliable it tends to be. Copies of most secular works often span hundreds, if not a thousand or more, years between the time the copy was written from the date of the original manuscript.[195]

The Bible is so accurate in its transmission from the originals to the present copies, that if you compare it to any other ancient writing, the Bible is light years ahead in terms of the number of manuscripts, accuracy, and close time proximity of the copy to the original. The New Testament alone is considered to be ninety-nine, point five percent textually pure. This means that of the 6,000 Greek copies (the New Testament was written in Greek) and the additional 21,000 copies in other languages, there is only one-half of one percent variation. Of this very slight number, the great majority of the variants are easily corrected by comparing them to other copies without "typos," or by simply reading the context. These variants are very minor. None of the variants affects doctrinal truth, and the words and deeds of Christ are superbly and reliably transmitted to us.[196]

### THE NEW TESTAMENT MANUSCRIPTS COMPARED TO OTHER ANCIENT MANUSCRIPTS

| AUTHOR | DATE WRITTEN | EARLIEST COPY | PERIOD | SURVIVING COPIES |
|---|---|---|---|---|
| Plato | 400 B.C. | 900 A.D. | 1300 yrs. | 210 |
| Homer | 800 B.C. | 400 B.C. | 400 yrs. | 1,757 |
| Caesar | 100 B.C. | 900 A.D. | 1000 yrs. | 251 |
| Aristotle | 300 B.C. | 1100 A.D. | 1400 yrs. | 5 |
| Tacitus | 100 A.D. | 900 A.D. | 1000 yrs. | 31 |
| Herodotus | 450 B.C. | 1000 A.D. | 1350 yrs. | 109 |
| N.T. Bible | 50-100 A.D. | 130 A.D. | 30-40 yrs. | 5,795 |

[197]

## What About Copy Errors Made by Scribes?

Professor Bruce Metzger of Princeton conducted a research project comparing the accuracy of the copies of the New Testament to other ancient works of history. He concluded that "the Hindu *Mahabharata* was copied with about 90% accuracy and Homer's *Iliad* was copied to 95% accuracy regarding the essential teachings of the originals. By contrast, scholars estimate that the New Testament was copied with up to 98.33 to 99.75% accuracy."[198] According to Metzger's findings, the New Testament we have today is extremely reliable.

R.T. France, a noted New Testament scholar and Principal of the London School of Theology, makes this compelling statement, "The student of the history of Jesus is, from the point of view of textual criticism, on vastly safer ground than the student of the life of Julius Caesar or indeed of any other figure of ancient history."[199]

The evidence from non-Christian sources is sufficient to lead all reputable historians to agree that a Jewish teacher named Jesus did live and die by crucifixion during the early part of the first century. As Professor Christopher Tackett writes in the *Cambridge Companion to Jesus*, "The fact that Jesus existed, that he was crucified under Pontius Pilate... seems to be part of the bedrock of historical Christian tradition." Tackett continues, "If nothing else, the non-Christian evidence can provide us with *certainty* on that score."[200]

Based on the early manuscript copies validating the historical person of Jesus, the evidence is much more numerous and far more compelling than for most other notable figures of history. The renowned New Testament scholar Bart Ehrman, a self-avowed agnostic, is highly skeptical of the reliability of the New Testament documents. Even Ehrman was compelled to admit that any manuscript variant or error by a copyist did not affect the central message or essential doctrine of the New Testament at all:

> It would be a mistake... to assume that the only changes being made were by copyists with a personal stake in the wording of the text. Most of the changes in our early Christian manuscripts have nothing to do with theology or ideology.[201]

Bart Ehrman, and his mentor Bruce Metzger, are recorded in their book *The Text of the New Testament* as saying:

> The textual critic compares numerous scriptural quotations used in commentaries, sermons, and other treatises written by early church fathers. Indeed, so extensive are the citations that if all other sources for our knowledge of the text of the New Testament are destroyed, they would be sufficient alone for the reconstruction of practically the entire New Testament.[202]

In other words, we are not left guessing about the literary content and accuracy of the New Testament original doctrine or message. "Because of the vast number of copies (5800), the original New Testament manuscripts are the most well-attested texts from the ancient world, based on the quality, quantity and early dates of copies."[203] We can be confident in the reliability of documents as consistent as these.

### Archaeological Evidence: The Dead Sea Scrolls

In 1947, a shepherd in the Qumran area on the northwest shore of the Dead Sea discovered a cave full of ancient documents stored in clay pots. Between 825-870 documents were retrieved from there out of 11 caves. The caves held the documents of all the books of the Hebrew Bible except for Esther and Nehemiah. These ancient documents were written from a period of 250 B.C. to 70 A.D.

The Book of Isaiah was written 700 years before the birth of Christ, yet Isaiah 53 predicts the crucifixion of Jesus and the exact way in which he would die. Psalm 22, which was written 1,000 years before Jesus' life, gives a detailed description of the Lord's trial, His crucifixion, and even that the soldiers would gamble for His garments. An interesting side note: The Roman use of crucifixion was not even invented or used until around the third century B.C. when the Phoenicians introduced it to the Romans.[204] Isaiah could not possibly have known what He was prophesying about, regarding the mode of execution that would be used to kill Jesus.

Yet, Isaiah accurately predicted the method of Jesus' death. Many liberal scholars and Bible critics have said that because Isaiah 53 and Psalm 22 make such accurate predictions about Jesus' death, those two chapters must have been written after the events in 33 A.D. However, using paleography and carbon 14 isotopic dating, historians were able to date the Dead Sea manuscripts between 125-100 B.C. According to Eugene Ulrich at Oxford University, "The scrolls have shown that our traditional Bible has been amazingly accurately preserved for over 2,000 years."[205]

The discovery of the Dead Sea Scrolls confirmed that both Isaiah and the Psalms were written 700-1000 years before Jesus' birth, life, and crucifixion. The most complete Dead Sea manuscript was that of Isaiah and its wording was almost exact to the modern Hebrew Bible with very few minor deviations.[206] What better evidence of authenticity can one ask for?

**Prophecy Proves the New Testament**

There are over 300 prophecies in the Old Testament that point directly to a coming Messiah. Was Jesus of Nazareth actually who the New Testament claims he was? Was he born of a virgin? Was he the Son of God? Did he live a sinless life? Was he crucified? Did he rise from the dead? These questions will be answered in the next few pages. George Carey declared "Jesus presented Himself throughout the Gospels, not first as a prophet, but as the *object of prophecy.*"

This section will investigate just eight prophecies to prove conclusively that Jesus of Nazareth was indeed the Jewish Messiah crucified under the Roman Governor of Judea, Pontius Pilate. Let's look at some of the prophetic Scriptures concerning Jesus' life.

| EVENT | PROPHESIED | FULFILLED |
|---|---|---|
| He would be born in Bethlehem. | Micah 5:2 | Matt. 2:1-6 |
| He would be born of a virgin. | Isaiah 7:4 | Matt. 1:18-25 |
| He would be a descendent of David. | Jer. 43:14-15 | Luke 3:23-31 |
| He would be betrayed for thirty pieces of silver. | Zech. 11:12 | Matt. 26:14 |
| He would be mocked and pierced. | Ps. 22:6-8 Ps. 22:16 | Matt. 27:27 |
| They would gamble for his garments. | Ps. 22:18 | Mark 15:24 |
| He would die with the wicked but be buried with the rich. | Isaiah 53:9 Isaiah 53:12 | Matt. 27:57-60 |
| He would be raised from the dead. | Ps. 16:8-10 | Matt. 28:7 |
| He would die for the sins of the world. | Dan. 9:26 | 1 Peter 2:23-25 |

Looking at just *eight prophecies* like the ones mentioned, what is the mathematical probability of these predictions coming true? Is it just an amazing coincidence, or could it be divine providence? Astronomer and mathematician Peter Stoner has studied the mathematical probability of Old Testament prophecies being fulfilled by Jesus' life and ministry. With just eight prophecies coming true by blind chance, Dr. Stoner's calculation put the probability to be 1 in $10^{17}$. That is the number "1," followed by 17 zeros (100,000,000,000,000,000). This would be equivalent to covering the entire state of Texas with silver dollars two feet deep, marking just one silver dollar with an X, and then letting a blindfolded person fly over in a helicopter, and on his very first attempt, pick the coin marked with the X.[207]

That number makes the chance of just eight prophecies coming true not only mathematically improbable but virtually impossible! Yet we know with historical certainty that over 300 prophecies have indeed come true regarding Jesus' birth, life, ministry, crucifixion, and resurrection. The fact that Jesus had no control over where he was born, how he would die, or where he would be buried indicates that the fulfillment of these prophecies *defies all-natural causes*.[208] The Old Testament prophecies provide overwhelming proof of the deity of Jesus and the reliability of the Bible as a trusted guide.

# CHAPTER SIX

## Did Jesus Claim to Be God?

"For a child will be born to us, a son will be given to us, and the government will rest on His shoulders; and His name will be called Wonderful Counselor, Mighty God, Eternal Father, Prince of Peace."

— Isaiah 9:6

In an age of conflicting religious views and confusion over truth claims, many philosophers and skeptics are still wrestling with the question about the deity of Jesus of Nazareth. Down through the ages, some believed Jesus was simply a great moral teacher. Some believed him to be a prophet, sent by God. Still, others contended that Jesus was a controversial Jewish teacher who became a political deliverer to liberate the Jewish people, by overthrowing the geopolitical power that Rome held over Judea.

### Lord, Liar, or Lunatic

Of all the world religions, only Christianity proclaims that God Himself became a man with the incarnation of Jesus. Of all the founders of the various world religions, Jesus of Nazareth was the only man who ever claimed to be God in the flesh! This is significant. Christian apologist C. S. Lewis wrote:

> A man who was merely a man and said the sort of things Jesus said would not be a great moral teacher. He would either be a lunatic - on a level with the man who says he is a poached egg - or else He would be the Devil of Hell. You must make your choice. Either this man was,

and is, the Son of God: or else a madman or something worse. You can shut Him up for a fool, you can spit at Him and kill Him as a demon, or you can fall at His feet and call Him Lord and God. But let us not come with any patronizing nonsense about His being a great human teacher. He has not left that open to us. He did not intend to.[209]

## More Than a Prophet

There were many religious Jews in Jesus' day that believed Jesus was like one of the great prophets of Israel recorded in the Old Testament. However, one of the most controversial and crucial topics in religious history surrounds the deity of Jesus. Did Jesus actually claim to be God? The second question is equally important. Did the writers of the New Testament *think Jesus was God?* The claims that Jesus made about himself were staggering, particularly in the light of the strict monotheistic teachings of orthodox Judaism in the first century.

In the Gospel of John, Christ is revealed as the *Logos Incarnate*, being both pre-eminent and eternal (John 1:1-3).[210] This claim that Jesus was one with God, signified equality with Yahweh. If Jesus openly claimed divinity for Himself, He was claiming the highest title reserved only for the God of Abraham, Isaac, and Jacob. According to New Testament sources, Jesus understood himself to be equal with God the Father, possessing the power to do things that only Deity could do.

Jesus claimed many God-like characteristics:

1. One in Essence with God the Father: John 10:30.

2. The Embodiment of the Truth: John 14:6.

3. Granted Eternal Life: John 3:16.

4. Lived a Sinless Life: John 8:46.

5. The Object of Faith: John 8:24.

6. The Power to Answer Prayer: John 14:13.

7. Worthy of Human Worship: Matthew 14:33.

8. Right to Judge the World: John 5:27,30.

9. Ability to Forgive Sin: Matthew 9:1-8.

10. Has all Authority on Earth: Matthew 28:18.

When we look at the Gospel accounts, we find that Jesus did indeed claim to be equal with God. Those who heard Jesus' assertions, understood Him to be claiming oneness with the Father.

## Jesus as the Great "I AM"

In the Gospel of John, we witness a religious showdown between the scribes and Pharisees testing Jesus about a woman allegedly caught in adultery. The self-righteous Pharisees were trying to trap Jesus to see how he would judge this difficult case of a woman, who by all Jewish laws, should be condemned and publicly stoned. Jesus knowing the trickery and deceit in their hearts challenged them, "He who is without sin cast the first stone" (John 8:7 KJV). "As the Pharisees, left the temple court one by one, Jesus said to her, 'Woman where are they? Did no one condemn you?' She said, 'No one, Lord.' And Jesus said, 'I do not condemn you either. Go. From now on do not sin any longer'" (John 8:10-11).

This incident set the stage for Jesus to rebuke the religiosity practiced by the scribes and Pharisees and to announce His true identity. The Gospel of John records, "'Your father Abraham rejoiced to see my day, and he saw it and was glad.' So, the Jews said to Him, 'You are not yet fifty years old, and have you seen Abraham?' Jesus said to them, 'Truly, truly, I say to you, before Abraham was born, *I AM*.' Immediately, they picked up stones to throw at Him, but Jesus hid Himself and went out of the temple" (John 8:56-59). When Jesus claimed that He existed before Abraham, the Jews' immediate reaction was to stone Him to death. They understood the implication of Jesus' claim of being "I AM."

The Old Testament punishment for blaspheming the name of the Lord was stoning. "Moreover, the one who blasphemes the name of the Lord shall surely be put to death; all the congregation shall certainly stone him" (Leviticus. 24:16). By claiming to be "I AM," Jesus was openly claiming equality with God by using the sacred name of Yahweh, the God of Abraham, Isaac, and Jacob. The Jews in the temple believed Jesus had openly blasphemed by claiming to be God.

The phrase "I AM" appears in the Old Testament in several places, with significant meaning. The origin of "I AM" can be traced to Exodus 3:14, where God was speaking to Moses and declared that His name was "I AM" or "I AM that I AM." In Isaiah 45:18 the phrase "I AM" represents "Jehovah." The expression was another way of saying, "I am Jehovah," and means "I am He." It is a way of expressing that He is the only God. In Isaiah "I am He," is only spoken by Jehovah. If anyone else used the phrase, it was viewed to be a false and blasphemous claim to be equal with God. By the time of the Prophet Isaiah, it had become a sacred and revered title. Jesus told the Jews in Jerusalem, "If you believe not that *I am He,* you shall die in your sins" (John 8:24).[211] Jesus left no doubt in the minds of those who heard Him. He was not just a prophet or great teacher, He openly claimed to be Deity.

**Power to Forgive Sins**

During His ministry on earth, Jesus claimed to have the power and authority to forgive the sins of others. In Mark's Gospel there is the story of a paralytic man being lowered through the roof by his four friends, in the attempt to avoid the crowd, and get him in front of Jesus. When Jesus saw the crippled man being lowered into the meeting, He pronounced, "Son, your sins are forgiven" (Mark 2:5). The Bible goes on to record that some of the scribes, upon hearing that statement, became indignant, "Why does this man speak that way? He is blaspheming! Who can forgive sins but God alone?" (Mark 2:7). The scribes who were there, immediately recognized that Jesus was exercising a divine prerogative, the ability to forgive sins.

The scribes were correct in their judgment. Only God has the authority to forgive sins! Without explanation, Jesus further validates His authority to forgive sins, by demonstrating His power to heal the paralytic's physical body as well. Jesus exhorted the paralytic, "'I say to you, get up, pick up your pallet and go.' And he got up and immediately picked up the pallet and went out in the sight of everyone so that they were all amazed and were glorifying God, saying, 'We have never seen anything like this'" (Mark 2:11-12).

CHAPTER SIX

## Judge of the Whole World

In Matthew 25:31-46, Jesus speaks of a day when He would judge the whole world. In this final judgment, Jesus clearly describes Himself sitting on the glorious throne, dividing the sheep from the goats. The authority to judge the world was a prerogative that only God could possess. Paul wrote to his young disciple, Timothy "I solemnly charge *you* in the presence of God and of Christ Jesus, who is to judge the living and the dead" (2 Timothy 4:1). Understanding the ramifications of Jesus' claims of Deity, the chief priests and elders hatched a plot to arrest Jesus and have Him killed (Matthew 26:4).

## Jesus Permitted Others to Worship Him

Jesus confirms His Deity by allowing people to openly worship Him. Of course, this would have been seen as idolatry for any orthodox Jew to receive worship from another person. The Jews were systematically taught to worship the one true God of Israel, "You shall fear the Lord your God; and you shall worship Him... You shall not go after other gods, the gods of the peoples who are all around you" (Deuteronomy 6: 13-14). Jesus even quoted this Scripture to Satan when He was being tempted to bow down and worship Him in the wilderness (Luke 4:8).

We see in Matthew's Gospel that Jesus miraculously heals the blind and the crippled as the people begin to worship him. In Psalms 8:2 miraculous healings had been prophesied hundreds of years earlier.

> And the blind and the lame came to Him in the temple, and He healed them. But when the chief priests and the scribes saw the wonderful things that He had done, and the children who were shouting in the temple, "Hosanna to the Son of David," they became indignant and said to Him, "Do You hear what these children are saying?" And Jesus said to them, "Yes, have you never read, 'Out of the mouth of infants and nursing babies You have prepared praise for Yourself'?" (Matthew 21:14-16).

A blind man receives his sight. "Jesus heard that they had put him out, and finding him, He said, 'Do you believe in the Son of Man?' He answered, 'Who is He, Lord, that I may believe in Him?' Jesus said to him, 'You have both seen Him, and He is the one who is talking with you.' And he said, 'Lord, I believe.' And he worshiped Him" (John 9:35-38).

## The Early Church Claimed Jesus as Deity

Recorded in Acts 2:21, we see Peter and the disciples preaching to the multitudes in Jerusalem. In his address to the people, Peter cites the Old Testament Prophet Joel 2:32, "Everyone who calls upon the name of the LORD will be saved." Peter is attributing the title of "LORD" to Jesus. In Joel's passage, the word for LORD is the same Hebrew word, "Yahweh." There is no doubt that Peter is declaring the resurrected Christ as LORD.

Jesus not only claimed deity for Himself but during the first century of Christianity, New Testament writers like Paul, viewed Jesus as fully divine. One of the clearest examples is in Paul's letter to the church in Philippi. Paul speaks of the humble sacrifice resulting in the ultimate exaltation of Jesus by God the Father. Jesus is given the name above all names, and at His name, "Every knee will bow and every tongue will confess that Jesus is Lord to the glory of the Father" (Philippians 2:10 -11). Paul writes to the church at Colossae, highlighting Jesus' nature as *God*, "For in Him all the fullness of Deity dwells in bodily form, and in Him, you have been made complete, and He is the head over all rule and authority" (Colossians 2:9-10.) Paul openly portrays Jesus as being of the same essence as, and one with God, the Father. Paul quotes the Old Testament Scripture written in Isaiah 45:23, which is a direct reference to Yahweh, the God of Abraham, Isaac, and Jacob. There can be no doubt in Paul's letter, Christ's exaltation is absolute and his Lordship is to be universally recognized.

Anglican theologian J. R. Stott wrote, Jesus saw His connection and identity with God as being one with the Father. Jesus stated that his divinity equaled that of God. Jesus claimed that to know Him, was the same as to know God (John 8:19;14:7). To see Jesus was also to see God (John 12:45; 14:9). To believe in Jesus was the same as believing in God (John 12:44; 14:1). To give honor to Jesus was synonymous with giving honor to God (John 5:23).[212]

"For this reason, therefore, the Jews were seeking all the more to kill Him, because He not only was breaking the Sabbath but also was calling God His own Father, making Himself equal with God" (John 5:18). When Thomas was informed by the other apostles that they had seen the risen Jesus, Thomas doubted and said he refused to believe unless he could put his hand on Jesus' hand witnessing the nail print made. Thomas insisted on seeing Jesus' side to examine where the spear pierced his crucified body. Jesus appeared soon afterward to all the apostles and invited Thomas to examine his hands and his side. Thomas responded, "My Lord and my God" (John 20:24-28). C.S. Lewis described his thoughts on the person of Jesus, by stating that Jesus is either the very incarnation of God sent to earth to redeem people from their sins and depravity, or he is the greatest fraud and deception ever introduced to humanity.

## Do All Religions Lead to God?

I have the opportunity to speak on university campuses on topics dealing with apologetics and worldviews. One of the seminars I present is an exposé of major world religions. The seminar's topic, "Do all Religions Lead to God?" During these seminars, it never ceases to amaze me, that the majority of the students who attend, assert that all major religions are basically the same and that they just use different names to describe the same god or gods.

Mahatma Gandhi, the Nobel Prize-winning lawyer who led a successful campaign to rid India from British Rule, once declared, "My position is that all the great religions are fundamentally equal." [213] This pluralistic idea claiming all religions are just slight variations of one another, representing different roads, leading up the same mountain to God, is known as *universalism*. Universalism suggests that all people will eventually be released from any penalty of sin, allowing all individuals to be admitted into God's presence in the afterlife (heaven). This notion may sound loving, inclusive, and culturally sensitive, but universalism is a contradiction of justice and is logically self-refuting.[214]

Many of the major world religions don't even try to claim that they ascend the mountain toward God. Upon closer investigation, all major world religions, except for Christianity, don't deal with historical facts or cognitive information, but rather operate exclusively in the domain of one's personal feelings. Instead of making it up the mountain to God, world religions fall off the precipice... advocating ideas like eternal reincarnation, melting into oneness with the vastness of the universe, or emptying one's consciousness to achieve *cosmic peace* or Nirvana.

Reincarnation, along with New Age mysticism, has grown popular in the last two decades in the West, but it is an Eastern concept found in both Hinduism and Buddhism. Reincarnation claims individuals don't really die spiritually but, their spiritual essence is recycled over and over again into the physical world until that person can rid themselves of their "bad karma" which they accumulated in their past life. The purpose is to earn one's purification by working off bad deeds with good deeds, hoping to eventually achieve perfection. For many of the world's major religions like Hinduism or Buddhism, having a relationship with the Creator God, or going to heaven is not even a part of their stated purpose.

Jesus said, "I am the way, and the truth, and the life; no one can come to the Father except through Me" (John 14:6). Jesus emphasized what is known in logic as a *universal negative*, "*No one* comes to the Father *except* through Me." This is an exclusive absolute claim made by Jesus. Two mutually exclusive statements cannot both be true in the same sense. If Jesus is the *only open channel* for salvation, by definition all other religious options must *be closed*. If multiple religious avenues can lead us to God, then Jesus' claims about being *the only way* is false! If Jesus deceived people about being the only way to God, it then becomes problematic to trust any of the other claims made by Jesus. Known liars should never be classified as *good moral teachers* or *prophets of God* in the manner that Jesus was recognized and acclaimed.

# CHAPTER SEVEN

# The Resurrection
## Historic Fact or Religious Fiction?

"Christ's resurrection can be proved with at least as much certainty as any universally believed and well-documented event in ancient history."

**— Peter Kreeft**

I remember talking to a student at the University of Florida who sincerely believed that he was "god." Furthermore, he went on to explain to me that all other people were gods too. According to this guy, "Most people just have not discovered their godhood yet." Anyone can claim to be God, but what kind of supernatural powers would be necessary to prove one's deity? What are the special credentials that someone would need to possess to prove to the world they were God in the flesh? In the Gospel of John, Jesus predicts his physical death and his bodily resurrection to the scribes and pharisees.

> The Jews then said to Him, "What sign do You show us as your authority for doing these things?" Jesus answered them, "Destroy this temple, and in three days I will raise it up." The Jews then said, "It took forty-six years to build this temple, and will You raise it up in three days?" But He was speaking of the temple of His body. So, when He was raised from the dead, His disciples remembered that He said this; and they believed the Scripture and the word which Jesus had spoken (John 2:18-22).

121

Andy Stanley, senior pastor at North Point Community Church once said, "Anyone who can accurately predict their own death and then prophesy being raised from the dead... and then pull it off, deserves to be listened to!"

## Without the Resurrection, There Would be No Christianity

If you want to disprove Christianity, it is very simple... disprove the resurrection of Jesus. If you can do that, Christianity would instantly crumble! The Bible is very clear on how essential the resurrection is to the Christian faith. The Apostle Paul wrote, "But if there is no resurrection of the dead, not even Christ has been raised; and if Christ has not been raised, then our preaching is vain, your faith also is vain" (1 Corinthians 15:13-14).

Richard Dawkins, the author of the bestselling book, *The God Delusion*, references professor George Wells at London University. According to Dawkins, "Professor Wells is an *expert*... who has called into question the literal existence of Jesus of Nazareth." Quoting Dr. Wells, Dawkins confidently asserts that the *historic Jesus* must have been a religious legend, conjured up as a part of a mythological creation.

What is not known by most readers and Dawkins fails to mention, is that Dr. Wells' academic expertise is in the *German Language*. Wells has absolutely no critical training whatsoever in classical history, archeology, or biblical studies. The fact that Dawkins and other atheists are happy to depend upon an unqualified language professor instead of a scholar in a relevant field like religious history or archaeology is very telling.[215] That's like asking an auto mechanic to diagnose and surgically remove an infected appendix from a patient. The mechanic may have some knowledge of and have an opinion about appendicitis, but he is not qualified to operate. By the same token, your medical doctor is unqualified to fix your car's faulty fuel injector, even though the doctor has driven cars all his adult life.

When one does consult a trained historian, there is a completely different response to the life, crucifixion, and resurrection accounts of Jesus. According to Professor Graeme Clarke, a renowned classicist (Historian) from The Australian National University and author of the chapter on Christianity in *The Cambridge Ancient History,* Professor Clarke says, "Frankly, I know of no ancient historian or biblical historian who would have a twinge of doubt about the existence of Jesus Christ, the documentary evidence is simply overwhelming."[216]

## The Minimal Facts for the Resurrection

How can we be sure Jesus rose from the dead? Many scholars and historians have wrestled with that same question. Dr. Gary Habermas, while writing his doctoral dissertation on the historicity of the Resurrection, developed what he calls, "The Minimal Facts Argument of the Resurrection." One of Dr. Habermas's criteria for selecting these *minimal facts* was that they had to be acknowledged and accepted by critical scholars and skeptics as being irrefutable and historically valid. These twelve facts are significant because they supply overwhelming historical evidence for Jesus' miraculous life, death, and resurrection.

1. Jesus died by crucifixion.

2. He was buried.

3. His death caused the disciples to despair and lose hope.

4. The tomb was empty (the most contested fact).

5. The disciples claimed to have seen the risen Jesus (the most important proof).

6. The disciples were transformed from fearful doubters to bold proclaimers.

7. The resurrection was the central message of first-century Christians.

8. They preached the message of Jesus' resurrection in Jerusalem.

9. The Christian Church was born and grew quickly.

10. Orthodox Jews, who believed Jesus was their Messiah, made Sunday their primary day of worship instead of the Jewish Sabbath.

11. James was converted to the faith when he saw the resurrected Jesus (James, the brother of Jesus, was a family skeptic).

12. Paul was converted to the faith when he encountered the risen Jesus (a hostile witness and persecutor of the Church).[217]

Remember, these historical facts are unanimously accepted by critical theologians and scholars who still intellectually dismiss miracles like Jesus' virgin birth, His walking on water, and His physical resurrection. Some people simply refuse to follow the evidence to its logical conclusion. Facts will always trump feelings no matter how sincerely one's feelings are held.

> As they were coming out, they found a man of Cyrene named Simon, whom they pressed into service to bear His cross. And when they came to a place called Golgotha, which means Place of the Skull, they gave Him wine to drink mixed with gall; and after tasting it, He was unwilling to drink. And when they had crucified Him, they divided up His garments among themselves by casting lots. And sitting down, they began to keep watch over Him there. And above His head, they put up the charge against Him which read, "THIS IS JESUS THE KING OF THE JEWS." At that time two robbers were crucified with Him, one on the right and one on the left (Matthew 27:32-38).

All four Gospels, as well as the book of Galatians, give an account of the crucifixion of Jesus (Matthew 27:32-38; Mark 15:21-32; Luke 23:26-46; John 19:16-27; Galatians 3:13). There is ample evidence from biblical references regarding Jesus' death, but we will also look at extra-biblical sources as well.

### Flavius Josephus (AD 37-103)

The Jewish historian Flavius Josephus, a Roman citizen, recorded considerable information confirming Jesus' Death in his famous work *Antiquities of the Jews.*

> At this time there was a wise man called Jesus, and his conduct was good, he was known to be virtuous. Many people among the Jews and the other nations became his disciples. Pilate condemned him to be crucified and to die. Those who had become his disciples did not abandon his discipleship. They reported that he had

appeared to them three days after His crucifixion and that he was alive. Accordingly, he was perhaps the Messiah, concerning whom the prophets have reported wonders. And the tribe of Christians, so named after him, has not disappeared to this day.[218]

This provides clear extra-biblical evidence supporting that Pilate had condemned Jesus and had Him executed in Jerusalem. Josephus also records that the disciples claimed Jesus appeared to them three days later, helping to solidify their belief in Jesus as the Messiah.

## Cornelius Tacitus (AD 56-117)

Tacitus was a senator and historian of the Roman Empire. He was governor of Asia in 112 A.D. His two major works are the *Annals* and *Histories*. Tacitus was alive and recorded events when Emperor Nero persecuted the Christians and blamed them for the burning of Rome.[219]

Christus from the name had its origin, suffered the extreme penalty during the reign of Tiberius at the hands of one of our procurator Pontius Pilate, and a mischievous superstition, thus checked for the moment, again broke out not only in Judea the first source of evil, but even in Rome.[220]

Tacitus explains the Christians derived their name from a historical figure named Christus (Christus is Latin for Christ). "As Tacitus puts it, Christus went on to suffer *the extreme penalty*, obviously referring to the Roman method of execution, which was crucifixion. Tacitus writes that this occurred during the reign of Tiberius and that he was sentenced by Pontius Pilate."[221]

Every sermon preached by the early Christ-followers in the first century focused on one key component, *the Resurrection of Jesus*. Paul wrote, "For I am not ashamed of the gospel, for it is the power of God for salvation to everyone who believes, to the Jew first and also to the Greek" (Romans 1:16). The gospel, by definition, is the "good news" that Jesus demonstrated to the world, that He was the Jewish Messiah by being raised from the dead!

Luke recorded in the Book of Acts, "As they were speaking to the people, the priests and the captain of the temple guard and the Sadducees came up to them, being greatly disturbed because they were teaching the people and proclaiming in Jesus the resurrection from the dead" (Acts 4:1-2). On one of his missionary journeys, Paul preached the gospel in Athens to the Greek Philosophers. The concept of the dead being raised, was so alien to them they thought Paul was teaching about *two new gods*, Jesus and *Anastasis* (Greek for "resurrection") (Acts 17:18).[222]

This proves how central the resurrection account was to the proclamation of the early gospel message. Paul E. Little confirms the centrality of Jesus' resurrection in the history of early Christianity.

> Jesus' supreme credential to authenticate His claim to deity was His resurrection from the dead. Five times in the course of his life he predicted he would die. He also predicted how he would die and that three days later he would rise from the dead and appear to his disciples.[223]

## Historical Evidence for the Resurrection

Lawyer, philosopher, and Lutheran theologian John Warwick Montgomery asserts that Christianity differs from other world religions in that it is testable. The truth of Christianity's essential claims rests squarely on certain historical facts open to ordinary investigation. Christianity is historically credible.[224] There are a host of foundational differences that separate Christianity from all the other world religions, but we will focus mainly on the historical event that specifically sets the Christian faith apart; the resurrection. All major religions are based on philosophical or theological systems, but Christianity is unique because it is based on real-life, verifiable historical events.

> The uniqueness and the scandal of the Christian religion rest in the mediation of revelation through historical events. Christianity is not a code for living or philosophy of religion; rather it is rooted in real events of history. To some, this is scandalous, because it means the truth

of Christianity is bound up with the truth of central historical facts, such that if those facts should be disproved, so would Christianity. But at the same time, this makes Christianity unique because, unlike most other world religions, we now have a means of verifying its Truth by historical evidence.[225]

To prove something is historically true there must be valid written or eyewitness testimony that corroborates the event beyond any *reasonable doubt*. We have overwhelming evidence for Jesus' resurrection. The Anglican theologian and missionary to India, Lesslie Newbigin once said:

> In speaking of the 'gospel,' I am referring to the announcement that in the series of *events* that have their center in the life, ministry, death, and resurrection of Jesus Christ *something has happened* (physical events occurring in the past) that alters the total human situation and must therefore call into question every human culture.[226]

Newbigin stated that the historical events of Jesus' life, his death, and especially the resurrection have altered and forever impacted all of human history. Historical facts must be acknowledged, made available, and taught to all people, just the way other facts of history are, like the invention of the printing press by Gutenberg in 1455, the discovery of penicillin by Louis Pasteur in 1895, or the signing of the American Declaration of Independence in 1776. No one ever doubts those events in history, even though they were not physically there to witness and confirm the event with their own eyes. They rely upon a knowledge of the past, based on reliable witnesses.

Newbigin was convinced that the Gospel of Jesus, which included His crucifixion and physical resurrection, were factual events that should be proclaimed to everyone in every culture. Newbigin viewed the crucifixion and resurrection of Jesus as actual events based in history that should be recognized, taught and communicated like any other *public truth of history*.

The Superintendent of Princeton Theological Seminary B.B. Warfield asserted, "Christ himself deliberately staked his whole claim to the credit of Deity upon His resurrection. When asked for a sign, He pointed to this sign as a single and sufficient credential."[227] In the early church, the apostolic kerygma (preaching) clearly indicates that the Christian faith was a *resurrection movement* since its inception. People joined the church because they believed in the resurrection. History confirms that early Christians willingly suffered for their conviction that Jesus rose from the grave.[228]

Brooke Foss Westcott (1825-1901) who served as the Bishop of Durham, was a noted biblical scholar and theologian. He was perhaps best known for co-editing The New Testament in the Original Greek. Dr. Westcott said, "Taking all the evidence together, it is not too much to say that there is no historic event better or more variously supported than the resurrection of Christ."[229]

Dr. Simon Greenleaf, a legal scholar at Harvard University and author of the classic forensic textbook, *A Treatise on the Laws of Evidence*, examined the resurrection of Jesus applying the principles of his analytical legal training. Contrary to what skeptics might have expected, Greenleaf concluded that according to the laws of legal evidence used in law courts, the evidence he discovered supported the claim that Jesus had indeed risen from the tomb. His conclusion, "There is more evidence for the historical fact of the resurrection than just about any other event in history."[230]

Paul records in his first letter to the Church at Corinth instructing them on how essential the resurrection was to the foundation of their faith.

> But if there is no resurrection of the dead, not even Christ has been raised; and if Christ has not been raised, then our preaching is vain, your faith also is vain. Moreover, we are even found to be false witnesses of God, because we testified against God that He raised Christ, whom He did not raise if in fact the dead are not raised. For if the dead are not raised, not even Christ has been raised; and if Christ has not been raised, your faith is worthless; you

are still in your sins. Then those also who have fallen asleep in Christ have perished. If we have hoped in Christ in this life only, we are of all men most to be pitied (1 Corinthians15:13-19).

As a result of His bodily resurrection, Jesus proved to be the Jewish Messiah by appearing to Paul, and then to over 500 people after His crucifixion and resurrection (1 Corinthians 15:6). Paul wrote about the devastating consequences for the Christ-follower if indeed there was no physical resurrection by Jesus (1 Corinthians15:20-26).

- Our testimony has been in vain... falsely claiming a resurrection.
- Your faith has been in vain.
- We are false witnesses because we testify that God raised Christ whom He did not raise.
- You are still in your sins.
- Those who have died in Christ, have perished eternally.
- If we have hoped in Christ, we are to be pitied, having been deceived.

The whole foundation of Christianity depends upon the historical fact that the resurrection of Jesus occurred in Jerusalem early in the first century. Jesus fulfilled all the Old Testament prophecies and proved to be the Jewish Messiah by defeating physical death. Therefore, Jesus' claims of divinity were miraculously validated by His resurrection.

German scholar Wolfhart Pannenberg, points to the rapid emergence of Christianity in the first century as proof of Jesus' resurrection. The Apostle Paul traced back the multiple appearances of the resurrected Christ to over five hundred witnesses. Pannenberg writes, "Within the earliest Christian community there must have been a reliable testimony to the empty tomb.[231] This would explain the rapid growth of the early church among Jewish converts, as well as, the setting aside the first day of the week Sunday (the day Jesus rose), as the official Christian day of worship. Pannenberg concludes that, for the Jews of Jesus' time, His resurrection would have signified deity.[232]

Former Professor of History at Oxford University, Thomas Arnold wrote regarding the historic validity of the resurrection:

> I know of no one fact in the history of mankind which is proved by better evidence of every sort, to the understanding of a fair inquirer, again from that great sign which God hath given us that Christ died and rose again from the dead.[233]

## The Resurrection: Five Possibilities

Let's take a look at the explanation that best fits the data detailing what happened in Jerusalem on that first Easter Sunday after Jesus' crucifixion. These five theories were previously put forth by Peter Kreeft.

1. Jesus Rose from the Dead: Jesus died and physically rose from the dead which leads to the supernatural origin of Christianity.

2. Myth Theory: The apostles were grieving and traumatized over the loss of their leader and later created a myth, not meaning it literally to be passed on.

3. Conspiracy Theory: The apostles were deceivers and started a conspiracy that Jesus rose from the dead, making Christianity the most successful lie in history.

4. Hallucination Theory: Jesus didn't rise and the apostles were delusional and imagined they saw Him alive.

5. Swoon or Resuscitation Theory: Jesus didn't really die, but survived the Roman crucifixion and somehow convinced his followers to propagate a deception, that He had risen from the dead.[234]

We will critically examine these five theories beginning with the least plausible and simplest one, and work up to the most difficult one.

## The Swoon Theory

The Roman crucifixion was one of the most effective and painful instruments of execution ever known to humanity. The physical trauma inflicted on the human body was severe. The crucified victim could die from a combination of physical complications like shock, suffocation, dehydration, cardiac arrest, massive loss of blood, or pulmonary edema (fluid on the lungs). The Roman empire's stock and trade was its ability to conquer and eliminate military enemies or criminals. The Roman soldiers in the ancient world were highly trained and proficient killers.

Jesus could not have survived the physical exertion of a crucifixion. Furthermore, Roman law pronounced the death penalty for any Roman soldier who allowed a convicted prisoner to escape. This would include mishandling or botching a crucifixion. Theologian and apologist Lee Strobel from his years of research says, "There is no historical record anywhere of any person *ever surviving* a Roman crucifixion."[235]

The Romans did not break Jesus' legs, a procedure used to speed up suffocation, ensuring the crucified person could not press upon his feet to breathe, thus prolonging the death sentence (John 19:31-33). Because Jesus' legs were not broken by the guards, it confirms the fact that the Roman soldiers believed Jesus was already dead. This was done in fulfillment of a Messianic prophecy, "He keeps all his bones, not one of them is broken" (Psalm 34:20).

John, who claimed to be an eyewitness, reported that he saw blood and water come from Jesus' heart as a Roman spear pierced his side (John 19:34-35). This discharge of water and blood would be medically consistent with fluid collecting around the heart and lungs (pericardial effusion and pleural effusion) during the crucifixion. According to *The Journal of American Medical Association*, "The weight of evidence indicates that Jesus was dead, even before the spear to his side was inflicted."[236] Jesus' physical body was taken down from the cross, wrapped in burial cloths, and entombed in a cave provided by Joseph of Arimathea (John 19:38-42).

Jewish authorities began spreading the story that the guards fell asleep and the disciples came in the night and stole the body (Matthew 28:11-15). Roman guards would not have jeopardized their lives and fallen asleep on the job. Even if they had fallen asleep, the big crowd and the commotion required to move a two-ton boulder would have roused the soldiers from their sleep.[237] Not only did the Romans lack motives for removing the body of Jesus, but the Jewish law also forbade moving a corpse when it was interred to the family tomb.[238]

How could a swooning, dehydrated, half-dead man, remove a huge stone from the door of the tomb? Who moved the stone if not an angel? We can eliminate the Roman soldiers, who would have been condemned to death, or the frightened disciples who were hiding from the Jewish authorities. If Jesus was resuscitated after coming down from the cross, where did He go to receive medical help and to escape notice?

If Jesus could have survived the cross, how did He convince His frightened, demoralized disciples to help spread an outrageous lie that he had risen from the dead? Why did all the disciples worship Jesus as the divine Lord, miraculously risen from the dead, if they knew He had faked his death? All the disciples would have faced rejection, floggings, imprisonment, and death themselves for defending their belief in Jesus' resurrection. It is simply not believable that any one of the disciples would have willingly sacrificed their lives for a known lie!

History confirms that all of Jesus' remaining apostles were eventually killed for their testimony, except for the apostle John. New Testament letters confirm that John lived to be an elderly man on the isle of Patmos (Revelation 1:9). Nothing proves sincerity like martyrdom. The Swoon Theory is not convincing. It cannot explain the rapid spread of Christianity with the dominant belief in Jesus' physical resurrection.

## The Hallucination Theory

The fact that individuals experience hallucinations during severe stress and trauma is a psychological fact. According to medical science, hallucinations are always private, individual, and subjective.[239] It is important to understand that common hallucinations are never experienced by groups (in mass) or by more than one individual at a time.

After Jesus' corpse was placed in the tomb there were many reported sightings of Him. These appearances were by both individuals and by groups of people. These sightings of the risen Jesus happened over a prolonged period of time, occurring in several geographical areas. The nature and frequency of these sightings do not qualify as hallucinations because of the multitude of witnesses and the similarity of sightings.

CHAPTER SEVEN

Christ's Post-Resurrection Appearances:

1. Jesus appeared to Mary Magdalene (Mark 16:9).

2. He appeared to His disciples except for Thomas (John 20:19-25).

3. He appeared once more to the disciples including Thomas (John 20: 26-29; John 21:1-12).

4. Jesus appeared to two disciples on the road to Emmaus (Luke 24:13-35).

5. Jesus appeared to His brother James (1 Corinthians 15:7).

6. Jesus appears to Saul of Tarsus (Acts 9:1-9).

7. Jesus appears to five hundred brethren (1 Corinthians 15:1-6).

If these were all hallucinations and nothing more, why didn't the Jewish authorities simply produce the corpse of Jesus and resolve the controversy instantly? According to medical cases, hallucinations only last for a few seconds. This one hung around for over forty days (Acts 1:3).[240]

## The Conspiracy Theory

The disciples could have conspired to make up the story of a risen Jesus. For several obvious reasons, this theory seems to be the least plausible of all. After Jesus' crucifixion, not only were the disciples discouraged, confused, and scattered; they were leaderless. Peter had denied Jesus on three separate occasions. Judas had betrayed Jesus for thirty pieces of silver and then he went out and hung himself. Thomas doubted and thought the other disciples were delusional when they reported they had seen Jesus risen. The rest of the Lord's disciples were cowering away hiding from the Jewish leaders. This rag-tag group was not psychologically or emotionally stable enough to fabricate such an elaborate conspiracy concerning Jesus' resurrection. Even if they did, there was no possible motive for them to advance such a fantastic lie.

Again, all the Jews needed to do was to produce the body of Jesus and the conspiracy gig would be up. According to William Lane Craig, the disciples could not have gotten away with proclaiming a concocted

133

resurrection story in Jerusalem just weeks after the crucifixion. There were Roman soldiers and other eyewitnesses who were present at the same time and at the same place as the disciples. This type of resurrection deception or conspiracy would have easily been debunked by the Jewish authorities or other witnesses.[241]

Conspiracies are always advanced for some selfish gain. What did the disciples stand to gain but shame, persecution, exile, and death? There is simply no motive for the disciples to have advanced such a lie. Secondly, the disciples were willing to die for their conspiracy. From the Scriptural accounts, the various individuals who encountered Jesus after the crucifixion acknowledged and worshipped him as the Jewish Messiah, the resurrected Lord (Matthew 28:9; Matthew 28:16-17; Acts 2:36; Acts 10:36-42). Again, it is highly unlikely that the disciples would sacrifice their lives to maintain a known deception that they themselves hatched. There is no credible evidence to accept this theory.

## The Myth Theory

A myth is any traditional story consisting of events that are ostensibly historical, though often supernatural, explaining the origins of a cultural practice or natural phenomenon. Myths are often stories that are currently understood as being exaggerated or fictitious.[242] Usually, myths and folklore are constructed long after the alleged event occurred and are presented mostly in a fanciful, fairytale nature. In the Star Wars Movie during the "opening crawl," we see a basic example, "A long time ago, in a galaxy far, far away." The Star Wars story represents the literary style of mythology.

According to Peter Kreeft, a professor of philosophy at Boston College:

> The style of the Gospels is radically and clearly different from the style of all the myths. Any literary scholar who knows and appreciates myths can verify this. There are no overblown, spectacular, childishly exaggerated events. Nothing is arbitrary. Everything fits in. Everything is meaningful.[243]

CHAPTER SEVEN

There was simply not enough time for a *mythological Jesus story* to emerge. The close time of proximity to the resurrection events, coupled with written and oral accounts of what happened in Jerusalem that first Easter, are the results of eyewitness accounts and realistic testimony. Any mystical version of the resurrection would have been quickly discredited because of the freshness of the events and the abundance of eyewitnesses still around.[244]

In his letter to the Corinthian Church, written about 55 AD, Paul reminds his readers of the events surrounding the miraculous resurrection of Jesus of Nazareth (1 Corinthians 15:3-5 NIV). Paul was raised a Pharisee and would have been very familiar with the creedal style of quoting and memorizing key doctrinal statements.[245] Paul recites the creed to the church and admits he is not the source of the creed and is putting it in circulation for others to read. Paul does emphasize the primary importance of these events that marked the rapid spread of the Christian faith.

Paul the Apostle wrote, *"For what I received, I passed on to you as of first importance."*

- Christ died.
- He was buried.
- He was raised on the third day.
- He appeared to Cephas, then to the Twelve.

Some scholars believe Paul received this creed around 31-32 A.D., others point to 33-34 A.D. when he spent fifteen days in Jerusalem while at the school of Tyrannis (Galatians 2:1-5).[246] Several critical scholars have openly rejected what this creed affirms, that "Jesus died for sins" and "that He rose again." They do, however, unanimously agree that the letter is to be dated approximately to the period immediately after the purported resurrection events themselves.[247]

Famous Oxford scholar and literary historian C.S. Lewis stated, "I am perfectly convinced that whatever else the Gospels are they are not legends. I have read a great deal of legends and I am quite clear that they are not the same sort of thing."[248] Peter Kreeft reminds us that the Myth

Theory does not supply a reasonable answer for historical events. There was not a sufficient lapse of time to justify the origins of a mythological resurrection. There is simply too much corroboration of historical evidence supporting the facts surrounding Jesus' life, crucifixion, and resurrection for it to be a myth.[249]

## Jesus Rose from the Dead

New Testament scholar at the University of St. Andrews, N. T. Wright asserts, "That is why, as a historian, I cannot explain the rise of Christianity, unless Jesus rose again leaving an empty tomb behind him."[250] Likewise, Peter Slezak, a professor of Philosophy of Science at the University of New South Wales declares, if God exists then miracles such as the resurrection are possible. "For God who is able to create an entire universe, the odd resurrection would be child's play."[251]

While many have asked, "Who is Jesus of Nazareth?" no one can escape the evidence that He was an historical person and that His life radically altered human history. As historian Jaroslav Pelikan describes Jesus' influence, "It is from His birth that most of the human race dates its calendars, it is by His name that millions curse, and in His name that millions pray."[252]

# CHAPTER EIGHT

## Why Does God Allow Evil and Suffering?
### Reconciling God's Goodness with a Broken World

"If God should have a reasonable defense for being the god who permits war, poverty, and disease, he (man) is ready to listen to it. The trial may even end in God's acquittal. But the important thing is that man is on the bench and God is in the dock."[253]

– C.S. Lewis

Probably the strongest argument hurled against God is concerning the *problem of evil*. The existence of evil is without a doubt one of the greatest obstacles contemporary society faces. I am writing this chapter amidst the COVID-19 pandemic. Whole nations have closed their borders to travel. People are advised to maintain social distancing while in public and are wearing masks to prevent further infection. Millions of people may die because of the coronavirus; thousands more are hospitalized with respiratory infections, fighting for their lives. The COVID-19 lockdown has forced millions of people worldwide to lose their jobs and livelihoods. It is easy to look out at our contemporary world and see many things in our society that are not as they should be. Just turn on your nightly evening news or consult your YouTube news feed, and you will be hit with a barrage of negative and disturbing events. The mainstream media reports news of sex trafficking, abortion, rioting, and looting in major cities, global pandemics, terrorist attacks, widespread childhood poverty, and political scandal. These events don't seem fair or just. These unfortunate situations provoke sympathy, anger, and despair all around the world.

Why would God, who allegedly is good and perfect, allow evil and suffering in the world? This is probably the most asked question throughout history when plagues, wars, or natural disasters happen. Why would a loving God ever allow so much human pain and suffering?

*Theodicy* answers the question about why a loving God permits the manifestation of evil and suffering in the world. The word *theodicy* comes from the Greek words *theos*, "God," and *dikē*, "justice."[254]

## Evil: The Universal Problem

Philosophers and theologians have wrestled with the problem of evil for many centuries. Our broken culture highlights the gap between what is and what *ought to be* in our world. Everyone knows that events in this world are not as they are supposed to be. Even young children playing together instantly recognize injustices committed by their playmates whenever the rules of a game are broken, "Hey! You're cheating, that's not fair!" For a distinction to be made about what is just and unjust, there must be overarching rules to distinguish fair play from unfair play, good from evil.

Perhaps the first to put the argument in words was the Greek philosopher Epicurus when he asked, "Is God willing to prevent evil, but not able? Then He is not omnipotent. Is He able, but not willing? Then He is malevolent. Is He both able and willing? Then whence cometh evil? Is He neither able nor willing? Then why call him God?[255] This is the rationale that many atheists and skeptics use to try to dismiss God's existence.

## The Truth About Evil:

In the beginning, God created humanity in His likeness with the power to make choices, thereby giving people the freedom to choose to love and honor Him as God, or choose not to love and honor Him. He also endowed humanity with the human agency to love, act and respond to others. The Bible confirms that the power of choice was freely granted to all humanity by an omnipotent God, who knew the *freedom of choice* would enable people to make bad decisions with evil consequences. Beings that are capable of choice have moral responsibility. Therefore, evil is a bi-product of humanity's prerogative to freely choose.

Free will is impossible without empowering people with individual volition and agency. Without the freedom to choose, we would be nothing more than robots following a preset program. I have the choice to love my neighbor or to despise and hate him. If humanity had been pre-programmed to automatically love God, such affection would not be true love, because freedom is indispensable to real love.

In the beginning, God created everything and called it Good (Genesis 1:31). Writing in his *Confessions*, St. Augustine stated that he at one time believed that evil was a kind of material substance, however, later on, he came to think that evil was not real, and it had no existence except as the absence of good. He explained, "Whatever things exist are good, and the evil into whose origins I was inquiring is not a substance, for if it were a substance, it would be good... evil does not exist at all." Augustine attributed the problem of evil in the world to the Fall of Humanity through disobedience towards God. Human depravity had a universal effect on creation. Accordingly, God did not create evil so much as to allow for the demonstration to the world of His love by bringing Christ to satisfy and redeem fallen humanity.[256]

According to Augustine, the manifestation of evil is not the opposite of good; it is the absence of good. Just as darkness becomes prevalent in the absence of light, so too does evil manifest in the absence of God's attributes. Evil is not a substance, but a corruption of the good substance God has made. Evil can be compared to the rust in a car or the rot of a tree trunk. It is the lack of a good thing. It is not a thing in itself.[257]

C.S Lewis once described the existence of evil in the following way:

> It demands that *good* should be original and *evil* a mere perversion; that good should be the tree and evil the ivy; that good should be able to see all around evil (as sane men understand lunacy) while evil cannot retaliate in kind; that good should be able to exist on its own while evil requires the good on which it is parasitic in order to continue its parasitic existence.[258]

*Evil* by definition is the *violation of an objective moral standard*. A rational person must realize that if evil exists, good must be presumed to exist also so that we can tell the difference between them. If good does exist, then some sort of moral law must be in place by which to measure it as good. We know that goodness originated with God's creation at the beginning of the universe (Genesis 1:10,12,18). Given its source in God, goodness is an original attribute. In contrast, evil is *the absence of good*. Good is necessary for the notion of evil to even manifest.[259]

We all know that people set up some kind of code of conduct by which they attempt to live. The universal human need for rules and boundaries points to the existence of a moral lawgiver. If a transcendent moral command exists then, there must be a *Moral Commander*. The following syllogism rationally supports the moral truth people can already know. If the answer to the first three premises is *yes*, then the conclusion must also *be true*.

- Does evil exist?

- Does good exist?

- Are there moral laws that can be used to differentiate between good and evil?

- If there exists a moral code of laws to gauge good and evil, where do they come from? There must be a moral lawgiver.

Rather than disproving God's existence, the problem of evil in the world logically confirms the necessity for God's existence. On May 25, 2020, George Floyd died in Minneapolis, Minnesota after a white police officer knelt on Floyd's neck for almost nine minutes while he was handcuffed face-down in the street. The video of Floyd begging the officers for help as he is suffocated is both shocking and wicked. The moral outcry of the entire nation in response to this occurrence acknowledged that George Floyd's death was unnecessary and morally deplorable. We all know that murder and racism are absolutely wrong, but why are they wrong? Actions like this are wrong because an absolute moral law given by a just lawgiver has made them wrong: God has embedded these moral truths in the human heart, "the seat of one's conscience."

For the atheist or skeptic to use the presence of evil as an excuse to dismiss God's existence is a logical contradiction. When addressing the problem of evil, most atheists conclude it is inconsistent for there to be a God whose character is good if indeed evil is allowed to exist. However, the existence of evil points to the evidence for God (an objective moral law-giver).

The problem atheists encounter by denying God's existence is the unwitting removal of any transcendent moral reference point by which to distinguish good from evil. If evil is nothing more than a personal preference, who am I to condemn someone who steals, rapes, or murders? As an atheist philosopher, Jean-Paul Sartre admitted, "Everything is indeed permissible if God does not exist."[260] If there are no objective standards left by which to judge right from wrong, all that remains are individual opinions and arbitrary human preference.

## If God Is All-Powerful... Why Doesn't He Stop Evil?

Later than Epicurus and earlier than Lewis, Enlightenment philosopher David Hume also wrote about the problem of evil. Hume believed that because evil is a reality, it proves that an omnipotent, just God described in the Bible cannot exist. Hume was a vocal advocate of a naturalistic approach to science and dismissed the rationality of religious belief. There are several practical problems with Hume's approach. I am reminded of a woman who was constantly angry at God and decided to become an atheist. At times, she would scream at God, accusing and blaming God for allowing certain bad things to happen in her life. Someone once asked this woman, "Who are you so mad at?" She replied, "God... and I don't believe in him anymore!" Her friend replied, "Then, why in the world, are you talking to someone who does not exist?" We all know it is not psychologically healthy or logically consistent to carry on discussions with beings that don't exist. If there is no God, the conclusion to our moral outrage must be that there is *no one left to complain to* about all of the bad things going on in our world.

The Problem of Evil Assaults the Character of God:
- God is all-powerful (Nehemiah 9:6; Psalm 33:9; Isaiah 44:24; Romans 1:20).

- God is all-good (Psalm 100:5; Psalm 145:17; Nahum 1:7; Mark 10:18).

- God is all-wise (Job 12:13; Proverbs 2:6-7; Daniel 2:20; Romans 16:27; James 1:5).

The problem of evil may pose questions about God's character, but it cannot disprove His existence. Hume's argument does not take into account what theologians call moral *evil,* a bi-product of human freedom, neither does it consider God's undisclosed reasons for allowing evil, given that His reasons transcend human understanding. Biblically, God has set aside a future time to judge all evils and enforce His justice for all eternity (Revelations 21:3-9). Evil will not win in the end! We will be able to better understand the concept of evil by placing evil into two categories; Natural and Moral Evil.

**Natural Evil** is defined to include natural disasters such as hurricanes, floods, earthquakes, tsunamis, or diseases that cripple and destroy human life. In this model, natural evil has been seen historically to be a punishment for sin or the result of the disturbance of the order of things through acts of moral evil, as I will go into below. A disturbance in the earth's ecology, for instance, might in this view be brought about by human greed and the exploitation of natural resources. Natural disasters and disease could be the by-product of the corrupting effects of sin on the physical planet.[261]

**Moral Evil** is the result of free human choices that negatively affect other people, evidenced by things such as stealing, rape, slander, murder, or any other wrongful act that harms another person. The majority of evil we see in our culture on social media or hear about on the evening news falls into this category of moral evil. People hurting other people is rampant in our culture. This type of evil occurs daily whenever people consciously or unknowingly commit acts that harm or violate others. When one's actions or decisions inflict pain and suffering on another, it is the result of individual choice. Our choices have consequences. This affects how we view a drunk driver recklessly crashing into another vehicle, killing a mother and father with three young children. Is it fate's fault, did God do it, or is the drunk person to blame because he chose to drive while intoxicated?

# CHAPTER EIGHT

## How Things Ought to Be

Honestly, a lot of suffering is brought on directly by the choices we make. The choice to abuse our own bodies can result in sickness and early death. Other people can suffer directly or indirectly because of our personal choices. Addictions can lead a person's family into poverty and public humiliation. With human free will, there will always be the inherent potential for evil.

Whenever God has acted to reduce, eliminate or punish evil, such as allowing for the death penalty for criminals or life-long incarceration for a murderer or rapists, many humanists and progressives violently protest God's intervention by crying, "inhumane," "unjust," "immoral!" Sadly, these same secular progressives call it a moral choice, whenever they cheer pregnant women on to abort their babies for the sake of their own convenience.

Ironically, most people see the problem of evil as existing *outside of themselves*. The reality could not be further from the truth. Scripture informs us that the origin of evil is in the *human heart*. Jesus said, "For out of the heart comes evil thoughts, murders, acts of adultery, other immoral sexual acts, thefts, false testimonies, and slanderous statments" (Matthew 15:19).

If God did eliminate evil, He would have to take away the human power of choice. Once I was talking to a college student who was troubled over the negative condition that the world was in. He asked me the obvious question, "Why can't God just rid the world of evil today?" I responded, "If God got rid of all the evil in the world, he would have to take away your freedom to choose and remove you and me from the planet! Carl Gustav Jung, a Swiss psychiatrist who founded analytical psychology, observed the source of the majority of the world's evil, "It is becoming more and more obvious that it is not starvation, not microbes, not cancer, but man himself who is mankind's greatest danger."[262] The reality that God does not immediately irradicate the presence of evil is explainable. To do so would mean God would have to eliminate all *free will*. Destroying someone's power to choose would take away human liberty and replace it with domination and control. Freedom of the will is indispensable to human choice.

**What is the Purpose for Evil?**

One last question before we delve into this topic. Does God in His infinite wisdom allow pain to bring about ultimate good? Does God work through evil to bring about His purposes? I remember taking my children to the dentist to remove their wisdom teeth when they were entering their teen years. This was a scary and painful ordeal for my daughter Rachael. Her wisdom teeth were impacting her molars and affecting her jaw alignment and chewing ability.

She did not enjoy having a big hypodermic needle repeatedly injected into her gums. As she sat in the chair, she was scared, with tears filling her eyes. Even though getting your wisdom teeth out may not qualify as an evil event, there certainly is pain involved. I had a good reason for allowing my daughter to experience temporary pain. Her pain yielded a beneficial outcome that she enjoys to this day.

Alvin Plantinga reasonably answers the atheist's claim regarding the presence of evil, "Why suppose that if God does have a good reason for permitting evil, the atheist would be the first to know? Perhaps God has good reasons, that transcends our limited ability to grasp or to understand with our finite minds."[263] God will one day defeat all evil in a way that preserves human choice, in that those who reject Him and commit acts of moral evil will be separated for ultimate justice. God will protect their right to choose eternal destruction if they so desire. If people choose not to live for God in this life, He will never force them to live with Him in heaven during the next.

Recently, I was driving near my home and noticed a large turtle crossing four lanes of busy traffic. Cars were swerving and screeching to a stop trying to miss this helpless creature. I carefully and quickly pulled over and ran to help him. It happened to be a big Florida Soft Shell, probably around 30 pounds in weight. As I picked up the turtle, it tried to bite me with its beak-like mouth. The turtle started frantically scraping its claws against my hands, trying to force me to let it go. The struggle lasted about three minutes until I finally got a secure hold on the turtle's shell, away from his mouth and claws. He was still very agitated, vigorously snapping at me, but I got him safely back to the small pond beside the road and released him. He took off like a flash, disappearing under the water. This must have been a very frightening ordeal for the poor turtle.

Many times, people can be like this hapless turtle. When God intervenes in our lives in a way that we perceive as difficult or painful, unknown to us, He is keeping us from greater evil and pulling us out of harm's way. At times, we may experience painful circumstances without fully understanding the dangerous situations God is protecting us from. God can protect us like I did the poor frightened turtle, allowing certain difficult events to promote our greater good and future wholeness.

God in His infinite wisdom and goodness, is providentially at work. God has good reasons for allowing unfortunate and difficult events to exist in our world, even though these reasons may transcend our limited understanding. The infinite love and perfection of God guarantee the eventual defeat of evil once and for all. Theologically, the temporary appearance of evil can be outlined using the following logical argument:

**Premise A: God is good and desires to defeat evil.**
**Premise B: God is all-powerful and can defeat evil.**
**Premise C: Evil is not yet defeated.**
**Conclusion: Therefore, evil will one day be defeated.**[264]

The appearance of evil does not prove that evil is more powerful than God; it simply indicates that God's ways are different than ours. Author and apologist Lee Strobel said, "God answers the question of pain and suffering not with *an explanation,* but with *His incarnation.*"[265] If anyone can identify with injustice, pain, and suffering, it is Jesus of Nazareth. Jesus came to earth as a sinless and perfect being. He demonstrated unconditional love, righteousness, justice, and forgiveness during His earthly ministry. He was falsely accused, beaten, and eventually crucified. As Jesus hung on the cross, the crowd began hurling insults at Him, challenging Him to come down off the cross. The same people He came to redeem mocked and rejected Him. Jesus' response was, "Father, forgive them; for they do not know what they are doing" (Luke 23:34).

Christianity, through the incarnation of Jesus Christ, is the only religion in the world that provides an adequate apologetic for human suffering and pain. The prophet Isaiah wrote that Jesus would be despised by men, a man of sorrows and acquainted with grief (Isaiah 53:3). During His earthly ministry, Jesus identified with human grief and suffering on a very personal level. The writer of Hebrews describes how Jesus willingly suffered injustice and death for our sake so that He could personally stand in place for humanity's sin and identify with humanity's grief.

> But we do see Him who was made for a little while lower than the angels, namely, Jesus, because of the suffering of death crowned with glory and honor, so that by the grace of God He might taste death for everyone. For it was fitting for Him, for whom are all things, and through whom are all things, in bringing many sons to glory, to perfect the Author of their salvation through sufferings (Hebrews 2: 9-10).

One day Jesus will return and make things the way they were originally intended by God to be. He will again make all the world the way it *ought* to be. God has an eternal plan that He is working out for His glory and for the good of His creation. Beyond our understanding, that plan includes permitting evil and suffering for some time. We do know that God permits evil that He may produce a *greater good* that will unfold to His greater glory. Our Christian hope is grounded in the belief that evil will not prevail and will one day be judged and destroyed to establish eternal justice and righteousness, "Behold the Lord, for He is coming to judge the earth; He will judge the world with righteousness and the people with equity" (Psalm 98:9).

> And I saw the holy city, new Jerusalem, coming down out of heaven from God, prepared as a bride adorned for her husband. And I heard a loud voice from the throne, saying, "Behold, the tabernacle of God is among men, and He will dwell among them, and they shall be His people, and God Himself will be among them, and He will wipe away every tear from their eyes; and there will no longer be any death; there will no longer be any mourning, or crying, or pain; the first things have passed away (Revelation 21:2-4).

# CHAPTER NINE

## Classical Apologetics
### Giving a Rational Defense for Christianity

The principal Scripture cited for the use of apologetics is found in 1 Peter 3:15, which declares, "But sanctify Christ as Lord in your hearts, always being ready to make a defense to everyone who asks you to give an account for the hope that is in you, yet with gentleness and reverence." Being ready *to give a defense* for what one believes can be as important as the belief itself. In the classic sense of the word, apologetics derives its meaning from the Greek word *apologia* which means *defense.*[266]

The belief in God's existence or the truth claims of the Bible when introduced can be misunderstood or seen as irrelevant or extreme to the average person. The Bible clearly states that the natural mind is hostile toward God, unwilling to subject itself to God's laws (Romans 8:7). The very notion of God is contrary to the secular mindset of twenty-first-century people. Therefore, some skeptics may require more rational or historical evidence to help them navigate through their lifetime of secular education and religious doubt.

Many people do come to believe in God *because of evidence.* Christianity is not *blind* faith, but rather, a very *reasonable* faith. Christianity is rationally compelling because when carefully examined its claims are factually supported. As witnesses of Jesus, we can use apologetic arguments to gain trust to validate through reasonable and adequate evidence what the Bible already states as truth. Although intellectually focused, there is only one goal and that is to bring people to a saving

147

knowledge of Christ. We do Christianity a great disservice if we field objections on various topics for the sake of debate only. Believers must remember that they are approaching carnal minds and hearts that are lost and resistant to the truth.

Do not get so caught up with peripheral arguments or you may miss the gravity of the most central issue at stake: introducing the person to Jesus. There are a variety of ways to engage our world with the truth of Christianity. We must always be sensitive to individual people and opportunities as they open up to us. It is important as Christians to remember why we are here and what we are called to do. C.S. Lewis once wrote:

> To be ignorant and simple now, not to be able to meet the enemies on their own ground, would be to throw down our weapons, and to betray our uneducated brethren who have, under God, no defense but us against the intellectual attacks of the heathen. Good philosophy must exist, if for no other reason because bad philosophy needs to be answered.[267]

God has given us the tools to evaluate and determine truth. The Bible is filled with many examples where God exhorts His people to use their reason to intellectually support the truth and to rationally defend their faith in a Creator God. For example:

1. Believers are exhorted to love the LORD with all their heart, mind (intellect), and strength.

As Deuteronomy 6:4-5 states, "Hear, O Israel! The LORD is our God, the LORD is one! You shall love the LORD your God with all your heart and with all your soul (mind) and with all your might."

2. Luke records eyewitness accounts of the events and teachings surrounding Jesus' ministry, resurrection, and ascension.

As Luke 1:2-4 states, "Just as they were handed down to us by those who from the beginning were eyewitnesses and servants of the word. It seems fitting for me as well, having investigated everything carefully from the beginning, to write it out for you in consecutive order, most excellent Theophilus; so that you may know the exact truth about the things you have been taught."

Acts 1:1-3, also written by Luke, states, "Until the day when He was taken up to heaven after He had by the Holy Spirit given orders to the apostles whom He had chosen. To these He also presented Himself alive after His suffering, by many convincing proofs, appearing to them over a period of forty days and speaking of the things concerning the kingdom of God."

3. Paul used reason (logic and evidence) to debate with the Jews in the synagogue and with the Greek philosophers on Mars Hill, winning many to Christ.

According to Acts 17:17, "So he was reasoning in the synagogue with the Jews and the God-fearing Gentiles, and in the marketplace every day with those who happened to be present." Also, in Acts 17:22, "So Paul stood amid the Areopagus and said, 'Men of Athens, I observe that you are very religious in all respects. For while I was passing through and examining the objects of your worship, I also found an altar with this inscription, 'TO AN UNKNOWN GOD.' Therefore, what you worship in ignorance, this I proclaim to you.'"

4. Paul urged Christians to destroy speculations and not be taken captive by false philosophies that conflicted with the truth of Christ.

As Colossians 2:8 states, "See to it that no one takes you captive through philosophy and empty deception, according to the tradition of men, according to the elementary principles of the world, rather than according to Christ."

5. Elders were instructed to be able to refute those who contradict the truth.

Titus 1:9 reads, "holding fast the faithful word which is in accordance with the teaching, so that he will be able both to exhort in sound doctrine and to refute those who contradict."

6. Jude urged the believers to contend earnestly for the faith that was originally preached to them.

Jude 3 states: "Beloved, while I was making every effort to write to you about our common salvation, I felt the necessity to write to you appealing that you contend earnestly for the faith which was once for all handed down to the saints."

God's truth along with a compassionate, well-equipped messenger can go a long way in blowing away the smoke of deception from a skeptic's eyes. The problem with deception is that the person doesn't realize they are deceived. If they did, they would reject the deception and accept the truth. Part of the apologist's job is to help the skeptic remove worldly speculations and false imaginations, which he has raised up against the knowledge of God (truth), bringing his thoughts to the obedience of Christ and His Word (2 Corinthians 10:5).

## Classical Apologetics

Apologetics stress rational arguments for the existence of God and historical evidence supporting the truth of Christianity. Some of the earliest arguments we have today were developed and presented by St. Anselm and Thomas Aquinas. These arguments can be extremely useful when trying to address legitimate questions that many non-believers have about God's existence and nature.

These arguments provide solid logical reasons that address common objections to Christianity. *Logic* is the study of methods and principles used to distinguish good (correct) from bad (incorrect) reasoning. Because God's existence is rationally provable via His creation, it is also logically reasonable to believe He is Sovereign over this universe, including the humanity which God made.[268]

## The Cosmological Argument: Cause and Effect

The Cosmological Argument sometimes referred to as the *Kalam Cosmological Argument,* presents two premises and one conclusion. In the field of logic, if both premises are recognized as true, the conclusion must necessarily be true, as well. This makes an argument valid. According to analytic philosopher William Lane Craig, the Cosmological Argument is as follows:

**Premise A: Everything that begins to exist has a cause.**

**Premise B: The universe began to exist.**

**Conclusion: Therefore, the universe has a cause for its beginning.**[269]

The cause for the beginning of the universe must, by definition, transcend all matter, space, and time because such a cause precedes all physical and spatial creation. It must possess intelligent agency. Additionally, it is physically impossible for *nothing* to cause *something*. Every effect must have a cause! Something can't create itself. Self-creation is a contradiction. This concept in cosmology is identified by the Latin phrase: Out of nothing... nothing comes (*ex nihilo nihil fit*).

We now know that the universe is not eternal as once believed. It came into existence in the ancient past. Thanks to Astrophysicist Edwin Hubble and his scientific discovery regarding the expansion of the universe in 1929, we know that distant nebulae or galaxies are retreating from one another in a linear manner.[270]

In other words, we know the universe is expanding, so if we rewind the cosmic clock back to the ancient past, we arrive at a singularity that somehow appeared, then became unstable and exploded, producing all the matter and energy we now experience in the known universe. This is the first evidence that the universe had a beginning, sometimes referred to as the *Big Bang*. Since we can trace back to the Big Bang as the beginning of all matter, energy, and space-time, we can conclude that whatever caused the Big Bang had to be immaterial, timeless, spaceless, all-powerful, and conscious. Such an entity would have had to exist before and beyond matter and time.

To get a Big Bang, there must be a necessary cause: an immaterial conscious mind (spiritual), timeless (eternal), and all-powerful (omnipotent). The cosmos is clearly the work of a designer of superintelligence. Centuries ago, the great Greek philosopher Aristotle called God the "Unmoved Mover." God is the uncaused cause, Creator of everything that exists in time and space.

Some skeptics try to discredit the Cosmological Argument by asking, "Who created God?" This question mistakenly assumes that God was created. By definition, God is infinite and uncreated. God is eternal, existing outside of time, space, and matter. God must necessarily be a conscious, all-powerful being, capable of bringing the entire universe into existence out of nothing. An eternal being of this kind needs no creation.

Remember, every effect must have a *necessary cause*. God is eternal and omnipotent and therefore uncaused. Atheists and secularists falsely assume that inorganic matter, plus chemistry, plus blind chance, gave rise to conscious minds (humans). It seems more reasonable to say that an intelligent Mind gave rise to matter and the conscious human mind. Dead matter has no way of spontaneously organizing itself, let alone achieving consciousness.[271]

In the world around us, we can see that there must be an intelligent agent at work to create and arrange matter into specifically ordered objects like computer software. It may be compared to the difference between a computer engineer who wrote the IBM Watson AI software to the sand writing of a six-year-old child scribbling on the beach, "I love Mommy." By comparing the engineers who made the IBM super-computer and designed its software to that of the scribblings of a child, the most reasonable explanation is that only advanced intelligence is able to produce sophisticated design and complexity.

## The Second Law of Thermodynamics

The second scientific proof regarding the universe's beginning is contained in The Second Law of Thermodynamics, which states that the universe is running out of usable energy. This is also known as the *law of entropy*. Imagine pouring yourself a cup of hot coffee in your kitchen. You go to your office to answer some emails. Two hours later, you return to the kitchen looking for your hot coffee. After two hours, the coffee is no longer hot. Strangely, it has cooled off to room temperature. That shift of energy describes how entropy works.

In the physical world plants, animals, and matter are all slowly deteriorating. Life is running down. People age, they get grey hair and wrinkled skin and die. Cars rust out. Clothes fade, get threadbare, and decay. With time, things don't get more ordered; they lose energy and move toward disorder. This is entropy at work. It is a universal law.

Understanding how entropy works, scientists know that the universe could not be eternal, because we still have usable energy available. Just like our cup of coffee, all the heat would be gone by now if our universe were eternal. The universe would have suffered heat death by burning up all of its usable energy. Since the universe still has an abundance of usable energy, it must have had a beginning in the finite past. Again, some scientists call this the Big Bang, others call it creation. Regardless, to get a Big Bang, you must have a *Big Banger!* Who could that be? An eternal, all-powerful, immaterial, conscious deity best fits the scientific evidence. Yes, that's right - God!

**The Fine-Tuning Argument**

Sir Fred Hoyle: an English astrophysicist who formulated the theory of stellar nucleosynthesis, wrote in great detail about the mathematical improbability of carbon-based life forms like humans randomly arising on the earth. Hoyle wrote,

> A commonsense interpretation of the facts suggests that a super-intellect has monkeyed with physics, as well as with chemistry and biology and that there are no blind forces worth speaking about in nature. The numbers one calculates from the facts seem to me so overwhelming as to put this conclusion almost beyond question.[272]

Theoretical physicist Paul Davies concludes, "There is for me powerful evidence that something is going on behind it all. It seems as though somebody has fine-tuned nature's numbers to make the universe." "The impression of design is overwhelming." The most logical and obvious explanation is that a super-intelligent agent has so ordered matter, chemistry, and information arranging it so precisely as to produce an ordered universe and biological life.

The universe is intricately and elegantly designed to a precision that defies human imagination. For example, the complexity and specificity of information stored in the human DNA are mind-boggling. DNA is the information storage unit that directs all cells and biological functions in the human body. Bill Gates, Microsoft's founder, described the amazing complexity of a DNA molecule, "DNA is like a computer program but far, far more advanced than any software ever created.[273] Human DNA consists of approximately 3.1467 billion base pairs. If the information were printed on average 8.5 x 11 size paper, single-sided, one would need 2,414 reams of paper to print out the human genome! The stack of printed information would stand 424.4 feet tall, approximately as tall as the Washington Monument.[274]

As previously mentioned with the Anthropic Principle, whenever scientists examine the complexity of our physical universe and the fine-tuning necessary for life to exist on earth, the chances of this randomly happening, without an intelligent agent, are impossible.[275] Physicist Roger Penrose has calculated the chance of undirected formation of our universe to be one part in $10^{123}$ power. This number is so wildly improbable that it eliminates undirected forces as the explanation for the origin of our ordered universe; as an explanation, the chance is not even a rational consideration.[276] The more scientists examine the universe and its delicate yet complex structure, the more it shows that the universe was specifically designed to accommodate plant, animal, and human life.

## The Teleological Argument: The Design Inference

*Teleo* means "beginning or design," so the Teleological Argument has to do with design and a necessary designer. The most famous example used to illustrate this argument is the watchmaker argument made by William Paley. It goes something like this: Because there is a watch (which has complexity and specific order), we know there had to be a watchmaker.[277] We have already established that one cannot get order and design from mindless chance or dead matter. There must be an intelligent agent to create things that have design and purpose. A watch not only has a design, but it has a specific function and purpose that the designer intended. The ancient Greek philosopher Plato is credited with saying, "An effect cannot be greater than the underlying cause."[278]

If you were to go home one evening and find a wonderful dinner prepared for you, sitting on the table with candles and flowers, you would realize that your thoughtful wife or roommate prepared it. The dinner is the effect you can see before you, but you know that this dinner, though delicious and nourishing, is not nearly as complex or intricately designed as your wife, the necessary cause. She was the one who shopped for the food at the store, organized the kitchen, prepared the table, cooked the dinner, and lit the dinner candles. Why do we so easily conclude this when we eat a meal? A dinner does not prepare itself. There must be an intelligent agent (in this case a cook) who exists and moves outside of the dinner to cook the food, set the table, and effectively bring the delicious meal into existence.

Imagining otherwise is like believing that an explosion at a printing press is capable of producing the *Encyclopedia Britannica*. We all know that explosions don't create order. The atheist and the materialist have got a real problem on their hands. There must be an intelligent agent (the cause) at work to create and arrange matter into specifically ordered objects like the *Encyclopedia Britannica* (the effect). Remember what was established earlier? The more complex the design, the more intelligent the designer. The elegant design and specific complexity observed in biological life and the biosystems that make life possible on planet earth are mind-boggling.

We have no evidence that suggests that non-rational, inanimate matter can give rise to rational, complex, conscious beings like humans. People are not just sophisticated biochemical machines. People possess emotions of all kinds. We can experience joy, fear, love, loneliness, and pain. People can create beautiful music, nuclear submarines, and inspiring art. People can feel a sense of purpose and personal worth. People also possess consciousness as self-aware beings, which is a metaphysical quality that cannot be explained by materialism.

All of God's creation gives overwhelming proof of His existence. If inanimate objects like cell phones, office buildings, or airplanes can point to human designers, how much more do living things like a newborn baby or a caterpillar transforming into a beautiful butterfly point to an intelligent agent behind them? All observers agree physical matter and complex life exist. There must be a supernatural, intelligent agent who is responsible for their existence. These qualities unmistakably point to the Hebrew God described in the Genesis account.

As the following verses demonstrate, the Bible points to God as the uncreated first cause:

- "In the beginning, God created the heavens and the earth" (Genesis 1:1).

- "In the beginning, You laid the foundations of the earth and the heavens are the works of Your hands" (Psalm 102:25 NIV).

- "Before the mountains were born or You gave birth to the earth and the world, even from everlasting to everlasting, You are God" (Psalm 90:2).

- "For by Him all things were created, both in heaven and on earth, visible and invisible, whether thrones or dominions, rulers or authorities, all things were created through Him and for Him. He is before all things, and in Him all things hold together" (Colossians 1:16-17).

- "Before Me there was no God formed, and there will be none after Me. I, even I, am the Lord, and there is no savior besides Me" (Isaiah 43:10-11).

- "Every house is built by someone, but the builder of all things is God" (Hebrews 3:4).

Bill Gates and the staff at Microsoft can create complex operating software for computers, but one does not need to look inside a computer to find Mr. Gates. Every design around us has a designer, and everything that comes into existence has a cause. In the same way, we don't find God by only examining what He has made. God is transcendent, existing outside of His creation. Just like you examine a computer, identifying the make and model, it is possible to discover it has a designer and manufacturer.

### The Moral Argument: Morality is Universal

Why is it that people always expect polite manners and respectful behavior from other people? Most people are taught from a young age, to say "please" and "thank you" to people they meet or work with. We are taught to treat people with respect and dignity because we want them to reciprocate precisely that same kind of behavior to us.

I have had the privilege of living in three different nations and have traveled to 40 different countries during my lifetime. When traveling,

I am always struck by the sense of civility, respect, and human courtesy that are shared by all these different nations and cultures. No matter what country, the common denominator is that all people seem to know the difference between basic good behavior and bad. There exists universal and basic ethics written on every human heart. We call the results of this sense of universal morality names like decency, fair play, respect, and justice. *Oughtness* is the state of being morally obligated to certain duties and moral responsibilities. This sense of oughtness is manifest in all people whether religious or secular. Another way of explaining it is, that human beings possess an innate *Moral Law* that we share across all times, and across all cultures. It points back to the Moral Lawgiver who put the law there.

The philosopher Immanuel Kant is known for formally recognizing this Moral argument. Kant wrote his *Categorical Imperative*, "Act as if the maxim of your action were to become through your will a general natural law."[279] This is just a philosophical way of reiterating exactly how Jesus commanded His followers to behave centuries before, "Do unto others, as you would have them to do unto you" (Luke 6:31 NIV). Our inbuilt moral sense provides powerful evidence of the existence of a transcendent intelligence who designed us to feel this way.

While I was living in New Zealand, I had the opportunity to travel to Tonga and Fiji. In 2007, I was invited to minister at several churches in those island nations. I did a little reading and discovered that the London Methodist Society had sent missionaries to the islands of Tonga in 1822 and Fiji after that. Before the Methodists came, many of the Islands of Polynesia engaged in widespread tribal warfare and cannibalism. According to legend, many Polynesian people believed that once you defeated an enemy, their special essence, spirit/power, or *Mana* could be spiritually absorbed by physically eating one's vanquished foe. Cannibalism was a part of the Polynesian warfare custom for centuries. After a generation of Christian missionary work, by the Presbyterians and Methodists, the practice of cannibalism was discouraged and eventually eradicated by the early twentieth century.

Traveling to Fiji, I was being hosted by a local pastor who related a story to me about the island's history. During World War II, a soldier met a Fijian guide who could speak English carrying a Bible. The soldier pointed to the Bible and grinned real big saying, "We educated people don't put much stock in that book anymore." The islander looked back, with a grin of his own, and said, "Well it's a good thing we do (while pointing at his stomach), or else you would be in here by now!"[280] As we can see from this example, some cultures teach, "Love your neighbor and do good to your enemies" (Matthew 5:43-48), and other cultures have taught, "Conquer your enemy and eat them." The real question is, do you have a preference of which culture you would like to live in? After the tour, the Australian visitor got the message: All people have a sense of universal morality, but not all cultures consistently practice those morals.

Paul wrote, "For when Gentiles who do not have the Law do instinctively the things of the Law, these, not having the Law, are a law to themselves, in that they show the work of the Law written in their hearts, their conscience bearing witness and their thoughts alternately accusing or else defending them" (Romans 2:14-15). The Creator has not left humanity alone to figure out the truth about life, morals, and purpose all by themselves. He has placed a knowledge of His divine presence, nature, and attributes in our consciences. God's timeless, transcendent reference points always orient people towards absolute moral truths.

# CHAPTER TEN

## Why We Persuade Others

*Some were being persuaded by the things spoken, but others would not believe.*

**− Acts 28:24**

In November of 2019, I was traveling internationally to several speaking engagements in Singapore, and then on to Brisbane, Australia. It had been a few years since I had visited Singapore, as well as, our Every Nation church in Brisbane which Renee and I planted back in 2012. I was thrilled to be able to minister in both these beautiful countries over a two-week period.

While in Australia, I was scheduled to do some evangelism training and Christian apologetics for another church in the city on Saturday evening. The hotel I was staying at was on the Brisbane River directly across the beautiful Southbank district. The Southbank had lush parklands, museums, a performing arts center, boutique restaurants and coffee shops along with stunning river views.

On Saturday morning, I went for a walk on the Southbank to grab a coffee and stroll along the river trying to beat jet lag. After about an hour, I came upon a flea market area that was buzzing with people. There were dozens of stalls with people selling everything from Aboriginal jewelry and Australian yogurt, to five-minute self-portraits. As I sat down on a bench, I noticed a booth where people were handing out fliers to individuals as they walked by. I went over to see what they were selling. This booth happened to be a New Age organization that was encouraging people to view God as part of all creation (Pantheism). The guy at the booth seemed like a friendly Aussie bloke, so I began to strike up a conversation with him about his beliefs, and he began to tell me about his worldview. He told me, "The physical reality that we see with our eyes, is not really real, and all people are on a path to ultimate unity with the divine." According to this guy, "All world religions are basically the same and have similar requirements to know the ways of God." He went on to say, "We don't need to say that one view is wrong and another view is right."

I then asked this young man if he would answer some questions for me. He cheerfully agreed, "Yeah mate, I will." I began asking him questions about the differences in world religions... and how could they all be true at the same time if they say opposite and conflicting things about God, sin, heaven, and salvation? I then asked him if he believed in Jesus. He acknowledged that he did. I then asked this fellow, "Do you believe that Jesus always told the truth?" Once again, he nodded in agreement. At that point, I showed him John 14:6 where Jesus made this exclusive statement, "I am the Way, the Truth, and the Life. No one comes to the Father but through Me." I asked, "Is Jesus telling us the truth about *being the only way to God*?" At that moment, I could tell he had no response to my question about the exclusive claims of Christianity. He began to backtrack a bit and say, "Well, I am not so sure about all the other religions... I'm... I'm kind of, ahhh... new at this stuff."

At that point, another New Age counselor walked up to listen to our conversation. He appeared concerned and even agitated that I was talking to his colleague. I told him, I was a Christian and we were discussing the truth merits of New Age Mysticism versus Christianity. He then declared to me that I was trying *to persuade* his friend to change his mind about his religious beliefs, saying that if I wanted to be *loving and tolerant of other beliefs,* I should not try to influence or persuade other people at all.

"Don't ever try to persuade other people at all?" I could not believe my ears! I tried hard not to laugh as I heard this guy trying *to convince me* that being persuasive was wrong! This was truly ironic. I smiled big and asked him, "Are you trying to persuade me now... not to persuade other people?" Do you realize that you are doing exactly what you are asking me not to do… be persuasive?" I then asked him why he and his organization were out on the Southbank of Brisbane handing out fliers to people advertising New Age beliefs? Was it not an attempt to convince other people to change their minds about their religious beliefs? If so, weren't they trying to persuade them?!? Both New Age counselors looked at me puzzled and speechless. I thanked the two guys for their time and continued on with my walk along the Brisbane River.

The English word *persuade* or *persuasion* occurs fifteen times in the New Testament. The Greek words that translate to persuade or persuasion are *peitho, peithos,* and *peimone.* Vines Expository Dictionary New Testament Words describes *peitho* as follows, "To prevail upon or win over, to bring about a change of mind by the influence of reason or moral consideration."[281]

The Oxford English Dictionary defines *to persuade* as follows, "Successfully urge to do; talk into or out of an action; attract in a particular direction; cause to believe a statement or truth; to urge strongly; try to convince; lead a person to believe by argument; to talk earnestly with a person to secure agreement; to carry conviction; be convincing."[282]

We are all in the business of exerting influence through the power of persuasion. Whether it is selling cars, life insurance, iPhones, cosmetics, or hamburgers. Marketing companies spend billions of dollars using every commercial medium available, to try to persuade people to change their minds about a product, a service, or an idea. They openly favor and prefer their own products over all the alternatives. They openly discriminate against all other competitors and products by using their influence to sway people to buy their products. It's called, "Free Market Economy." People are free to pick and choose what they want, as well as, have the ability to change their minds if they perceive a better option or a better product arises.

A former missionary to India and general secretary of the World Council of Churches, Lesslie Newbigin talks about our responsibility and obligation to help influence and persuade people to believe in and to obey the Gospel of Jesus Christ. Newbigin brilliantly observed that real faith is always obligatory.

Anyone who has a faith that he believes, whether he is a Marxist or a Muslim or a disciple of Maharishi, wants to persuade others to believe it too. If you do not want to share it with others, it is not your real faith.[283]

If a medical doctor recommends a new cancer treatment to a cancer patient, he must have confidence that the new drug can help his suffering patient. The cancer patient may not be aware of or want to use this new drug, so therefore, the doctor sincerely tries to influence his patient to change their mind. The more the doctor is convinced of the drug's medical benefit, the more persuasive he will be! If people are going to venture out and try to convince others about particular claims or ideas, they must first be convinced that they are true and assured that they possess the remedy for whatever ails those people they interact with.

## The Power of Persuasion

Persuasion is a critical word when trying to understand and establish the ministry of evangelism and apologetics. Paul the Apostle informed the Christians in Corinth, "Therefore, knowing the fear of the Lord, *we persuade men*," (2 Corinthians 5:11). Paul wanted to rationally influence and convince the people regarding the truth concerning Jesus being the Messiah, stating that one of his motivating factors was, "the fear of God."

Also, on the Day of Pentecost, Peter persuaded the people to listen to his message. "He testified with many other arguments and was exhorting them, "Save yourselves from this corrupt generation." Those who accepted his message were baptized, and about three thousand persons were added that day" (Acts 2:40-41). The gospel message appeals not just to the heart of a person, but also to the will, emotions, conscience, and intellect. We must keep this fact in mind if we want to become effective Christian witnesses.

The Book of Acts is full of examples of how Paul used reason and persuasive evidence to convince people of Jesus' physical resurrection and His deity, "And he (Paul) reasoned in the synagogue every Sabbath, and *persuaded* both Jews and Greeks" (Acts 18:4). "(Paul was) arguing *persuasively* about the kingdom of God" (Acts 19:8). King Agrippa's reply to Paul's conversion testimony, "You almost persuaded me to become a Christian" (Acts 26:28). Paul's Gospel presentation was demonstrated by a persuasive argument, trying to influence and convince his audience it was factually true and should be accepted as such. "Persuasion is the art of speaking to people who, for whatever reason, are indifferent or resistant to the message we have to say."[284] One of Christianity's main features, as an absolute truth claim, is the necessity to inform and persuade others of that truth. So often in contemporary evangelism, the emphasis is on the proclamation and explanation of the gospel, neglecting to persuade people that Christianity is historically factual and scientific and therefore intellectually credible.

As we have demonstrated in this book, one of the major taboos in our pluralistic society is to believe you have absolute truth and then try and convince another person that their religious perspective may be false. Thomas Paine once said, "He who dares not offend cannot be honest." Truth, conviction, and honesty are at the core of why we do evangelism. If indeed Christianity is true, we must be honest about it and present this truth to others. Present-day postmodernism, political correctness, and tolerance fly directly in the face of the words of Jesus Christ. The Great Commission directs Christians to take the gospel message to the whole world and teach all people to obey it (Matthew 28:18-20).

## Using Apologetics to Persuade

Within the task of offering a defense for the Christian faith, there are two distinct aspects of apologetics that emerge, the *destructive* and the *creative*. The *destructive aspect* attempts to dismantle or explain-away arguments leveled against Christianity (2 Corinthians 10:3-5; Titus 1:9-11). The *creative aspect* offers evidence to confirm and support the truthfulness of Christian claims (Acts 1:3; Luke 24:39; Romans 1:19-20).[285]

The use of apologetics has been endorsed and demonstrated by believers throughout Scripture (Jude 3; Colossians 2:8; Isaiah 1:18; Acts 17:17-34). Apologetics has provided a valuable and necessary tool serving as a catalyst in the preservation, establishing, and expansion of the Christian faith throughout history. Apologetics aims to offer the reasonableness of the Christian faith to those who are ignorant to its truth. You don't have to suspend your reason in order to put your faith in God. Paul wrote to the church in Rome about his *debt* (moral obligation) to preach the gospel to both Jews and Greeks (Romans 1:14-16). As Christians, we cannot be neutral or detached concerning the truth. We are obligated to speak biblical truth to others. Today many Christians lack the confidence and the scriptural knowledge base to present an effective gospel presentation.

Being persuasive is central to the proclamation of the gospel message, as well as, defending the truth claims of the Christian Faith. Proclamation and persuasion must never be separated.[286] However, Christian persuasion must always be conscious of and show that the decisive power to convince and influence others, does not rest in our ability, but in God's ability. Jesus reminded His disciples, "But when He, the Spirit of truth, comes, He will guide you into all the truth" (John 16:13). It is the *Spirit of Truth* that does the essential work in the heart of the listener.

Whenever people are closed, indifferent, or hostile to the Gospel they may require added persuasion and prayer. In those situations, apologetics can help. As previously mentioned, apologetics can be used to offer a rational, logical defense for the truthfulness, divine origin, and the authority of Christianity. Paul told the Philippians that he was personally responsible not just for the proclamation, but for the *defense of the gospel*, "Some, to be sure, are preaching Christ even from envy and strife, but some also from goodwill; the latter do it out of love, knowing that I am appointed for the defense of the gospel" (Philippians 1:15-16).

## People Have Real Doubts

With the rise of secularism in the culture, many times the spiritual dimension of the evangelistic and apologetic enterprise can be fuzzy. In his book, *Thinking About Christian Apologetics,* Todd Daly addresses not just rational human doubt and skepticism, but some of the spiritual or emotional causes of unbelief.

While apologetics often focuses exclusively on the numerous intellectual causes of unbelief, it too often ignores the affective and spiritual causes of unbelief that often defy rational argumentation. One's emotional and relational quotients are probably more valuable than one's intelligence (IQ), though this should not be an excuse for shoddy argumentation. In short, one's character matters more than one's arguments.[287]

Resistance to the proclamation, as well as, to the receptivity of the Christian message, can happen on both the intellectual and spiritual fronts of the human experience. It makes it easy for non-believers to dismiss one's message if the Christian's lifestyle is contrary to their message. Hypocrisy easily spoils receptivity in others.

Paul addressed spiritual delusion when he wrote to the believers at Corinth, "And even if our gospel is veiled, it is veiled to those who are perishing, in whose case the god of this world has blinded the minds of the unbelieving so that they might not see the light of the gospel of the glory of Christ, who is the image of God" (2 Corinthians 4:3-4).

## Not Private Spirituality… Public Truth

The Apostle Paul, while on trial before Festus, used this apologetic approach, "For the king knows about these matters, and I speak to him also with confidence, since I am persuaded that none of these things escape his notice; for this has not been done in a corner" (Acts 26:26). Paul confidently informs Festus that the events of the gospel were public knowledge and could be corroborated by eyewitness accounts. This common ground was based on a rational and intellectual level without dismissing the fundamental doctrines of Christianity. This method remained faithful to the Scriptures, as well as, intellectually stimulating for skeptical people to consider.[288] In other words, faith in God and belief in the Bible are reasonable (not a blind leap of faith) and can be demonstrated as such to people who don't necessarily believe. Even the Old Testament prophet Isaiah points to the use of reason as a means to come to a valid belief in God, "Come now, and let us reason together," says the Lord, "Though your sins are as scarlet, they will be as white as snow; though they are red like crimson, they will be like wool" (Isaiah 1:18). According to Princeton theologian J. Gresham Machen:

> False ideas are the greatest obstacles to the Gospel. We may preach with all the fervor of a reformer and yet succeed only in winning a straggler here and there. If we permit the whole collective thought of the nation or the world to be controlled by false ideas. . . without presenting the irresistible force of logic, then we prevent Christianity from being regarded as anything more than a harmless delusion.[289]

## Is Christianity Tolerant?

In the twenty-first century there has been a subtle, but ominous change in the definition of the word tolerance. Instead of the original rendering "allowing *the existence of* different views," the new definition has changed to the *acceptance of different views!* In the old Oxford English Dictionary, the word *tolerate* is defined as "To endure, sustain pain or hardship; To allow to exist or to be done or practiced without authoritative interference or molestation; to permit." The new definition of tolerance suggests that affirming another's position to hold an alternate opinion, equates to believing that position is *true*. Under this new definition of tolerance, to accept a belief or position means that you are no longer in opposition to it since it is assumed true.[290]

*True tolerance* means to respectfully disagree with someone or endure the difference, not endorse their view. Sadly, we seem to have lost the art of respectful disagreement in our culture. Pluralism and relativism want to erase all disagreements under the guise of tolerance and inclusion to mandate a uniformity of thought. Dealing with the public's false understanding and definition of tolerance might be the most critical place our society has ever been in.[291]

We see that tolerance is not tacit agreement, acceptance, or forced compliance of an idea. Instead, it is making accommodation for an idea to be voiced, while allowing its merits to be debated, scrutinized, and sometimes even rejected and dismissed by others. This subtle cultural slide towards *conformity* and *groupthink* present a real challenge for any truth claim. In understanding the true meaning of tolerance, the French philosopher Voltaire has been quoted as saying, "I disapprove of what you say, but I will defend to the death your right to say it."[292]

There are some ideas we don't tolerate. If you were to witness the gang rape of a young woman taking place, you would not be passive or tolerant towards the people who were physically violating her. You would do whatever you could to stop the violent act from taking place! Why are some acts and beliefs considered intolerable and others tolerated?

We don't hire illiterate people to be chancellors of universities or serve as the CEO of large corporations. We don't tolerate pedophiles operating childcare centers or teaching children in elementary school. We don't tolerate cigarette smoking on planes, buses, subways, or other public venues. It is painfully obvious that some ideas and behaviors are harmful and can never be permitted under any circumstances. Some behaviors are simply not tolerated because of the potentially destructive consequences to the individual or to others. We have laws and moral codes that discriminate against destructive or harmful conduct, not the individuals, per se.

No matter how deviant or absurd the idea or lifestyle is, according to this *New Tolerance*, it can be *deemed true* if... the idea is *sincerely held* by the individual. Notice the operative word is *personal sincerity*. In this post-truth culture, sensitivity and sincerity can override facts and truth, automatically validating their beliefs, so that they must be accepted as "their truth" and therefore *embraced by everyone*.[293] To not do so would be perceived as being *cruel* and *unloving!*

The foundations of *the New Tolerance* are bolstered by three basic assumptions:

- All opinions are equal in value.
- All worldviews have equal worth.
- All stances are equally valid.

Not only are these three assumptions contradictory and self-refuting, but they also are not livable in the real world! Ironically, to even question this postmodern axiom is deemed as *intolerant* and *narrow-minded*. Professor Leslie Amour, at the University of Ottawa, highlights the absolute ridiculousness of this notion when she wrote, "Our idea to be a virtuous citizen is to tolerate everything except intolerance."[294]

The new tolerance is the social commitment to treat all ideas and people as equally right, except, of course, those people who disagree with this view of tolerance. According to Jay Budziszewski, "The new tolerance will not allow any dissenting point of view. If you possess a different opinion, you will be conveniently *canceled out.*" This shows exactly how bizarre and unhinged Political Correctness has become.[295]

## Is Christianity Exclusive?

One of the most common concerns about Christianity is its claims of exclusivity. Many world religions and postmodern philosophies consider this to be the height of *arrogance*. In this present culture, it is common for Christians to be labeled *exclusive, narrow-minded, arrogant, hateful, and intolerant.* Our postmodern environment has given rise to the, *you be you,* and *don't criticize anyone's lifestyle* sentiment. Amid this "judgment-free" and "live-and-let-live environment," we are confronted with some challenging and exclusive statements made by Jesus to His followers. Most secularists and a growing number of church-going Millennials and Gen Z-ers (those born between 1997-2015) are very troubled by what they perceive as the *exclusivity of Christianity*. This is one of the negative effects of pluralistic thinking, which wants to reject any hint of an exclusive truth claim. Unfortunately, many contemporary Christians now view biblical assertions of *truth claims* as being *mean-spirited* and out-of-step with *love and mercy.*

Paul wrote to Timothy,

"This is good and acceptable in the sight of God our Savior, who desires that all men to be saved and to come to the knowledge of the truth. For there is one God, and one mediator also between God and men, the man Christ Jesus" (1 Timothy 2:3-5).

Likewise, Luke records, "And there is salvation in no one else; for there is no other name under heaven that has been given among men by which we must be saved" (Acts 4:12).

The Bible clearly identifies Jesus exclusively as *the only way to God*. If one accepts these claims, does that make Christianity intolerant and bigoted? In the past few decades, multiculturalism has been widely propagated and is being taught in many educational institutions. Along with multiculturalism comes the pluralistic pressure to accommodate various cultural and world religious ideologies. In the name of inclusion, diversity, and equality all beliefs and lifestyle choices are to be considered permissible. It is against this backdrop that Christianity has been labeled "exclusive."

According to apologist Walter Martin, "A truth by definition is exclusive." If truth were all-inclusive, nothing would be false." When a truth claim is made... the opposite of that claim must be *necessarily false!* Two mutually exclusive claims cannot both be true! A person cannot be sitting in their living room in Chicago and flying in an airplane over the Pacific Ocean at the same time. That fact does not make the statement *prejudiced or bigoted*. If a truth claim matches objective reality, it is considered factually accurate. Exclusivity in this context simply means that not all possibilities can be correct at the same time.[296]

1. Christian truths are made for all people, of all nations, of every culture, and for all time. Christianity speaks to the 'world' and not a specific people group or nation. In this sense, Christianity is radically inclusive.

2. Jesus of Nazareth's truth claims necessarily exclude other contrary claims.

## Christianity's Appeal is for All People Everywhere

The ministry and mission of Jesus were always intended to extend salvation to people from every tribe, tongue, and nation freely offering the gift of redemption and the forgiveness of sin.

- There is no distinction between Greek and Jew, circumcised and uncircumcised, barbarian, Scythian, slave, free; but Christ is all and in all (Colossians 3:11).

- For all have sinned and fall short of the glory of God, being justified as a gift by His grace through the redemption which is in Christ Jesus (Romans 3:23-24)

- Therefore, having overlooked times of ignorance, God is declaring to men that all people everywhere should repent (Acts 17:30).

- He gave His only begotten Son, that whoever believes in Him should not perish, but have everlasting life (John 3:16 KJV).

Paul's writing to Timothy confirmed Jesus' uniqueness, "For there is *one God*, and there is *one mediator* between God and men, the man Christ Jesus" (1 Timothy 2:5). If the biblical claims concerning Jesus being *the only way to God the Father* is true, then all alternative religions and worldviews cannot possibly be correct.

> Because Christianity is open and available to all people in every culture, non-believers could logically say, "The claims of Jesus are false," but they cannot claim "Christianity to be exclusive!" The gospel message has a universal appeal which makes it applicable to all peoples, cultures, and races. This *inclusive feature* is seen throughout the Scriptures. However, the core doctrines of the Christian faith are exclusive truth assertions.[297]

Previously, we gave solid evidence showing the Christian Faith to be not only logically plausible, but also evidenced by science, and historical record. If the Christian religion is true, it would still be true even if no one ever believed in it. If it were false and everyone still believed in it, it would not change its factual quality or essence. The objective certainty of Christianity is fixed in reality no matter if anyone believes in it or not. Jesus said to His disciples, "Enter through the narrow gate; for the gate is wide and the way is broad that leads to destruction, and there are many who enter through it. For the gate is small and the way is narrow that leads to life, and there are few who find it" (Matthew 7:13-14).

Nurtured by the truths of historical evidence, archeology, and Bible prophecy which unanimously confirm Jesus' amazing life, death, and miraculous resurrection, there are no logical reasons to doubt Jesus' central message to the world. If people insist on accusing Christianity of being narrow and exclusive by virtue of its truth claims, it will just have to remain "narrow!" The truth of Christianity cannot deny its own, self-evident, internal veracity.

# CONCLUSION

"The driver on the highway is safe not when he reads the
signs, but when he obeys them."

**– A. W. Tozer**

We live in an age of religious pluralism and secularism which
has tried to dilute and obscure the truth for the sake of self-expression,
hedonism, and personal autonomy. Words like inclusion, tolerance, and
diversity are being weaponized to achieve their secular agenda. These so-
called *progressive values* have been adopted by our syncretistic society while
canceling out or shaming into submission any absolute truth claims. If
our society continues to drift on this path away from transcendent points
of truth, this confusion will continue.

In this book we have established the following truths:

1. God Exists.

2. Truth is Real and Knowable.

3. Miracles Do Occur (The creation of the universe and the
   origins of all biological life on earth out of nothing: The
   incarnation, death, and resurrection of Jesus Christ).

4. The Bible is God's Revelation to all Humanity.

These truths establish a fixed point from which to navigate from.
There is hope if we defend and establish the universal Lordship of Jesus
Christ with reliance upon God's Word, as the bedrock of truth! The
material in this book is aimed to give real-life evidence that is intended
to help fortify one's confidence so that all believers can contend
earnestly and persuasively for their faith. My desire has been to provide
readers with pertinent information and historical evidence to help them
confidently confront the false ideologies and anti-God worldviews that

are plaguing our society. Whether you are a believer, seeker, or skeptic, I have provided answers for the most common objections being hurled at the Christian faith, such as "Why does God permit evil?" "Is the Bible reliable?" and "Did Jesus resurrect from the dead?" I have sincerely tried to frame the cultural obstacles that the majority of Christians are facing while living in the twenty-first century.

As mentioned in the introduction, Antony Flew, the once infamous atheist, was cited for publicly renouncing his atheism. After close examination, he claimed that the scientific evidence for God's existence was simply overwhelming and could not be ignored by serious investigators. Dr. Flew offered the world a simple solution for finding the truth, *"We will follow the evidence to wherever it leads."*

This author has attempted to provide a compelling amount of historical, scientific, and bibliographic evidence to confirm the reasonableness of the Christian Faith to any *sincere, objective inquirer.* Truth must never be taken for granted. Truth is precious and must be identified and appropriately taught to others. It has been demonstrated that God's Word is true and there is no reasonable cause to deny God's existence nor the veracity of Jesus' life, death, resurrection, or deity. We must leave behind our excuses and personal preferences, follow Flew's advice, and be willing to follow the truth no matter where it leads!

All serious believers must learn to develop a love for God's truth because it provides a moral compass for successfully negotiating life's realities. Making *the quest for truth* one's primary goal in life means at times we must go against the grain of this confusing world. By earnestly pursuing truth, one will automatically be in pursuit of the transcendent God and His wisdom. This is why truth is so important. It allows people to acknowledge it, and then to cooperate with reality whether spiritual or physical. Understanding and living the Christian worldview regarding truth puts us back in touch with the author of all truth, God. The Prophet Isaiah reminds us, "He who is blessed in the earth will be blessed by the God of truth, and he who swears in the earth will swear by the God of Truth" (Isaiah 65:16).

Christians are finding themselves more and more on the defensive. Living in the midst of our secular, post-truth society. We must try to regain our balance and apply our energies toward reclaiming the eternal truth claims of God. Presbyterian minister and New Testament scholar J. Gresham Machen wrote:

> Christian religion flourishes not in the darkness but in the light. Intellectual slothfulness is but a quack remedy for unbelief; the true remedy is the consecration of intellectual power to the service of the Lord Jesus Christ.[298]

I believe what Machen wrote more than eighty years ago is prophetically relevant for all Christians living today. Believers must take up the truth of God's word, *the Sword of the Spirit* (Ephesians 6:17), and become proficient at using it against the lies and falsehoods deceiving our world. It has been true in the past and will continue to be accurate in the future. God's truth and light are totally sufficient to overcome and dispel all darkness and deception from every human heart.

In almost every area of our existence, contemporary society stands in sharp contrast to the morality and truth presented in the Bible. John's Gospel further reveals Jesus' true essence.

> In the beginning, was the Word, and the Word was with God, and the Word was God. He was in the beginning with God. All things came into being through Him, and apart from Him, nothing came into being that has come into being" (John 1:1-3). And the Word became flesh, and dwelt among us, and we saw His glory, glory as of the only begotten from the Father, FULL OF GRACE AND TRUTH [emphasis added] (John 1:14).

Notice that John emphasizes Jesus' nature as being *full of grace and truth*. Probably the single most important question a person can ask in our present culture is, "What is truth?" The night Jesus was betrayed, Pontius Pilate posed that same question to Jesus. What is truth? Whether he was aware of it or not, Pilate was looking directly at truth personified in Jesus. Pilate went away and declared to the Jewish accuser, "I find no guilt in Him" (John 18:39).

The Bible describes the nature of the spiritual struggle that we encounter in this life. A major battle continues to rage between what God declares is true versus the counter-claims of the world, the flesh, and the devil. In the very beginning, God revealed His truth only to have it challenged and violated by the first humans. Satan told Adam and Eve that they would not die if they ate of the forbidden fruit as God had warned, but instead, they could become like God Himself, having their eyes opened, able to discern good and evil (Genesis 3:4-7). The individual's quest to determine what is good or evil, right or wrong, apart from God… has always been at the root of the fallen human condition.

Paul wrote to the church in Rome, "They exchanged the truth of God for a lie… and worshipped and served the creature rather than the Creator, who is blessed forever, Amen" (Romans 1:25). There is a spiritual battle going on between God's overarching, eternal truths and the deception operating in this fallen world system. The Christian's responsibility is not to be argumentative, but with gentleness offer truthful answers so that others may come to receive the truth themselves. "With gentleness correcting those who are in opposition, if perhaps God may grant them repentance leading to the KNOWLEDGE OF THE TRUTH, and they may come to their senses and escape from the snare of the devil, having been held captive by him to do his will" (2 Timothy 2:25-26).

The root of the problem of humanity's ills has been the attempted *suppression* and the *redefinition* of truth itself. Whenever words can be neutered or made meaningless, they lose their power. Wisdom demands that we expose and uproot these dangerous trends that are trying to eliminate or reduce biblical truth claims. To resist our secular, post-truth culture, believers must follow the instructions given by God, the author of all truth. Paul's exhortation to the Roman Christians captures that instruction, *"Let God be found true, though every man be found a liar"* (Romans 3:4).

Christianity cannot be limited to a private compartment of one's life. We are compelled to see Christianity as the all-encompassing truth, objectively real, and historically accurate. It is the ultimate reality.[299] Jesus is the Alpha and the Omega. All things have been created through Him and for Him. Life does not make sense apart from Him. "He Himself will come to have first place in all things" (Colossians 1:18).

# GLOSSARY OF TERMS

**Absolute:** Free from exception, qualification, or conditional limitations; operating or existing in full under all circumstances without variation or exception.

**Agnosticism:** (Literally; *without knowledge*) The belief that one cannot, or at least does not, know reality, or especially God.

**Apostasy:** The act of leaving the church and/or rejecting the core claims of Christianity after once affirming them.

**Autonomy:** The right of *self-government*. Self-directing freedoms and especially moral independence; an emphasis on a personal choice regarding values and ethics.

**Atheism:** A system of thought based on the non-existence of God. The belief that God does not exist, or that the evidence for His existence is inadequate.

**Canon:** A ruler or measuring rod; a list of books accepted as genuinely inspired and authoritative.

**Christian Apologetics:** The discipline of defending the veracity of Christianity against contradictory ideas by employing philosophical thinking to form a logically coherent defense.

**Logic:** The study of valid thinking and argument.

**Enlightenment:** A period of European intellectual history that covers roughly the 18th century and is characterized by great optimism in the triumph of reason over tradition and religious authority. Human reason and rationality became the "religion" of many, particularly in France, England, and Germany.

**Ethics:** The study of standards of conduct and moral judgment; the system or code of morals of a particular person, religion, group, or culture; the overarching sense of what one *ought* to do.

**Fact/Value Divide:** When secular concepts elevate all scientific and empirical knowledge for acceptance in the public domain while relegating religious values and morality to the private domain. Also referred to as, the *sacred/secular dichotomy*.

**Fallacy:** A logical error of inference, relationship, or conclusion.

**Empiricism:** The practice of relying on observation and experimentation, especially in the natural sciences; the idea that all knowledge is gained through sensory perception.

**Postmodernism:** A prevailing ideology within Western culture that presupposes the impossibility to attain true metaphysical knowledge. The rejection of anyone's world view or explanation of reality, as well as, a rejection of any notion of truth.

**Hedonism:** An ethical system based on the pursuit of pleasure and the avoidance of pain.

**Humanism:** A system of thought based on the nature, dignity, interests, and ideals of man; specifically, a modern, nontheistic, rationalistic movement that holds humanity supreme and capable of self-fulfillment, ethical conduct, without recourse to a transcendent, supernatural deity.

**Presupposition:** The foundational element of a world view; a belief held due to its "self-evident" nature.

**Pragmatism:** The philosophy that makes practical consequences the sole criterion for truth.

**Relativism:** The system of thought based upon the interrelatedness of all things; a philosophy that holds to no transcendent or objective truth for all people, places, and times.

**Rationalism:** A world view that holds reason itself to be the ultimate source of knowledge and superior to sense perceptions alone.

**Materialism:** The belief that all of reality is material (matter), that no spiritual entities, such as the human soul, angels, or God exists.

**Macro-evolution:** The idea that all biological organisms observed today, have descended directly from a single common ancestor from the ancient past. This claim became known as the theory of universal common descent or *The General Theory of Evolution*.

**Micro-evolution:** This refers to minor changes occurring in the features or structure of a specific animal species; the evidence of physical changes that may occur due to environmental conditions over a short period within a particular species. Also, known as *The Special Theory of Evolution.*

**Naturalism:** The belief that the universe is all there is; everything operates by natural laws (without miracles).

**General Revelation:** The self-disclosure of God through the created universe (a revelation derived via nature's existence sometimes referred to as *Natural Revelation*).

**Skepticism:** The belief that one should doubt or suspend judgment on philosophical questions.

**Syllogism:** A concise and deductive argument, consisting of two premises and a conclusion.

**Special Revelation:** God's self-disclosure in history through the scriptures and through the life, death, and resurrection of Jesus Christ.

**Scientism:** The belief that science is the highest form of knowledge and has authority over all other domains of knowledge.

**Syncretism:** The combining or merging of different beliefs or various schools of thought. Syncretism involves the assimilation of various religions, thus asserting an underlying unity and allowing for an inclusive approach to divergent belief systems.

**Theodicy:** Deals with the problem of how to reconcile a just God with a world containing evil.

**Religious Pluralism:** The idea that all religions lead to God; that there are many valid approaches to God or salvation, thus discounting the significance of differences in belief among world religions.

**The Church:** The aggregate of believers who claim to be disciples of Jesus Christ.

**The Gospel:** The truth claims that salvation and redemption are attained solely through faith in Jesus Christ.

**The West:** Refers to the geopolitical region of North and South America, Europe, and Australia.

**Secularism:** The belief that religion should not be involved with the ordinary social and political activities of a country. The term has also been used since the 1850s in a pragmatic and philosophical sense to refer to a self-reliant humanism invoking the exclusion of belief in God from matters of ethics and morality.

**Universal:** That which is true at all times and all places. The general concept or idea of a thing, as opposed to a particular instance or example.

**Worldview:** The sum total of our beliefs about the world. "The big picture" that directs our daily decisions and actions. All worldviews can be analyzed by answering the following three questions. 1) Where did we come from *(origins)*? 2) What has gone wrong with the world *(human depravity)*? 3) What can be done to fix it *(redemption)*?

# ENDNOTES

## INTRODUCTION

1. New American Standard Bible (NASB), (Grand Rapids, MI: Zondervan Press, 1995).

2. Blaise Pascal, *Pensees*, ed. Alban Krailsheimer (New York, NY: Viking, 1966), 697/383, 247.

3. David Kinnaman and Mark Matlock, *Faith for Exiles: 5 Ways for a New Generation to Follow Jesus in Digital Babylon* (Grand Rapids, MI: Baker Books, 2019), 49.

4. Phillip Johnson, *Reason in the Balance: The Case Against Naturalism in Science, Law & Education* (Downer Grove, IL: InterVarsity Press, 1995), 41.

5. Hans Boersma, "Therapeutic Revolution," *First Things* (Ft. Collins, CO: Ignatius Press, May 2021): 51.

6. Wayne House and Joseph Holden, *Charts of Apologetics and Christian Evidences* (Grand Rapids, MI: Zondervan Press, 2006), Chart 25.

7. David Noebel, *Understanding the Times: The Religious Worldview of Our Day and a Search for Truth* (Eugene, OR: Harvest House Publishers, 1992), 546.

8. J.P. Moreland, *Love God with all Your Mind: The Role of Reason in the Life of the Soul* (Colorado Springs, CO: NavPress, 2012), 145.

9. Francis Bacon, accessed December 15, 2020, https://www.goodreads.com/quotes/8067672.

10. C.S. Lewis, *Mere Christianity* (New York, NY: Macmillan Publishing, 1952), 38-39.

11. Brian K. Morley, *Mapping Apologetics: Comparing Contemporary Approaches* (Grand Rapids, MI: InterVarsity Press, 2015), 190.

12. J.P. Moreland, *Scaling the Secular City* (Grand Rapids, MI: Baker Books, 1987), 149.

13. Wayne House and Joseph Holden, *Apologetics and Christian Evidence* (Grand Rapids, MI: Zondervan Press, 2006), 1.

# CHAPTER 1

## WHATEVER HAPPENED TO RIGHT AND WRONG?

14. Norman Geisler, *Baker Encyclopedia of Christian Apologetics* (Grand Rapids, MI: Baker Books, 1999), 741.

15. Ralph Earle, *Word Meanings in the New Testament* (Grand Rapids, MI: Baker Book House, 1986), 82.

16. Mark Rutland, *Most Likely to Succeed: A Graduate's Guide to True Success in Work and Life* (Lake Mary, FL: Charisma House Publishing, 2001), 105.

17. David Kinnaman and Mark Matlock, *Faith for Exiles: 5 Ways for a New Generation to Follow Jesus in Digital Babylon* (Grand Rapids, MI: Baker Books, 2019), 49.

18. Ravi Zacharias, *Jesus Among Other Gods: The Absolute Claims of the Christian Message* (Nashville, TN: Thomas Nelson Publishing, 2000), 8, 151.

19. Josiah Cook, "The Nobility of Knowledge," *Popular Science* (March 5, 1974): 621.

20 Robert A. Sirico, *A Moral Basis for Liberty* (Grand Rapids, MI: Action Institute, 2012), 16.

21. Julie A. Ruben, *The Making of the Modern University: Intellectual Information and the Marginalization of Morality* (Chicago, IL: The University Chicago Press, 1996), 1, 17.

22. R.C. Sproul, *Not A Chance: The Myth of Chance in Science and Modern Cosmology* (Grand Rapids, MI: Baker Books, 1994), 94-95.

23.Walter Lippman, accessed May 15, 2021, https://www.goodreads.com/author/quotes/74615.

24. Nancy Pearcey, *Total Truth* (Wheaton, IL: Crossway Books, 2004), 34.

25 Davie Noebel, *Understanding the Times: The Religious Worldview of Our Day and a Search for Truth* (Eugene, OR: Harvest House Publishers, 1992), 543.

26. Abdu Murray, *Saving Truth: Finding Meaning and Clarity in a Post-Truth World* (Grand Rapids, MI: Zondervan, 2018), 12-13.

27. Dallas Willard, accessed December 8, 2021, https://renovare.org/articles/truth-and-reality-do-not-adapt-to-us.

28. J.P. Moreland, *Christianity and the Nature of Science* (Grand Rapids, MI: Baker Book House, 1989), 143.

29. J.P. Moreland and William Lane Craig, *Philosophical Foundations for a Christian Worldview* (Downer Grove, IL: Intervarsity Press, 2003), 142-144, https://www.barna.com/research/millennials-oppose-evangelism/.

30. Barna Research, "Almost half of practicing Christians think that evangelism is wrong," (February 5, 2019), accessed December 15, 2021, https://www.barna.com/research/millinneals-oppose-evangelism/.

31. C.S. Lewis, *Mere Christianity* (New York, NY: Macmillan Publishing, 1952), 45.

32. L. Russ Bush, *Classical Readings in Christian Apologetics: A.D. 100-1800* (Grand Rapids, MI: Zondervan Publishing House, 1983), 197.

33. R.C. Sproul, Ligonier Ministries, accessed September 11, 2020, https://thestateoftheology.com.

34. Abraham Kuyper, *Christianity: A Total World and Life System* (Marlborough, NH: Plymouth Rock Foundation, 1996), 39-40.

35. Ellen C. White, *Counsel to Writers and Editors* (Nashville, TN: Nashville Southern Publishing, 1946), 37.

36. Mary Poplin, *Is Reality Secular? Testing the Assumptions of Four Major Worldviews* (Downers Grove, IL: InterVarsity Press, 2014), 57.

37. Alvin Plantiga, *Where the Conflict Really Lies: Science, Religion, and Naturalism* (Oxford, UK: Oxford University Press, 2011), 271.

38. Oprah Winfrey, accessed July 7, 2021, https://www.goldenglobes.com/articles/your-truth-most-powerful-tool-oprahs-globes-speech-full.

39. Nancy Leigh DeMoss, ed., *The Rebirth of America* (West Palm Beach, FL: Arthur S. DeMoss Foundation, 1986), 36.

40. Douglas Groothuis, *Truth Decay: Defending Christianity Against the Challenge of Postmodernism* (Downer Grove, IL: InterVarsity Press, 2000), 152, 208.

41. Richard Dawkins, *River out of Eden* (London, UK: Weidenfeld and Nicholson, 1995), 133.

42. CruMinistries, *Obstacles to Faith*, accessed June 23, 2021, https://www.cru.org/us/en/train-and-grow/share-the-gospel/obstacles-to-faith.html.

43. Nancy R. Pearcey, *Love Thy Body: Answering Hard Questions about Life and Sexuality* (Grand Rapids, MI: Baker Books, 2018), 31.

44. Blaise Pascal, *Pensees*, Trans. A.J. Krailsheimer (London, UK: Penguin Books, 1966), 285.

45. Kenneth R. Samples, *7 Truths that Changed the World: Discovering Christianity's Most Dangerous Ideas* (Grand Rapids, MI: Baker Books, 2012), 185.

46. G.K. Chesterton, accessed July 12, 2021, https//www.chesterton.org/quotations-of-g-k-Chesterton/.

47. E. Michael Jones, *Degenerate Moderns: Modernity as Rationalized Sexual Misbehavior* (San Francisco, CA: Ignatius Press, 1993), 47.

48. Nancy Leigh DeMoss, ed., *The Rebirth of America* (West Palm Beach, FL: Arthur S. DeMoss Foundation, 1986), 83.

49. LifeSiteNews.com, accessed, June 19, 2019, http://www.lifesitenews.com/news/teacher-traumatizes-6-year-old-girl-source.

50. Art Lindsley, *True Truth: Defending Absolute Truth in a Relativistic World* (Downers Grove, IL: Intervarsity Press, 2004), 125.

## CHAPTER 2

## SECULARIZING KNOWLEDGE

51. Cambridge English Dictionary, accessed September 23, 2021, http://dictionary.cambridge.org/us/dictionary/english/secularism.

52. D. A. Carson, *Christ and Culture Revisited* (Grand Rapids, MI: Wm. B. Eerdmans Publishing, 2008), 116.

53. Norman L. Geisler, *Baker Encyclopedia of Christian Apologetics* (Grand Rapids, MI: Baker Books, 1999), 342.

54. Richard Dawkins, "Is Science A Religion?" *Humanist* (January/February 1997).

55. David Kinnaman and Gabe Lyons, *Good Faith: Being a Christian When Society Thinks You're Irrelevant and Extreme* (Grand Rapids, MI: Baker Books, 2016), 41.

56. Ibid., 222.

57. Hemant Mehta, "Where Did the Term 'Nones' Come From?" accessed March 9, 2020, https://friendlyatheist.patheos.com/2013/01/11/Where-did-the-term-nones-come-from/.

58. "Former Labor Secretary Predicts Religious Wars in America," (July 1, 2004), accessed May 14, 2020, https://www.christianitytoday.com/ct/2004/julyweb only/7-5-51.0.html.

59. Alister E. McGrath, *Science and Religion* (West Sussex, UK: Blackwell Publishers, 2010), 227.

60. Nancy Pearcey, *Total Truth* (Wheaton, IL: Crossway Books, 2004), 101.

61. David W. Henderson, *Culture Shift: Communicating God's Truth to Our Changing World* (Grand Rapids, MI: Bakers Books, 1998), 125, 153.

62. David Barton, *Original Intent: The Courts, The Constitution & Religion* (Aledo, TX: Wall Builder Press, 1997), 13.

63. Ibid., 14.

64. Rev John Armstrong, accessed October 3, 2021, http:// www.therepublic.com/2018/08/04/todays_question_is_secular_ progressivism_a_religion/.

65. William J. Federer, *America's God and Country* (St Louis, MO: Ameri-search Inc., 2000).

66. David Barton, *Original Intent* (Aledo, TX: Wall Builder Press, 2000), 81.

67. Stephen McDowell, *The Bible: America's Source of Law and Liberty* (Charlottesville, VA: Providence Foundation, 2016), 60.

68. John Dewey, *A Common Faith* (New Haven, CT: Yale University, 1934), 65.

69. Ibid., 157.

70. Christopher Dawson, "Man and Civilization," *The Listener* (August 23, 1933): 281.

71. Francis A. Schaeffer, *How Should We Live: The Rise and Decline of Western Thought and Culture* (Wheaton, IL: Crossway Books, 1976), 160.

72. Brian K. Morley, *Mapping Apologetics: Comparing Contemporary Approaches.*

73. Mary Poplin, *Is Reality Secular? Testing the Assumptions of Four Major Worldviews* (Downers Grove, IL: InterVarsity Press, 2014), 105-106.

74. Engel vs.Vitale, *Thompson Gale Legal Encyclopedia,* accessed October 12, 2021, Answers.com (2006). https://www.uscourts. gov/educational-resources/educational-activities/facts-and-case-summary-engel-v-vitale.

75. Celine Dion Song Banned, "Too Christian for School," (June 8, 2003), www.wnd.com/news/article, asp? ARTICLE...ID=32973.

76. Pew Research, accessed March 9, 2020, http://www.pewresearch. org/fact-tank/2016/08/24/why-MWEIXn-.

77. Walter Kaufman, ed., "The Gay Science," in *Portable Nietzsche* (New York, NY: Viking Press, 1954), 515.

78. Friedrich Nietzsche, *Beyond Good and Evil* (New York, NY: Random House, 1989), 54.

79. Phillip E. Johnson, *Reason in the Balance: The Case Against Naturalism in Science, Law & Education* (Downers Grove, IL: InterVarsity Press, 1995), 40.

80. Cornelius Plantinga Jr., *Engaging God's World: A Christian Vision of Faith, Learning, and Living* (Grand Rapids, MI: Wm. B. Eerdmans Publishing, 2002), 122.

81. J.P. Moreland, *Love Your God with All Your Heart and Mind: The Role of Reason in the Life of the Soul* (Colorado Spring, CO: NavPress, 2012), 28.

82. David Noebel, *Understanding the Times: The Religious Worldview of Our Day and a Search for Truth* (Eugene, OR: Harvest House Publishers, 1992), 154-201.

83. Harry Blamires, *The Christian Mind: How Should a Christian Think?* (Ann Arbor, MI: Servant Publications, 1978), 107.

84. Will and Ariel Durant, *The Lessons of History* (New York, NY: Simon and Schuster, 1968), 40.

85. Aldous Huxley, *Aldous Huxley's Complete Essays: 1936-1938*, ed. Ivan R. Dee (2001).

86. Julie Lanham, "The Greening of Ted Turner," *The Humanist* (November/December 1989): 30.

87. Chuck Colson and Nancy Pearcy, *How Now Shall We Live?* (Wheaton, IL. Tyndale Publishing, 1999), 13.

88. Will and Ariel Durant, *The Story of Civilization: Part IX, The Age of Voltaire* (New York, NY: Simon and Schuster, 1965), 615.

89. Jimmy Long, accessed May 12, 2021, https://jimmylong.net/2013/11/23/the-undeniable-depravity-of-the-human-heart/.

90. James Madison, *Federalist Papers,* no. 51 (New York, NY: Pocket Books, 1964), 122.

91. Nancy Pearcey, *Saving Leonardo* (Nashville, TN: B and H Publishing Group, 2010), 38.

92. Stephen Jay Gould, "Non-overlapping magisterial," accessed December 17, 2021, http//www.stephenjaygould.org/library/gould/_noma. HTML.

93. Richard Dawkins, *The Blind Watchmaker* (New York, NY: W.W. Norton, 1987), 6.

94. David Kinnaman and Gabe Lyons, *Good Faith: Being a Christian When Society Thinks You're Irrelevant and Extreme* (Grand Rapids, MI: Baker Books, 2016), 41.

95. Art Lindsley, *True Truth: Defending Absolute Truth in a Relativistic World* (Downers Grove, IL: InterVarsity Press, 2004), 17.

96. Lesslie Newbigin, *Truth to Tell: The Gospel Versus Public Truth* (Grand Rapids, MI: Wm. B. Eerdmans Publishing, 2006), 2.

97. Mark A. Beliles and Stephen K. McDowell, *America's Providential History* (Charlottesville, VA: The Providence Foundation, 1989), 178.

98. Harry Blamires, *The Christian Mind: How Should a Christian Think?* (Ann Arbor, MI: Servant Books, 1978), 27.

99. Francis Schaeffer, *The God Who Is There* (Downer Grove, IL: InterVarsity Press, 1968), 13.

100. Probe Ministries, *College Mind Games: College Survival Course* (Richardson, TX: Probe Ministries, 1996), 4.

101. Walter A. Elwell, ed., *Evangelical Dictionary of Theology* (Lansing, MI: Baker Books, 1984), 96.

102. Rice Broocks, *Man, Myth, Messiah: Answering History's Greatest Question* (Nashville, TN: Thomas Nelson, 2016), 10.

103. State of Maryland v. Roy R. Torcaso, 367, U.S. 495 (June 19, 1961).

104. Matt Ridley, *Discoverer of the Genetic Code*, rev. Nicholas Wade, *New York Times* (July 18, 2006), 155.

105. P.Z. Myers, "Chat with PZ Myers HERE," accessed March 16, 2020, http://ravingatheists.com/forum/sjpwtje read/PHP ?t=13602/page=2.

106. Ibid., 3.

107. Michael Denton, *A Theory in Crisis*, accessed May 14, 2021, https://www.semanticscholar.org/paper/Evolution%3A-A-Theory-in-Crisis-Denton.

108. Fyodor Dostoyevsky, *The Brothers Karamazov* ( New York, NY: Forestairs and Giroux Publishing 1990), 593.

109. Probe Ministries, *Mind Games: College Survival Course* (Richardson, TX: 1996), 5.

110. Steve Kumar, *Christianity for Sceptics* (Italy: John Hunt Publishing Ltd., 2000), 25.

111. https://practicalphilosophy.org.au/Blaise Pascal.

112. Probe Ministries, *College Mind Games* (Richardson, TX: 1996), 5.

113. David Kinnaman and Gabe Lyons, *Good Faith: Being a Christian When Society Thinks You're Irrelevant and Extreme* (Grand Rapids, MI: Baker Books, 2016), 53.

114. C.S. Lewis, *God in the Dock: Essays on methodology and Ethics*, (Grand Rapids. MI: William B. Eerdmans 1970), 52-53.

115. Christopher Dawson, "Christianity and European Culture," ed. Gerald J. Russello, *The Historic Reality of Christian Culture* (Washington, D.C. Catholic University of America Press, 1998), 97.

## CHAPTER 3

## HAS SCIENCE BURIED GOD?

116. Alister E. McGrath, *Science and Religion* (West Sussex, UK: Blackwell Publishers, 2010), 3.

117. James Hannam, *The Genesis of Science: How the Christian Middle Ages Launched the Scientific Revolution* (Washington, D.C. Regency Publishing Inc., 2011), 18.

118. Del Ratzsch, *Science and Its Limits: The Natural Sciences in Christian Perspective* (Downers Grove, IL: Intervarsity Press, 1986), 14.

119. March of Progress, accessed May 27, 2020, https://yalealumnimagazine.com/articles/3977-march-of-progress.

120. Daniel Dennett, *Darwin's Dangerous Idea: Evolution and the Meaning of Life* (New York, NY: Simon Schuster, 1995), 63.

121. John G. West, *Darwin's Corrosive Idea: The Impact of Evolution on Attitudes about Faith, Ethics and Human Uniqueness* (Seattle, WA: Published Discovery Institute, 2016), 1-2.

122. Stephen Jay Gould, accessed May 13, 2020, https://genius.com/Stephen-jay-gould-the-meaning-of-life-annotated.

123. Richard Dawkins, *River out of Eden* (London, UK: Weidenfeld and Nicholson, 1995), 133.

124. Lyall Watson, "The Water People," *Science Digest* Vol. 90 (May, 1982): 44.

125. Ann Gauger, Douglas Axe, and Casey Luskin, *Science and Human Origin* (Seattle, WA: Discovery Institute Press, 2012), 46.

126. Ibid.

127. Francisco Ayala, "The Myth of Eve: Molecular Biology and Origins of Humans," *Science* 270 (1995): 193-196.

128. Ann Gauger, Douglas Axe, and Casey Luskin, *Science and Human Origin* (Seattle, WA: Discovery Institute Press, 2012), 46.

129. John Reader, *Missing Links*, "Whatever Happened to Zinjanthropus?" *New Scientist* 26 (March 1981): 802.

130. Frank Spencer, *Piltdown: A Scientific Forgery*, (Claimed the forger was anthropologist Sir Arthur Keith). (New York, NY: Oxford University Press, 1990), 272.

131. Henry F. Osborn, "Hesperopithecus: The First Anthropoid Primate Found in America," *Science*, Vol. 60. No.1427 (May 5, 1922): 463.

132. William K. Gregory, "Hesperopithecus: Apparently Not an Ape nor a Man," *Science*, Vol. 66, No. 1720 (December 16, 1927).

133. Peter R. Grant and B. Rosemary Grant, "Hybridization of Bird Species," *Science* 256 (1992): 193-197.

134. *Evolution in Action*, accessed May 27, 2020, https://www.biointeractive.org/sites/default/files/FinchGraph-Educator-act.pdf.

135. J.A. Coyne, "Not Black and White," *Nature* 396 (6706) (1998): 35–36.

136. Jonathan Wells, *Zombie Science: More Icons of Evolution* (Seattle, WA: Discovery Institute Press, 2017), 66.

137. Benjamin Wiker, *The Darwin Myth: The Life and Lies of Charles Darwin* (Washington, DC: Regency Publishing, 2009), 139.

138. Charles Darwin, *The Origin of Species* (1859), accessed September 15, 2020, www.literature.org/author/darwin-charles/the-origin-of-species.

139. Charles Darwin, "Doubt About his Theory," accessed September 15, 2020, https://www.goodreads.com/quotes/344545-if-it-could-be-demonstrated-that-any-complex-organ-existed.

140. Dave Hunt, *Cosmos, Creator and Human Destiny: Answering Darwin, Dawkins and the New Atheists* (Bend, OR: Berean Call Publishing, 2010), 59.

141. Stephen Jay Gould, "Punctuated Equilibrium: An Alternative of Phyletic Gradualism," ed. Thomas J.M. Schopf, *Models in Paleobiology* (1972), 84.

142. Robert Carter, *Evolution's Achilles' Heels* (Powder Springs, GA: Creation Book Publishers, 2014), 128.

143. J. Shreeve, "Argument Over a Woman," *Discover* (1990), accessed July 5, 2020, https://answersingenesis.org/theory-of-evolution/quotes/singing-bones.

144. Jim Nelson Black, *The Death of Evolution: Restoring Faith and Wonder in a World of Doubt* (Grand Rapids, MI: Zondervan Publishing, 2010), 119.

145. G. Richard Bozarth, "The Meaning of Evolution," *American Atheist* (February 1978): 30.

146. Bruce L. Gordon and William A. Dembski, *The Nature of Nature: Examining the Role of Naturalism in Science* (Wilmington, DE: International Studies Institute, 2011), 3.

147. Paul Weston, *Lesslie Newbigin: Missionary Theologian: A Reader* (Grand Rapids, MI: Wm. B. Eerdmans Publication, 2006), 157, 257.

148. Richard Lewontin, accessed June13, 2022, www.nybooks.com/articles/1997/01/09/billions-and-billions-of-demons/.

149. "Free People from Superstition," *Freethought Today* (April 2000), accessed April 14, 2021, http://wwww..fffg.org/legacy/fttoday/2000/weinberg.html.

150. John Locke, *The Reasonableness of Christianity, As Delivered in the Scriptures,* Britannica Edition of the Works of John Locke, ed. John C. Higgins-Biddle (Oxford, UK: Oxford University Press, 2018), 86.

151. Thomas Nagel, accessed June 16, 2021, http://thewaytheballbounces.blogspot.com/2013/03/the-lost-atheist-thomas-nagels.

152. Robert Carter, *Evolution's Achilles' Heels* (Powder Springs, GA: Creation Book Publishers, 2014), 20.

153. Alister E. McGrath, *Science and Religion* (West Sussex, UK: Blackwell Publishers, 2010), 15.

154. Daniel Lapin, *Thou Shall Prosper: Ten Commandments for Making Money* (Hoboken, NJ: John Wiley and Sons Publication, 2010), 48.

155. Ibid.

156. Mark Hartwig and Paul Nelson, *Invitation to Conflict: A Retrospective Look at the California Science Framework* (Colorado Springs, CO: Access Research Network, 1992), 6, 20.

157. J.P. Moreland, *Love Your God with All Your Heart and Mind: The Role of Reason in the Life of the Soul* (Colorado Spring, CO: NavPress, 2012), 39.

158. Rodney Stark, *The Victory of Reason: How Christianity Leads to Freedom, Capitalism, and Western Success* (New York, NY: Random House Inc., 2005), 7.

159. Ibid., 22.

160. Alister E. McGrath, *Science and Religion* (West Sussex, UK: Blackwell Publishers, 2010), 59.

161. Norman Geisler, *Baker Encyclopedia of Christian Apologetics* (Grand Rapids, MI: Bakers Books, 1999), 725.

162. R.J Berry, *Science and Christianity: The Lion Handbook* (Oxford, UK: Wilkinson house, 2012), 271.

163. Alister E. McGrath, *Science and Religion* (West Sussex, UK: Blackwell Publishers, 2010), 29.

164. Francis A. Schaeffer, *How Should We Then Live? The Rise and Fall of Western Thought and Culture* (Old Tappan, NJ: Fleming H. Revell Publishing, 1976), 138.

165. Richard Howe and Thomas Howe, *I Want to Believe But* (Charlotte, NC: Southern Evangelical Seminary, 2016), 10.

166. Albert Einstein, "Physics and Reality," (1936) in *Ideas and Opinions*, trans. Sonja Bargmann (New York: NY, 1954), 292.

167. R.J Berry, *Science and Christianity: The Lion Handbook* (Oxford, UK: Wilkinson House, 2012), 61.

168. Francis Schaeffer, *How Shall We Live? The Rise and Decline of Western Thought and Culture* (Old Tappan, NJ: Fleming H. Revell Company, 1976), 138.

# CHAPTER 4

## ORIGINS: HOW DID WE GET HERE?

169. J.P. Moreland, *Science and Secularism* (Wheaton, IL: Crossway Publishing, 2018), 145-147.

170. J.P. Moreland, *Christianity and the Nature of Science* (Grand Rapids, MI: Baker Book House, 1989), 215.

171. "Spontaneous Generation," accessed August 12, 2021, https://creationstudies.org/operationsalt/spontaneous-generation.html.

172. Gerald Schoreder, *The Hidden Face of God: Science Reveals the Ultimate Truth* (New York, NY: Simon and Schuster, 2001), 58.

173. Robert Carter, *Evolution's Achilles Heel* (Powder Springs, GA: Creation Book Publishers, 2014), 96.

174. Ibid., 84.

175. Dr. Dean Kenyon, accessed February 17, 2020, https://www.youtube.com/watch?v=jrXf8KCJLMg.

176. William Dembski, *Intelligent Design: The Bridge Between Science & Theology* (Downer Grover, IL: InterVarsity Press, 1999), 159-161.

177. Sir Fred Hoyle and Chandra Wickramasinghe, *Evolution from Space* (New York, NY: Simon and Schuster, 1983), 19-21.

178. Jim Nelson Black, *The Death of Evolution: Restoring Faith and Wonder in a World of Doubt* (Grand Rapids, MI: Zondervan, 2010), 42.

179. The Discovery Institute: The Center for Science and Culture, *Educator's Briefing Packet* (Seattle, WA: Discovery Institute Press, 2016): 4.

180. Robert Jastrow, *God and the Astronomers* (New York, NY: Norton & Company Publishing, 1987), 87.

181. Ronald. H. Nash, *Worldviews in Conflict* (Grand Rapids, MI: Zondervan Publication, 1992), 38.

182. William B. Provine, *Origins Research* 16, accessed May 22, 2021 (1994): 9.

183. Michael Ruse, accessed September 26, 2019, https://creation.com/michael-ruse-evolution-is-a-religion.

184. Del Ratzsch, *Science and Its Limits: Natural Sciences in a Christian Perspective* (Downer Grove, IL: InterVarsity Press, 2000), 164.

185. Michael Ruse and E.O. Wilson, *The Evolution of Ethics: Religion and the Natural Sciences* (New York, NY: Harcourt Brace Jovanovich, 1993), 210.

186. Malcolm Muggeridge, *The End of Christendom* (Grand Rapids, MI: Wm. B. Eerdmans Publishing, 1980), 59.

187. Walter A Elwell, *Evangelical Dictionary of Theology* (Grand Rapids, MI: Baker Books, 1984), 558.

188. Bruce Shelley, *Church History in Plain Language* (Nashville, TN: Thomas Nelson Publishing, 1982), 66-67.

## CHAPTER 5

## IS THE BIBLE RELIABLE?

189. Walter A Elwell, *Evangelical Dictionary of Theology* (Grand Rapids, MI: Baker Books, 1984), 141.

190. David Alexander and Pat Alexander, ed., *Eerdmans Handbook of the Bible* (Grand Rapids, MI: Lion Publication, 1980), 74.

191. Norman Geisler and Ronald M. Brooks, *When Skeptics Ask: A Handbook on Christian Evidences* (Grand Rapids, MI: Baker Books, 2008), 144.

192. Ibid., 145.

193. Walter A. Elwell, *Evangelical Dictionary of Theology* (Lansing, MI: Baker Books, 1984), 887.

194. Joseph M. Holden and Norman Geisler, *The Popular Handbook of Archaeology and the Bible: Discoveries that Confirm the Reliability of Scripture* (Eugene, OR: Harvest House Publishers, 2013), 135-137.

195. Joseph M. Holden and Norman Geisler, *The Popular Handbook of Archeology and the Bible* (Eugene, OR: Harvest House Publishers, 2013), 102-103.

196. Matt Slick, accessed December 10, 2019, https://carm.org/is-the-bible-reliable.

197. *The Bibliographical Test Updated*, accessed January 9, 2020, "Christian Research Journal," Vol. 35, no. 03 (2012), http://www.equip.org.

198. Joseph M. Holden and Norman Geisler, *The Popular Handbook of Archeology and the Bible* (Eugene, OR: Harvest House Publishers, 2013), 127.

199. R.T. France, accessed October 10, 2021, https://www.tektonics.org/lp/nttextcrit.php.

200. Christopher Tackett, *Cambridge Companion to Jesus* (Cambridge, UK: Cambridge University Press, 2001), 124.

201. Bart Ehrman, *Misquoting Jesus: The Story Behind Who Changed the Bible and Why* (New York, NY: Harper Publication, 2005), 55.

202. Bruce Metzger & Bart Ehrman, *The Text of the New Testament: Its Transmission, Corruption, and Restoration,* 4th ed. (New York, NY: Oxford University Press, 1992), 101.

203. Ibid., 103.

204. F.P. Retief and L. Cilliers, *The History and Pathology of Crucifixion,* accessed January 13, 2021 (December 2003): 93, https://www.ncbi.nlm.nih. South African Med Journey.

205. Ulrich, Eugene C., *The Dead Sea Scrolls and the Origins of the Bible,* Eugene Ulrich, Chief editor of the Oxford Series *Discoveries in the Judaean Desert* (Grand Rapids, MI: Wm. B. Eerdmans Publishing, 1999).

206. P.R. Davis, G.J. Brooks, and P.R. Callaway, *The Complete World of the Dead Sea Scrolls* (London, UK: Thames and Hudson, 2002), 75.

207. *Is Jesus the Messiah?* http://www.bibletimelines.net/article/24/article-brief-and-to-the-point/jesus-is-he-really-the-messiah.

208. J. E. Hunter, *Let Us Go on To Maturity* (Grand Rapids, MI: Zondervan, 1978), 13.

## CHAPTER 6

## DID JESUS CLAIM TO BE GOD?

209. C.S Lewis, *Mere Christianity* (New York, NY: Macmillan Publishing, 1952), 13.

210. RC Sproul, *Essentially Truths of the Christian Faith* (Wheaton, IL: Tyndale House Publishing, 1992), 71, 160.

211. Shannon M. Stubbs, "Jesus' Claim to Singularity with Yahweh: An Exegetical Study of "I Am" Sayings in the Synoptic Gospels," Order No. 1495891, (Oral Roberts University, 2011), https://search.proquest.com/docview/873577254?accountid=36664.

212. J.R. Stott, *Basic Christianity* (Chicago, IL: InterVarsity Press, 1964), 26.

213. Fritz Ridenour, *So What's the difference?* (Glendale, CA: Regal Publishing, 1969), 99.

214. Walter A. Elwell, ed., *Evangelical Dictionary of Theology* (Lansing, MI: Baker Books, 1984), 1130.

## CHAPTER 7

## THE RESURRECTION

215. John Dickson, *Investigating Jesus: An Historian's Quest* (Oxford, UK: Wilkinson Publishing, 2010), 7.

216. Gary Habermas, *Minimal Facts on the Resurrection that Even Skeptics Accept,* accessed April 6, 2020, https://ses.edu/minimal-facts-on-the-resurrection-that-even-skeptics-accept.

217. Ibid.

218. Flavius Josephus, *Antiquities of the Jews,* accessed April 26, 2020, http://www.perseus.tufts.edu/hopper/text?doc=J.%20AJ%2018.5&lang=original.

219. Tacitus, Annuls, XV 40; see Appendix 2, accessed April 26, 2020, http://www.perseus.tufts.edu/hopper/text?doc.

220. Ibid.

221. Ibid.

222. Peter Kreeft and Ronald K. Tacelli, *Handbooks of Christian Apologetics* (Downers Grove, IL: InterVarsity Press, 1994), 176.

223. Paul E. Little, *Know Why You Believe* (London, UK: Scripture Union, 1968), 21.

224. Brain K. Morley, *Mapping Apologetics: Comparing Contemporary Approaches* (Downer Grove, IL: InterVarsity Press, 2015), 311.

225. William Lane Craig, *Reasonable Faith: The Christian Truth and Apologetics* (Wheaton, IL: Crossway Books, 2008), 207.

226. Lesslie Newbigin, *Foolishness of the Greeks: The Gospel and Western Culture* (Grand Rapids, MI: Wm. B. Eerdmans Publishing, 1986), 3.

227. B.B. Warfield, *The Person and Work of Christ* (Philadelphia, PA: Puritan Reformed, 1950), 537.

228. William C. Weinrich, *Spirit and Martyrdom: A Study of the Work of the Holy Spirit in Contexts of Persecution and Martyrdom in the New Testament and Early Christian Literature,* accessed May 3, 2020, https://www.cambridge.org/core/journals/church-history/.

229. Brooke Wescott, *"The Gospel of the Resurrection: Thoughts on Its Relation to Reason and History,"* accessed April 23, 2020, https://www.azquotes.com/author/21721-Brooke_Westcott.

230 Simon Greenleaf, accessed April 23, 2020, *Harvard Law Professor Puts Jesus' Resurrection on Trial,* https://y-jesus.com/simon-greenleaf-resurrection/.

231. Wolfhart Pannenberg, "Dogmatic Thesis on the Doctrine of Revelation," in *Revelations as History* (New York, NY: Macmillan, 1969), 134, 161.

232. Ibid.

233. Thomas Arnold, *Christian Life, Its Hopes, Its Fears, and its Close* (London, UK: G. Woodfall and Son, 1859), 15-16.

234. Peter Kreeft & Ronald K. Tacelli, *Handbook of Christian Apologetics* (Downers Grove, IL: InterVarsity Press, 1994), 182.

235. Lee Strobel, "4 Proofs of the Resurrection," in *The Case for Christ*, accessed April 28, 2020, http://bit.ly/1R7GZEs#lee Strobel #thecaseforchrist #easter.

236. Ibid.

237. Peter Kreeft, accessed April 29, 2020, http://www.peterkreeft.com/topics-more/resurrection-evidence.htm.

238. "Did Jesus Rise from the Dead?" Part Two, accessed April 28, 2021, https://www.reasonablefaith.org/did-jesus.

239. Peter Kreeft and Ronald K. Tacelli, *Handbook of Christian Apologetics* (Downers Grove, IL: InterVarsity Press, 1994), 186.

240. Ibid., 187.

241. William Lane Craig, *Knowing the Truth About the Resurrection: Our Response to the Empty Tomb* (Ann Arbor, MI: Servant Publications, 1988), 48.

242. Glenn Siniscalchi, "Early Christian Worship and the Historical Argument for Jesus' Resurrection," accessed May 1, 2020, https://www.jstor.org/stable/43251681?searchText=(Jesus%27%20Resurrection).

243. Peter Kreeft and Ronald K.Tacelli, *Handbook of Christian Apologetics* (Downers Grove, IL: InterVarsity Press, 1994), 186.

244. Ibid., 190-191.

245. John Dickson, *Investigating Jesus: An Historian's Quest* (Oxford, UK: Wilkinson Publishing, 2010), 99.

246. Ibid.

247. G. Lüdemann, *What Really Happened to Jesus: A Historical Approach of the Resurrection* (Westminster, UK: John Knox Press, 1995), 14-15.

248. C.S. Lewis, "What Are We to Make of Jesus Christ?" in *C.S. Lewis Essay Collection*, 40.

249. Peter Kreeft and Ronald K. Tacelli, *Handbook of Christian Apologetics* (Downers Grove, IL: InterVarsity Press, 1994), 190.

250. "Did Jesus Rise from the Dead?" accessed April 28, 2020, https://www.reasonablefaith.org/did-jesus.

251. Ibid.

252. Jaroslav Pelikan, *The Christian Tradition: A History of the Development of Doctrine* (Chicago, IL: University of Chicago Press, 1977), 162.

# CHAPTER 8

# WHY DOES GOD ALLOW EVIL AND SUFFERING?

253. C.S. Lewis, *God in the Dock: Essays on Theology and Ethics* (Grand Rapids, MI: Wm. B. Eerdmans Publishing, 2014), 28.

254. Walter A. Elwell, ed., *Evangelical Dictionary of Theology* (Lansing, MI: Baker Books, 1984), 1083.

255. *The Problem of Evil*, accessed January 24, 2021, https://www.namb.net/apologetics/resource/the-problem-of-evil/.

256. *Theodicy: The Problem of Evil*, accessed May 10, 2020, https://www.theopedia.com/problem-of-evil.

257. Norman Geisler, *Baker Encyclopedia of Christian Apologetics* (Grand Rapids, MI: Bakers Books, 1999), 221.

258. C.S. Lewis, *God in the Dock: Essays on Theology and Ethics* (Grand Rapids, MI: Wm. B. Eerdmans, 1970), 23.

259. C.S. Lewis, *Mere Christianity* (New York, NY: Macmillan Publishers, 1960), 53.

260. Jean-Paul Sartre, *Jean-Paul Sartre: Basic Writings,* ed. Stephen Priest (New York, NY: Routledge Publishing, 2001), 32.

261.Define *Theodicy*, accessed June 6, 2021, https://www.britannica.com/topic/theodicy-theology.

262. Carl Jung, accessed December 22, 2021, https://www.brainyquote.com/authors/carl-jung-quotes.

263. Brian K. Morley, *Mapping Apologetics: Comparing Contemporary Approaches* (Grand Rapids, MI: InterVarsity Press, 2015), 135.

264. Norman Geisler, *Baker Encyclopedia of Christian Apologetics* (Grand Rapids, MI: Bakers Books, 1999), 221.

265. "Does God Allow Tragedy?" accessed May 14, 2021, https://www.christianitytoday.com/pastors/2012/july.

# CHAPTER 9

# CLASSICAL APOLOGETICS

266. Walter Elwell, ed., *Evangelical Dictionary of Theology* (Grand Rapids, MI: Baker Books Publishing, 1997), 68.

267. C.S. Lewis, *Weight of Glory* (New York, NY: Harper Collins Publication, 2001), 34.

268. Irving M. Copi and Carl Cohen, *Introduction to Logic* (New York, NY: MacMillan Publishing, 1990), 3.

269. *The Kalam Cosmological Argument,* accessed September 12, 2021, http://www.reasonablefaith.org/writings/popular-writings/existence-nature-of-god/the-kalam-cosmological-argument.

270. Edwin Hubble, accessed September 12, 2021, https://www.nasa.gov/content/about-story-edwin-hubble.

271. Norman Geisler, *Christian Apologetics* (Grand Rapids, MI: Baker Book House, 1976), 234.

272. Fred Hoyle, *The Universe: Past and Present Reflection,* accessed May 17, 2020, http://hyperphysics.phy-astr.gsu.ed/Nave-html/Faithpathh/Hoyle.html.

273. Bill Gates, *The Road Ahead* (New York, NY: Viking Publishing, 1995), 42.

274. Paul Davies, accessed May 26, 2020, http://www.reasonalblefaith.org/finetuning.

275. Ibid., 163.

276. Roger Penrose, *The Emperor's New Mind* (Oxford, UK: Oxford University Press, 1989), 344.

277. "The Teleological Argument," https://plato.stanford.edu/entries/teleological-arguments/.

278. "Cause and Effect," accessed May 13, 2020, https://www.reddit.com/r/Physics/comments/4c4k84/no_effect_can_be_greater_than_its_cause/.

279. Immanuel Kant, accessed July 18, 2021, https://plato.stanford.edu/entries/kant/.

280. James C. Hefley and Marti Hefley, *God's Tribesman: The Rochunga Pudaite Story* (Dallas, TX: Accelerated Christian Books, 1969), 76.

# CHAPTER 10

## WHY WE PERSUADE OTHERS

281. Defining *Persuasive*, accessed February 8, 2021, https://www.studylight.org/dictionaries/eng/ved/p/persuasive-persuasivness.html.

282. Define *persuade*, accessed February 8, 2021, https://www.oxfordlearnersdictionaries.com/us/definition/english/persuade?q=Persuade.

283. Leslie Newbigin, *The Gospel in a Pluralistic Society* (Grand Rapids, MI: Wm. B. Eerdmans Publishing, 1989), 92.

284. H. Wayne House and Joseph M. Holden, *Zondervan Charts of Apologetics and Christian Evidences* (Grand Rapids, MI: Zondervan Press, 2006), 12.

285. Os Guinness, *Fools Talk: Recovering the Art of Christian Persuasion* (Downer Grove, IL: InterVarsity Press, 2015), 16.

286. Ibid., 27.

287. Todd T. Daly, Ph.D. "Thinking about Christian Apologetics: What it is and Why we do it," *Ethics & Medicine* 29, no. 2 (Summer 2013): 128, https://search.proquest.com/docview/1366045146?accountid=36664.

288. Brian K. Morley, *Mapping Apologetics: Comparing Contemporary Approaches* (Downers Grove, IL: Intervarsity Press, 2015), 148.

289. J. Gresham Machen, *What is Christianity?* (Grand Rapids, MI: Wm. B. Eerdmans Publishing. 1951), 162.

290. Defining *Tolerance*, accessed December 12, 2021, https://www.oxfordlearnersdictionaries.com/us/.

291. Cathryn Buse, *Teaching Others to Defend Christianity: What Every Christian Should Know* (Rapid City, SD: Cross Link Publishing, 2016), 62.

292. Evelyn Beatrice Hall (aka: Stephen G. Tallentyre), *The Friends of Voltaire* (London, UK: Smith Elder Company, 1906), 24.

293. D. A. Carson, *The Intolerance of Tolerance* (Grand Rapids, MI: Wm. B. Eerdmans Publishing, 2012), 11.

294. Ibid., 12.

295. Jay Budziszewski, *True Tolerance: Liberalism and the Necessity of Judgment* (New York, NY: Routledge Taylor and Francis Publishing. 1992), 67.

296. *Is Christianity Exclusive?* accessed April 15, 2021, https://evangelicalbible.com/apologetics/is-christianity-an-exclusive-religion/.

297. Ibid.

## CONCLUSION:

298. J. Gresham Machen, "Education, Christian and the State," ed. John W. Robbins, (Jefferson, MD: Trinity Foundation, 1987): 34.

299. Ibid.

# SELECTED BIBLIOGRAPHY

Arnold, Thomas. *Christian Life, Its Hopes, Its Fears, and Its Close*. London, UK: Forgotten Books, 2017.

Alexander, David, and Pat Alexander, eds. *Eerdmans Handbook of the Bible*. Grand Rapids, MI: Lion Publications, 1980.

Ayala, Francisco. "The Myth of Eve: Molecular Biology and Origins of Humans." *Science 270* (1995).

Barrett, Justin. *Born Believers: The Science of Children's Religious Beliefs*. New York, NY: Simon and Schuster, 2012.

Barton, David. *Original Intent: The Courts, The Constitution & Religion*. Aledo, TX: Wall-builder Press, 1997.

Beliles, Mark A., and Stephen K. McDowell. *America's Providential History*. Charlottesville, VA: The Providence Foundation, 1989.

Berry, R.J. *Science and Christianity: The Lion Handbook*. Oxford, UK: Wilkinson House, 2012.

Black, Jim Nelson. *The Death of Evolution: Restoring Faith and Wonder in a World of Doubt*. Grand Rapids, MI: Zondervan Press, 2010.

Blamires, Harry. *The Christian Mind: How Should a Christian Think?* Ann Arbor, MI: Servant Publications, 1978.

Boersma, Hans. "Therapeutic Revolution." *First Things*. Ft. Collins, CO: Ignatius Press, May 2021.

Bozarth, G. Richard. "The Meaning of Evolution." In *The American Atheist*. February, 1978.

Broocks, Rice. *Man, Myth and Messiah: Answering History's Greatest Question*. Nashville, TN: Thomas Nelson, 2016.

Brooke and Westcott. "The Gospel of the Resurrection: Thoughts on Its Relation to Reason and History." Accessed June 12, 2021. https://www.azquotes.com/author/21721-Brooke,Westcott.

Browne, Thomas. *Religion Medici, Hydriotaphia, and The Garden of Cyrus.* Edited by Robin Robbins. Oxford, UK: (1982) 16.

Budziszewski, Jay. *True Tolerance: Liberalism and the Necessity of Judgment.* New York, NY: Routledge Taylor and Francis Publications, 1992.

Buse, Cathryn. *Teaching Others to Defend Christianity: What Every Christian Should Know.* USA: Cross Link Publishing, 2016.

Bush, L. Russ. *Classical Readings in Christian Apologetics: A.D. 100-1800.* Grand Rapids, MI: Zondervan Press, 1983.

Cairns, Earle. *Christianity through the Centuries: A History of the Christian Church.* Grand Rapids, MI: Zondervan Publishing, 1981.

Calvin, John. "Battles in the library of Christian Classics." In *Institutes of Christian Religion.* Edited by John T. McNeil. Philadelphia, PA: Westminster, 1960.

Cambridge English Dictionary. Accessed September 23, 2017. http://www.dictionary.cambridge.org/us/dictionary/english/secularism.

Carson, D. A. *The Intolerance of Tolerance.* Grand Rapids, MI: *Wm. B.* Eerdman Publishing, 2012.

------.*Christ and Culture Revisited.* Grand Rapids, MI: Wm. B. Eerdman Publishing, 2008.

Carter, Robert. *Evolution's Achilles' Heels.* Powder Springs, GA: Creation Book Publishers, 2014.

Cass, Gary, Sam Kastensmidt, and Anthony Urti. *The Bible and the Blackboard: Biblical Solutions for Failing Schools.* Fort Lauderdale, FL: Coral Ridge Publishing, 2007.

Chesterton, G.K. *St. Thomas Aquinas: The Dumb Ox.* New York, NY: Double-Day Publishing, 1956.

Clarke, G.W. "The Origins and Spread of Christianity." In *Cambridge Ancient History.* Vol. X. Cambridge University Press, 1996.

Colson, Chuck, and Nancy Pearcy. *How Now Shall We Live?* Wheaton, IL: Tyndale Publishing, 1999.

Cook, Josiah. "The Nobility of Knowledge." *Popular Science.* Month 5 (1874).

Coyne, J.A. "Not Black and White: Melanism, Evolution in Action in Peppered Moth." Review by Michael E.N. Majerus. *Nature.* (1998): 396 (6706).

Craig, William Lane. *Knowing the Truth About the Resurrection: Our Response to the Empty Tomb*. Servant Publications, 1988.

------.*Reasonable Faith: The Christian Truth of Apologetics*. Wheaton, IL: Crossway Books, 2008.

------."The Indispensability of Meta-Ethical Foundations for Morality." *Foundations 5*(1997)

Craig, William Lane, and J.P. Moreland. *Philosophical Foundations for a Christian Worldview*. Downer Grove, IL: InterVarsity Press, 2003.

Daly, Todd T. "Thinking about Christian Apologetics: What it is and Why we do it." *Ethics & Medicine*. no. 2 (Summer 2013): 29.

Darwin, Charles, *The Origin of Species*, 1859, Literature Org. Accessed June 24, 2021. http://www.literature.org/author/darwin-charles/the-origin-of-species.

Davis, P.R., G.J. Brooks, and P.R. Callaway. *The Complete World of the Dead Sea Scrolls*. Thames and Hudson, 2002.

Dawkins, Richard. "Is Science a Religion?" *Humanist*. (January/February 1997).

------.*River out of Eden*. London, UK: Weidenfeld & Nicholson, 1995.

------.*The Blind Watchmaker*. New York, NY: W.W. Norton Publications, 1987.

Dawkins, Richard, and Lawrence Krauss. *Something From Nothing*. Lecture. Accessed April 19, 2012. https://www.youtube.com/watch?v=YUe0_4rdj0U.

Dawson, Christopher. "Man and Civilization." *The Listener*. August 23, 1933.

------."The Historic Reality of Christian Culture."In *Christianity and European Culture*. Edited by Gerald, J. Russello. Washington, DC: Catholic University of America Press, 1998.

Dee, Ivan R. *Complete Essays: 1936-1938*. Aldous Huxley, 2001.

DeMoss, Nancy Leigh. *The Rebirth of America*. Arthur DeMoss Foundation, 1986.

Dennett, Daniel. *Darwin's Dangerous Idea: Evolution and the Meaning of Life*. New York, NY: Simon and Schuster, 1995.

Dewey, John. *A Common Faith*. New Haven, CT: Yale University Press, 1934.

Dickson, John. *Investigating Jesus: An Historian's Quest*. Oxford, UK: Wilkinson Publishing, 2010.

Dion, Celine. "Too Christian for School." Song banned June 8, 2003. Accessed October 12, 2021. https://freerepublic.com/focus/f-news/925462/posts.

Discovery Institute: The Center for Science and Culture. *Educator's Briefing Packet*. Seattle, WA: Discovery Institute Press.

Dostoyevsky, Fyodor. *The Brothers Karamazov*. New York, NY: Farrar, Strais and Giroux Publications, 1990.

Durant, Will and Ariel. *The Lessons of History*. New York, NY: Simon and Schuster, 1968.

------. *The Story of Civilization: Part IX, The Age of Voltaire*. New York, NY: Simon and Schuster, 1965.

Earle, Ralph. *Word Meanings in the New Testament*. Grand Rapids, MI: Baker Books, 1986.

Elwell, Walter A. *Evangelical Dictionary of Theology*. Lansing, MI: Baker Books, 1984.

Einstein, Albert "Physics and Reality"(1936). In *Ideas and Opinions*. Trans. Sonja Bargmann. New York, NY: Bonanza, 1954.

Engel vs. Vitale, Thompson Gale Legal Encyclopedia. Accessed October 12, 2021. Answers.com 2006. https://www.uscourts.gov/educational-resources/educational-activities/facts-and-case-summary-engel-v-vitale.

Ehrman, Bart. *Misquoting Jesus: The Story Behind Who Changed the Bible and Why*. New York, NY: Harper Publications, 2005.

Federer, William J. *America's God and Country*. St Louis, MI: Amerisearch, 2000.

France, R.T., and Wenham Davis. *Gospel Perspectives*. Vol. III. Studies in Midrash and Historiography. Wipf & Stock, 2003.

Gallup, George Jr., and Jim Castelli. *The People's Religion: American Faith in the Nineties*. New York, NY: Macmillan, 1989.

Gates, Bill. *The Road Ahead*. New York, NY: Viking Books, 1995.

Gauger, Ann, and Douglas Axe, and, Casey Luskin. *Science and Human Origin*. Seattle, WA: Discovery Institute Press, 2012.

Geisler, Norman L. *Baker Encyclopedia of Christian Apologetics*. Grand Rapids, MI: Baker Books, 1999.

Geisler, Norman, and Ronald M. Brooks. *When Skeptics Ask: A Handbook on Christian Evidences*. Grand Rapids, MI: Baker Books, 2008.

Giller, Geoffrey, and Richard Conniff. https://yalealumnimagazine. com/search?site_search=Evolution%3A+March+of+Progress&commit=Search.

Gingerich, Owens. *God's Universe*. Cambridge, MA: Harvard University Press, 2006.

Gopnik, Alison. *See Jane Evolve:* Picture Books Explain "Darwin, Mind and Matter." *Wall Street Journal.* April 18, 2014.

Gould, Stephen Jay. "Non-overlapping Magisterial." Accessed October 14, 2021. https://www.academia.edu/37048682/A_Critique_of_Stephen_Goulds_Non_Overlapping_Magisteria.

Gordon, Bruce L., and William A. Dembski. *The Nature of Nature: Examining the Role of Naturalism in Science*. Wilmington, DE: International Studies Institute, 2011.

Grant, Peter R., and B. Rosemary Grant. "Hybridization of Bird Species." *Science* (1992): 256.

Gregory, William K. "Hesperopithecus: Apparently not an Ape nor a Man," *Science.* Vol. 66 (December 16, 1927): 1720.

Grossan, John Dominic. "Death of the Soul: From Descartes to the Computer." Garden City, NY: Anchor/Doubleday, 1986.

Groothuis, Douglas. *Truth Decay: Defending Christianity Against the Challenge of Postmodernism*. Downer Grove, IL: InterVarsity Press, 2000.

Guinness, Os. *Fool's Talk: Recovering the Art of Christian Persuasion*. Downers Grove, IL: InterVarsity Press, 2015.

Habermas, Gary. "Minimal Facts on the Resurrection that even Skeptics Accept." http://www.garyhabermas.com/articles/Habermas_Minimal%20Facts%20STR%202012.pdf. Accessed October 14, 2021.

Hannam, James. *The Genesis of Science: How the Christian Middle Ages Launched the Scientific Revolution*. Washington, DC: Regency Publishing, 2011.

Hartwig, Mark, and Paul Nelson. *Invitation to Conflict: A Retrospective Look at the California Science Framework.* Colorado Springs, CO: AbeBooks Publishing, 1992.

Hefley, James C. *God's Tribesman: The Rochunga Pudaite Story.* Elgin, IL: David C. Cook, 1969.

Henderson, David W. *Culture Shift: Communicating God's Truth to Our Changing World.* Grand Rapids, MI: Bakers Books, 1998.

Holmes, Arthur. *All Truth is God's Truth:* Grand Rapids, MI: Wm. B. Erdman Publishing, 1977.

Holden, Joseph M., and Norman Geisler. *The Popular Handbook of Archeology and the Bible.* Eugene, OR: Harvest House Publishers, 2013.

House, Wayne, & Joseph Holden. *Charts of Apologetics and Christian Evidences.* Chart 25. Grand Rapids, MI: Zondervan Press, 2006.

Howe, Richard, and Thomas Howe. *I Want to Believe But.* Charlotte, NC: Southern Evangelical Seminary, 2016.

Hoyle, Sir Fred, *The Universe: Past and Present Reflections.* Accessed November 1, 2021. https://www.annualreviews.org/doi/abs/10.1146/annurev.aa.20.090182.000245.

Hoyle, Sir Fred and Chandra Wickramasinghe. *Evolution from Space: A Theory of Cosmic Creationism.* New York, NY: Simon and Schuster, 1983.

Hunt, Dave. *Cosmos, Creator and Human Destiny: Answering Darwin, Dawkins and the New Atheists.* Bend, OR: Berean Call Publishing, 2010.

Jastrow, Robert. *God and the Astronomers.* New York, NY: Norton & Company Publishing, 1987.

Johnson, Phillip E. *Reason in the Balance: The Case Against Naturalism in Science, Law & Education.* Downers Grove, IL: InterVarsity Press, 1995.

Jones, E. Michael, *Degenerate Moderns: Modernity as Rationalized Sexual Misbehavior.* San Francisco, CA: Ignatius Press, 1993.

Josephus, Flavius, *Antiquities of the Jew.* Accessed November 1, 2021. https://www.britannica.com/topic/The-Antiquities-of-the-Jews.

Kant, Immanuel. "Critique of Practical Reason" (1788). In *Critique of Practical Reason and Other Writings in Moral Philosophy.* Edited and translated by L. W. Beck, 1949.

Kaufman, Walter. "The Gay Science." In *Portable Nietzsche.* New York, NY: Viking Press, 1954.

Kinnaman, David, and Gabe Lyons. *Good Faith: Being a Christian When Society Thinks You're Irrelevant and Extreme*. Grand Rapids, MI: Baker Books, 2016.

------.*Unchristian: What a New Generation Really Thinks about Christianity... and Why It Matters*. Grand Rapids, MI: Baker Books, 2007.

Kinnaman, David & Mark Matlock. *Faith for Exiles: 5 Ways for a New Generation to Follow Jesus in Digital Babylon*. Grand Rapids, MI: Baker Books, 2019.

Kreeft, Peter, and Ronald K, Tacelli. *Handbooks of Christian Apologetics*. Downers Grove, IL: InterVarsity Press, 1994.

Kumar, Steve. *Christianity for Sceptics*. Italy: John Hunt Publishing Ltd, 2000.

Kuyper, Abraham. *Christianity: A Total World and Life System*. Marlborough, NH: Plymouth Rock Foundation, 1996.

Lanham, Julie. "The Greening of Ted Turner." *The Humanist*. (November/December 1989).

Lapin, Daniel. *Thou Shall Prosper: Ten Commandments for Making Money*. Hoboken, NJ: John Wiley and Sons Publication, 2010.

Lennox, John C. *Gunning for God: Why the New Atheists are Missing the Target*. Oxford, UK: Lion Hudson, 2011.

Lewis, C.S. *Mere Christianity*. New York, NY: Macmillan Publishing, 1952.

------.*The Abolition of Man*. New York, NY: Harper Collins Publishers, 1974.

------.*Miracles*. San Francisco, CA: Harper Collins Publishers, Rev. ed., 2015.

------.*Weight of Glory*. New York, NY: Harper Collins Publication, 2001.

------."What Are We to Make of Jesus Christ?" In *C.S. Lewis Essay Collection*.

Lindsley, Art. *True Truth: Defending Absolute Truth in a Relativistic World*. Downers Grove, IL: InterVarsity Press, 2004.

Lipka,Michael.https://www.pewresearch.org/fact-tank/2016/08/24/why-americas-nones-left-religion-behind/.

Little, Paul E. *Know Why You Believe*. London: UK: Scripture Union, 1968.

Locke, John. *The Reasonableness of Christianity: As Delivered in the Scriptures.* Clarendon Edition of the Works of John Locke: Edited by John C. Higgins-Biddle. Oxford, UK: Oxford University Press, 2018.

Lüdemann, Gerd. *What Really Happened to Jesus: A Historical Approach of the Resurrection.* Westminster, UK: John Knox Press, 1995.

Machen, J. Gresham. *Education, Christianity, and the State.* Edited by John W. Robbins. Jefferson, MD: Trinity Foundation, 1987.

------.*What is Christianity?* Grand Rapids, MI: Wm. B. Eerdmans Publishing, 1951.

Madison, James. *Federalist Papers.* no. 51. New York, NY: Pocket Books, 1964.

Magee, Bryan. *The Story of Philosophy: The Essential Guide to the History of Western Philosophy.* New York, NY: DK Publishing, 1998.

Mehta, Hemant. "Where Did the Term 'Nones' Come From?" Accessed October 18, 2021. https://friendlyatheist.patheos.com/2013/01/11/where-did-the-term-nones-come-from/.

Metzger, Bruce, & Bart Ehrman. *The Text of the New Testament: Its Transmission, Corruption, and Restoration.* (4th Edition). New York, NY: Oxford University Press, 1992.

McDowell, Stephen. *The Bible: America's Source of Law and Liberty.* Charlottesville, VA: Providence Foundation, 2016.

McGrath, Alister E. *Science and Religion.* West Sussex, UK: Blackwell Publishers, 2010.

Miller, Stanley. https://evolutionnews.org/2008/01/darwins_failed_predictions_sli_11/.

Moreland, J.P. *Christianity and the Nature of Science.* Grand Rapids, MI: Baker Books, 1989.

------.*Love God with all Your Mind: The Role of Reason in the Life of the Soul.* Colorado Springs, CO: NavPress, 2012.

------.*Scaling the Secular City.* Grand Rapids, MI: Baker Books, 1987.

------.*Science and Secularism.* Wheaton, IL: Crossway Publishing, 2018.

Moreland, J.P. and Tim Muehlhoff, *The God Conversation: Using Stories and Illustrations to Explain Your Faith.* Downer Grove, IL: InterVarsity Press, 2007.

Morley, Brian K. *Mapping Apologetics: Comparing Contemporary Approaches*. Downers Grove, IL: InterVarsity Press, 2015.

Muggeridge, Malcolm. *The End of Christendom*. Grand Rapids, MI: Wm. B. Eerdman Publishing, 1980.

Murray, Abdu. *Saving Truth: Finding Meaning and Clarity in a Post-Truth World*. Grand Rapids, MI: Zondervan Press, 2018.

Myers, P.Z. "Chat with PZ Myers HERE!" Accessed October 24, 2021. https://evolutionnews.org/2013/10/pz_myers_the_happy_atheist/.

Nagel, Thomas. *The Last Word*. Oxford, UK: Oxford University Press, 1997.

Nash, Ronald. H. *Worldviews in Conflict*. Grand Rapids, MI: Zondervan Publishing, 1992.

Newbigin, Lesslie. *Foolishness to the Greeks: The Gospel and Western Culture*. Grand Rapids, MI: Wm. B. Eerdman Publishing, 1986.

------.*The Gospel in a Pluralistic Society*. Grand Rapids, MI: Wm. B. Eerdmans Publishing, 1989.

------.*Truth to Tell: The Gospel Versus Public Truth*. Grand Rapids, MI: Wm. B. Eerdmans Publishing, 2006.

(NASB Bible). Grand Rapids, MI: Zondervan Press, 1995.

Nietzsche, Friedrich. *Beyond Good and Evil*. New York, NY: Random House Publishing, 1989.

Noebel, David. *Understanding the Times: The Religious Worldview of Our Day and a Search for Truth*. Eugene, OR: Harvest House Publishers, 1992.

Orwell, George. https://www.goodreads.com/quotes/8204871--the-further-a-society-drifts-from-the-truth-the-more.

Osborn, Henry F. *Hesperopithecus*. "The First Anthropoid Primate Found in America." *Science* Vol. 60, No. 1427 (May 5, 1922).

Pannenberg, Wolfhart. "Dogmatic Thesis on the Doctrine of Revelation." In *Revelations as History*. New York, NY: Macmillan, 1969.

Pascal, Blaise. *Pensees*. Edited by Alban Krailsheimer. New York, NY: Viking Press, 1966.

Pearcey, Nancy. *Total Truth*. Wheaton, IL: Crossway Books, 2004.

------. *Saving Leonardo.* Nashville, TN: B & H Publishing Group, 2010.

Pelikan, Jaroslav. *The Christian Tradition: A History of the Development of Doctrine.* Chicago, IL: University of Chicago Press, 1977.

Penrose, Roger. *The Emperor's New Mind.* Oxford, UK: Oxford University Press, 1989.

Plantiga, Alvin. *Where the Conflict Really Lies: Science, Religion, and Naturalism.* Oxford, UK: Oxford University Press, 2011.

Plantinga, Cornelius Jr. *Engaging God's World: A Christian Vision of Faith, Learning, and Living.* Grand Rapids, MI: Wm. B. Eerdmans Publishing, 2002.

Poplin, Mary. *Is Reality Secular? Testing the Assumptions of Four Major Worldviews.* Downers Grove, IL: InterVarsity Press, 2014.

Probe Ministries. *College Mind Games: College Survival Course.* Richardson, TX: Probe Ministries, 1996.

Provine, William B. "No Free Will." In *Catching up with the Vision.* Edited by M.W. Rossiter. Chicago, IL: University Press, 1999.

Pyeatt, Matt, "ACLU Demands California School to Drop 'God Bless America' Display," Oct. 15, 2001. Accessed October 2, 2021. htpp://www.scr.itgo.com/aclu.html.

Ratzsch, Del. *Science and Its Limits: The Natural Sciences in Christian Perspective.* Downers Grove, IL: InterVarsity Press, 1986.

Reader, John. "Whatever Happened to Zinjanthropus?" *New Scientist.* (March 26, 1981).

Reich, Robert. Former Labor Secretary Predicts Religious Wars in America July 1, 2004. Accessed May 14, 2020. https://www.christianitytoday.com/ct/2004/julyweb-only/7-5-51.0.html.

Ridenour, Fritz. *So, What's the Difference?* Glendale, CA: Regal Publishing, 1969.

Ridley, Matt. *Discoverer of the Genetic Code.* Review. by Nicholas Wade. *New York Times* (July 18, 2006).

Ruben, Julie A. *The Making of the Modern University: Intellectual Information and the Marginalization of Morality.* Chicago, IL: University Chicago Press, 1996.

Ruse, Michael, and E.O. Wilson. *The Evolution of Ethics: Religion and the Natural Sciences: The Range of Engagement.* New York, NY: Harcourt Brace Jovanovich, 1993.

Rutland, Mark. 2001, *Most Likely to Succeed: A Graduate's Guide to True Success in Work and Life*. Lake Mary, FL: Charisma House Publishing.

Samples, Kenneth Richard. *7 Truths That Changed the World: Discovering Christianity's Most Dangerous Ideas*. Grand Rapids, MI: Baker Books, 2012.

Sartre, Jean-Paul. *Jean-Paul Sartre: Basic Writings*. Edited by Stephen Priest. New York, NY: Routledge University Press, 2001.

Schaeffer, Francis A. *How Should We Live: The Rise and Decline of Western Thought and Culture*. Wheaton, IL: Crossway Books, 1976.

*The God Who Is There*. Downer Grove, IL: InterVarsity Press, 1968.

Schaeffer, Franky. *A Time for Anger: The Myth of Neutrality*. Wheaton, IL: Crossway Books, 1982.

Schopf, J.M. "Punctuated Equilibria: An Alternative of Phyletic Gradualism." *Models in Paleobiology*. Edited by Stephen Jay Gould. 1972.

Schoreder, Gerald. *The Hidden Face of God: Science Reveals the Ultimate Truth*. New York, NY: Simon and Schuster, 2001.

Sirico, Robert A. *A Moral Basis for Liberty*. Grand Rapids, MI: Action Institute, 2012.

Slick, Matt. Accessed June 20, 2021. https://www.carm.org/is-the-bible-reliable.

Spencer, Frank. *Piltdown: A Scientific Forgery*. New York, NY: Oxford University Press, 1990.

Sproul, R.C. *Not A Chance: The Myth of Chance in Science and Modern Cosmology*. Grand Rapids, MI: Baker Books, 1994.

*Essentially Truths of the Christian Faith*. Wheaton, IL: Tyndale House Publishers, 1992.

Stubbs, Shannon M. "Jesus' Claim to Singularity with Yahweh: An Exegetical Study of "I Am" Sayings in the Synoptic Gospels," Order No. 1495891. Oral Roberts University, 2011. Accessed October 15, 2021. https://search.proquest.com/docview/873577254?accountid=36664.

Stark, Rodney. *The Victory of Reason: How Christianity Leads to Freedom, Capitalism, and Western Success*. New York, NY: Random House Publishing, 2005.

Stokes, Phillip. *Philosophy: 100 Essential Thinkers*. London, UK: Arcturus Publishing, 2002.

Stott, J.R., *Basic Christianity*. Chicago, IL: InterVarsity Press, 1964.

Strobel, Lee. "Four Proofs of the Resurrection." In *The Case for Christ*. Accessed October 20, 2021. https://www.youtube.com/watch?v=FT4Cj-Pi4m0.

Tackett, Christopher. *Cambridge Companion to Jesus*. Cambridge, UK: Cambridge University Press, 2001.

"The Bibliographical Test Updated." Christian Research Journal. Vol. 35, No. 03 (2012). Accessed January 20, 2021. http://www.equip.org.

Tozer A.W. *The Pursuit of God*. Columbia, SC: TheBiblePeople.com., 2020.

Turner, Steven. *Up to Date*. London, UK: Hodder and Stoughton, 1985.

Watson, Lyall. Anthropologist, *The Water People Science Digest*. Vol. 90 (May 1982).

Weinrich, William C. "Spirit and Martyrdom: A Study of the Work of the Holy Spirit in Contexts of Persecution and Martyrdom in the New Testament and Early Christian Literature." Accessed May 12, 2021. https://www.cambridge.org/core/journals/church-history/.

Wells, Jonathan. *Zombie Science: More Icons of Evolution*. Seattle, WA: Discovery Institute Press, 2017.

West, John G. *Darwin's Corrosive Idea: The Impact of Evolution on Attitudes about Faith, Ethics and Human Uniqueness*. Seattle, WA: Discovery Institute (November 2016).

Weston, Paul and Lesslie Newbigin. *Missionary Theologian: A Reader*. Grand Rapids, MI: Eerdman Publications, 2006.

White, Ellen C. *Counsel to Writers and Editors*. Nashville, TN: Nashville Southern Publishers, 1946.

Wienrich, William C. *Spirit of Martyrdom: A Study of the Work of the Holy Spirit in Contexts of Persecution and Martyrdom in the New Testament and Early Christian Literature*. Lanham, MD: University Press of America, 1983.

Wiker, Benjamin. *The Darwin Myth: The Life and Lies of Charles Darwin*. Washington, DC: Regency Publishing, 2009.

Willard, Dallas. Accessed December 8, 2021. https://renovare.org/articles/truth-and-reality-do-not-adapt-to-us.

Zacharias, Ravi. *Jesus Among Other Gods: The Absolute Claims of the Christian Message*. Nashville, TN: Thomas Nelson Publishing, 2000.

# ABOUT THE AUTHOR

Dr. Ken Dew has traveled and ministered in over forty nations worldwide. Ken has spoken on over 130 university campuses nationally and internationally.

Ken and his wife Renee have been married for thirty-two years. In 2000, Ken and his family moved from Nashville, Tennessee to Auckland, New Zealand, and planted the first Every Nation Church in the South Pacific. Since that first Auckland plant, there have been eight Every Nations Churches established in the Oceania region.

Ken also developed and directed Every Nation Leadership Institute (ENLI) in Auckland and Wellington, New Zealand, as well as in Melbourne and Sydney, Australia. The Dews are the Founding Pastors for Every Nation Church Auckland, New Zealand, and Every Nation Brisbane, Australia.

Ken is the author of two books: *Engaging the Culture: Why Sharing your Faith is No Longer an Option*, as well as, Ken's new book, *The Certainty of Christ: Confident Faith in a Confused World.* (New Release Date: Mar 2023)

Ken has a B.S. in Education from Tennessee Tech University and received a Master's Degree in Theology from Luther Rice University (2005). Ken earned a Doctor of Ministry Degree (D. Min. 2022) in Christian Leadership and Strategic Growth from Manna University.

After living on the mission field for 14 years, Ken and Renee now reside in Tallahassee, Florida where he serves as a Church Consultant, Equipping Evangelist, and Christian Apologist.

www.ingramcontent.com/pod-product-compliance
Lightning Source LLC
Chambersburg PA
CBHW031503120626
46545CB00005B/1731